Racisms

Racisms

an introduction

Steve Garner

Los Angeles | London | New Delhi
Singapore | Washington DC

First published 2010

SAGE Publications Ltd
1 Oliver's Yard
55 City Road
London EC1Y 1SP

SAGE Publications Inc.
2455 Teller Road
Thousand Oaks, California 91320

SAGE Publications India Pvt Ltd
B 1/I 1 Mohan Cooperative Industrial Area
Mathura Road, Post Bag 7
New Delhi 110 044

SAGE Publications Asia-Pacific Pte Ltd
33 Pekin Street #02-01
Far East Square
Singapore 048763

Library of Congress Control Number 2009925653

British Library Cataloguing in Publication data

A catalogue record for this book is available from the British Library

ISBN 978-1-4129-4580-6
ISBN 978-1-4129-4581-3 (pbk)

Typeset by C&M Digitals (P) Ltd, Chennai, India
Printed by CPI Antony Rowe, Chippenham, Wiltshire
Printed on paper from sustainable resources

Mixed Sources
Product group from well-managed
forests and other controlled sources
www.fsc.org Cert no. SGS-COC-2953
© 1996 Forest Stewardship Council
FSC

Contents

Acknowledgements

First, a big thank you to the people at Sage for their patience, especially Jai Seaman, Chris Rojek and Katherine Haw. Second, thanks to my family, who as usual suffer neglect as a result of my writing activity – Annie, Dani, Gabriel and Morganne – you're the best. Thirdly, this text is based on my interpretation of other people's hard work, so it really is, in a way, a collective project.

Teaching can, paradoxically, be a lonely old business in the middle of a crowd: trying to make epiphanies happen in the minds of strangers. Sometimes it can get depressing, or boring. Sometimes you may even think you have made a string of poor choices that lead you to a particular classroom, teaching a particular subject at a particular time, when you could instead have been coaching your favourite sport, watching fabulous jungle animals through a camera lens, saving somebody's life in an emergency room, or doing something demonstrably exciting and/or more fun for a living. At other times, on those rare occasions when you set another person on a course that they recognise is a direction in which they would not have travelled were it not for you, then I can't think of anything much better. I have an email I read when I'm feeling particularly low, in which a former student thanks me for teaching a module on racism. The last part reads: 'It was the only area of study I have undertaken that made me completely change the way I thought about the world'.

This text is dedicated to all the teachers to whom that sentence should be addressed, and more often, but whose former students are having too much fun to get round to telling them so.

List of Boxes, Tables and Figures

Boxes

Tables

Figures

Introduction

There are some splendid resource books for teaching 'race' and ethnicity in the social sciences. However, having taught specialist undergraduate modules for a decade, I have never been able to fully endorse buying a textbook because those available suppose too much knowledge. They are ideal for use with postgraduates and for referencing segments of larger works, but undergraduate social scientists just don't generally have enough background in the subject to make enough use of them properly. This is not a failing on the students' part. There has to be a period in which they acquire the knowledge that helps them fit these well-known works into some kind of a theoretical framework. It has taken me more than 20 years, and there is not a day that passes without me adding more knowledge. So this text is designed for undergraduates who are interested in this topic, primarily in the UK and the USA, which is why material from those two countries is prioritised here. It is a textbook to use either as the basis for a course, or to dip into as a set of free-standing chapters.

Academic colleagues who know this area will immediately be able to come up with a set of chapters for the topics I did not cover here. I agree: the choice is idiosyncratic. I could suggest an 'omitted chapters' list myself: anti-semitism; anti-nomadic racism; indigenous land rights; Transatlantic slavery; Far-right politics; criminology and the racialisation of minorities; concentrations on other historical periods and geographical locations. All of these areas and more could have been covered in this book, but then where would all the topics already in here have gone? Any student textbook has to cover what I understand to be the basics, which in this case comprises theories of 'race', racisms, racialisation, how class and gender articulate with 'race', what 'mixed-ness' means, and the role of science in making and sustaining the creative fiction that is 'race'. Particularly relevant examples for me of how issues can be racialised are asylum and Islamic religion in the West, hence the coverage of those two. Finally, there are the connected issues of the racialisation of white identities and of the establishment, over the last three decades or so, of 'new' forms of racism that emphasise culture more than phenotype in public and private discourse. If the publishers ask me to do another edition, I will certainly include something different. However, I stand by this choice of topics. It offers one possible route into the truly gigantic corpus.

I am often pushed to say 'what I know' about racism and in fact the more knowledgeable I get, the more I realise that I am getting further from, not closer to, some state of expertise. The more you know, the more you know what there is to know (and that is always more than one person can hope to know). So if you really want to know what the story is, then the following will help you begin.

'Race' is a fiction that we turn into a social reality every day of our lives. It lies at the heart of the complex, historical and multifaceted sets of social relationships to which we attach the label 'racism'. This is a historical process, a set of ideas and a set of outcomes (benefits for some, disadvantages for others). This can be anything from a promotion ahead of someone else who is just as good at what they do as you are, to being hunted like an animal and dying a protracted and painful death at the hands of someone who thinks 'race' is so real it authorises your murder with impunity.

The forms in which these social relationships play out are so diverse that I think 'racism' is too small a word to contain them, hence my choice of a plural in the title. If you are interested in struggling against racism, you have to be interested in more than just 'race'. You must also be a student of gender, class, nation states, culture, history and science. I encourage students to follow up by reading the work referred to in each chapter, at the next level of study. This text is merely a starting point, a marshalling of some arguments and an incitement to think that racism is a complicated part of the social world, rather than an aberration of individuals. I hope that someone who reads this text will end up contributing to the struggle … which unfortunately won't be ending any time soon.

1 The Idea of 'Race' and the Practice of Racisms

What is race? The striking element of all scholarly attempts to understand what 'race' is seems to be the impossibility of providing a definition. We think we know, obviously, who is in what 'race', even though we may try very consciously not to attach any further importance to it as an identity when we deal with other people. Clearly, dividing up people into 'races' is an act of categorisation. Yet when we look more closely at the kinds of assumptions this form of categorisation is based on, they do not hold water. We think 'race' is about physical appearance and has been a characteristic of humanity for centuries. But how many 'races' are there and what are they called? If you watch American crime shows, you may think 'Caucasian', 'African American' and 'Hispanic' are the main ones. Yet there are a number of problems with this understanding. First, these labels are all relatively new. 'Caucasian' was not used before the 1940s; 'African American' has only come into use since the 1990s; and 'Hispanic' has only been used since the 1970 Census. Second, the world really is bigger than the USA. What separates people's understandings of who is who in one place, at one time, is not necessarily the same logic that applies elsewhere at other times. Third, and we will come back to this many times, pursuing the idea that the world can be divided into 'races' requires a special suspension of logic. What are the physical attributes we are really talking about in the discussion of 'race'? Skin colour, hair type and colour, eye colour, shape of eyes, shape of nose. Are there any more? Yet let's think for a moment about all the ways in which two human bodies could differ from one another. If you had to make a list of such elements, that list would be very long. Once you have proportions of limbs to body, shape of head, distance between eyes and muscle definition, I am sure you could come up with 20 before you have even started to struggle. That's just the external (phenotypical) differences. If we then start to think about genetic differences, the scale of the sleight of hand involved in dividing the world up into 'races' on the premise of biology becomes apparent. In Box 1.1, we can see some information derived from contemporary science about the various ways in which human bodies could be grouped together: and it is counter-intuitive for people whose culture encourages the normalization of 'race'.

Box 1.1 Race and genes

While each human being has around 25,000–30,000 genes, the largest difference between two individuals seems to be in the region of 1 per cent. Although the biological basis of 'race' suggests distinct groups of people with more shared genetic heritage than genetic discrepancy,

(Continued)

(Continued)

research into genetic differences shows that this is a false claim. The science does not stand up. Indeed, often there are geographical, social and medical reasons for the relatively small differences in genetic structure between people.

Example 1 – *Sickle cell anaemia*: often seen as a disease for which people of African origin exclusively are at high risk. The cluster of genes that means a person is likely to develop this form of anaemia is concentrated among groups of people whose ancestors came from sub-Saharan Africa, the Mediterranean, the Middle East and India. Thus, it is not solely a black people's disease but rather closely linked to malaria: hence the geographical concentration of the pathology. Malaria exacerbates the illness, and so where malaria is not present, the rate of sickle cell sufferers drops. African Americans' rate is below that of West Africa, and falling as malaria has been eradicated in the USA.

Example 2 – *IQ testing*: the controversy about psychometric testing for Intelligence Quotient is ongoing. Introduced in the early twentieth century in the USA, its objective was to screen for intelligence among recruits for the armed forces. It was then used as a screening test for immigrants. The claims of those who advocate such tests are that different ethnic and racial groups score at different rates – even when environmental factors are taken into consideration. Those who disagree argue that there are a host of social class and culture-related issues around what is counted as intelligence and what is actually measured in these types of test. People can score at higher rates with training in the types of question asked, and in the case of immigrants, after longer exposure to the culture of the country in which the test is administered (Duster, 1990, 2006; Herrnstein and Murray, 1994; Fraser, 1995).

Ultimately, the judgement of science on 'race' as a way of definitively organizing the human population into discrete groups, according to genetic make-up, is unequivocal: 'Modern genetics does in fact show that there are no separate groups within humanity (although there are noticeable differences among the peoples of the world) … Individuals – not nations and races – are the main repository of human variation for functional genes. A race, as defined by skin colour, is no more a biological entity than is a nation, whose identity depends only on a brief shared history' (Jones, 1994: 246).

This is not to say that people do not share characteristics such as complexion, hair type, eye colour, etc., but instead it should draw our attention to the relatively tiny proportion of physical features that we use as criteria for our understanding of 'race': skin colour, hair type, eye colour, shape of mouth, shape of eyes, etc. Why, out of all the biological differences there *could* be between two people, do we only focus on half a dozen at most? Moreover, biological genetic similarity within a supposed racial group, and its distinction from another, represent only half the story: 'race' has always been about linking culture and behaviour to physical appearance. How we think about 'race' is to assume, for example, that Person X is part of group A, therefore she behaves in a certain way. There is more in this book about how the links were originally made, and on the idea of culture later, but here, we just need to underline the fact that the idea of 'race' is not merely about bodies looking similar to or different from one another, but about the ideological labour we put into collectively interpreting those similarities and differences.

So, if we accept that there are many physical differences possible, yet when we think about 'race', there are only half a dozen or so features that we are interested in, the problem for us becomes, 'why is this the case?' Moreover, the terms we use, like 'white', 'black', 'yellow', 'red', etc. are not even descriptions of what they claim to describe. Nobody living is actually white. Nobody is really 'black' in the sense of the ink on this page, although there are some people with very dark complexions indeed. Certainly, nobody's skin is yellow or red – unless they are sunburnt or suffering from particular diseases. So the conclusion must be that such terms have social meanings but not biological ones. The same could be said for the idea of 'race'. Our social worlds are full of ways to distinguish between one group and another in a specific context, and 'race' is one form of categorisation. The interpretations of physical differences that we make in our societies are determined not by the indisputable fact of racial difference, but by the social imperatives that enable us to do so. In other words, the social world provides us with tools specific to both our culture and our period of history, which we then use to read 'race' from the bodies of human beings. We are bombarded with ways of admitting that 'race' is a *natural* part of our social world, one of the legitimate ways in which we try to make sense of difference. 'We hold these truths', it appears, 'to be self-evident': all people are created racial.

Indeed, 'race' has never been the object of consensus because of this slippery relationship to the facts. Throughout this book, we will examine geographical and historical contexts in which the interpretations afforded to 'race' differ. Michael Omi's conclusion is valid not just for the USA:

> ... the meaning of race in the United States has been and probably always will be fluid and subject to multiple determinations. Race cannot be seen simply as an objective fact, nor treated as an independent variable. (Omi, 2001: 244)

Paul Silverstein's anthropological perspective is that 'race' is a 'cultural category of difference that is contextually constructed as essential and natural – as residing within the very body of the individual' (Silverstein, 2005: 364). So, making sense of such clues, which we are primed to do in our cultures, is labelled a 'social construction' in the social sciences. Sociologists have long argued that 'race' is a social construction, but that the meanings attributed to it have concrete impacts on social relations. Although there might be strategic reasons why 'race' could be retained, as a basis for solidarity (Gilroy, 1987), I am convinced that as far as academic practice goes, Stephen Small's rationale (1994: 30) is the correct one. Contrary to the focus on 'race relations', he maintains, which first 'assumes that "races" exist and then seeks to understand relations between them', racialisation directs our attention to 'how groups not previously defined as "races" have come to be defined in this way and assesses the various factors involved in such processes'. These processes result in 'race' becoming a salient factor in the way social resources are allocated and how groups are represented, that is, racialised.

DIFFERENT PLACES, DIFFERENT 'RACES'?

As we said, these readings differ from one place to another and at different moments in time. Let's take an example of a person whom we shall hypothetically move from place to place. Using the racial terminology available to us in our understanding of the world seen through the lens of 'race', her mother is white and her father is black (UK), or Caucasian and African American (USA). This makes her either African American or bi-racial (USA) or black or 'mixed race' (UK). If we take this fictitious person with light brown skin to Brazil, there are at least four ways to categorise her racially: *parda*, *preta*, *morena* and *negra*. Each of these has different connotations, and the degree to which one is not white often affects your life chances in terms of education, employment, etc. Returning to the Caribbean via Latin America, she would pass through a set of cultures where the gradations between black, white and native American origins have an elaborate terminology: there would certainly be a term to describe her, possibly *mulatta* or *morena*, for example, and when she gets to somewhere like Jamaica, she might be referred to as 'red' or 'yellow'.

If we take her back to South Africa between 1948 and 1994, when the system called Apartheid was in place, she would have been 'Coloured'. This meant you were restricted to living in particular areas, barred from others, and this, in turn, meant restricted access to education, employment and other resources, in a context where the entire population was identified by 'race' and governed on that basis.

In such systems of attributing social value, therefore, everyone has a set of physical attributes that can get you categorised. However, in this form of categorisation, the outcomes are unequal. If you look like this person in the USA, South Africa, Latin America or Brazil, particular openings are closed off to you. Yet should she stay in a country where the vast majority of people are black, let's say Nigeria, her identity is much more likely to relate to religion, region of origin, language, professional status, etc. Lastly, if we took her back to 1930s Germany, she would have been a candidate for the forced sterilisation programme. After the First World War, the Rhineland (the industrial region bordering France) was occupied by American troops. Several of the French African soldiers had children with German women, and from 1937 onwards, as part of the 'racial hygiene' programme led by Dr Eugen Fischer, these 400 children were sterilised in order that they did not contaminate the Aryan gene pool. In each of those settings, the social and political distinctions between people have their own histories; the words used to describe groups of people based on culture and physical appearance have different meanings and refer the individuals concerned to different positions of relative power in the society. 'Race' is therefore not a universal concept, but a particular and contingent one.

There are some significant elements to note from this small set of examples:

- 'Race' in biological terms (of simply what people look like) matters a lot. For example, it bears importantly on the way resources are made more or less accessible.

- It is not individuals alone, but also important institutions like the State, which have input in determining the meaning of 'race'.

- Different social systems and their cultures attach different types of meaning to physical appearance.

- It is not simply a case of some people being denied access to goods and resources, but of the corresponding easier access for others. Racism, as we shall define it below, is a social relationship. This means that there is always an imbalance of power, expressed through access to resources.

DEFINING RACISM

What *isn't* racism?

The systems of Nazi Germany, South Africa under apartheid (1948–94), and the segregated southern states of the USA ('Jim Crow') placed racial discrimination very obviously at the heart of the way that government and everyday life were carried out. We will return to these historical examples throughout this book, but it is important also to recognise that they are not paradigms (examples that serve as models) but rather extreme points on a continuum. A common misperception of racism is that it is only the severe examples that constitute the whole, in other words only violence, verbal abuse and deliberate segregation are actually racist; nothing else counts. In the course of this book, an argument will be presented that the phenomenon is far broader and more complex than such a view would suggest. Indeed, the term has been bandied around in so much public discourse, particularly since the 1960s, that it appears to have lost some of its explanatory power. It gets divorced from power relations, so that terms such as 'reverse racism' gain currency. Such a concept is derived from perceptions that pro-grammes ranging from affirmative action to multiculturalism in the public arena end up placing white people at a *systematic* disadvantage in the realms of educa-tion and employment especially. Finally, there is also a view that racism is caused by continually addressing 'race' per se, and that there is really not a problem until activists and academics make a fuss about it. One such definition is that of Mike Adams (a University of North Carolina–Wilmington professor, writing as a columnist):

> Racism – is a pathological tendency to interject race into situations where it is not relevant, merely for personal gain. (Adams, 2006)

From this emerges a broader, popular understanding that racism is both 'natural' (people sticking together and preferring their own kind) and distributed equally, so that any member of a given group can be racist about a member of another group. However, through the interplay of claim and counter-claim about who is racist, the term comes to occupy a particular role. It is asked to serve as a normative description of something it is not – a level playing field (Doane, 2006). While it is perfectly possible that individuals have discriminatory opinions, the point of racism is that it constitutes much more than just personal opinions. What sociology has contributed to understandings of racism is that there are different levels of the phenomenon, some of which are to do with historical legacies and social formations that are not within an individual's capacity to alter. Like all forms of discrimination, racism is primarily an unequal *collective* power relationship, which we shall look at throughout this book.

In addition, there are the terms 'institutional racism', 'individual racism', 'cultural racism', 'indirect racism', and a host of other adjectives that qualify the noun. Faced with these competing understandings of what racism is, how can we take a step back and focus on the field as developed in the social sciences? Different expressions are used for phenomena, for groups and for outcomes in different periods. Indeed, terms like 'racialism' and 'race prejudice' were used in previous eras to describe more or less what the field of study is here.

We need a working definition to help us navigate this very broad terrain. My suggestion involves a two-part strategy. The first comprises looking at some existing definitions that undergraduates might find particularly helpful, and the second is an attempt to set out some criteria by which we can assess competing claims, and therefore, implicitly, develop our working definition.

Michael Banton (1997: 28) asks whether it 'is possible to discuss the sociology of race relations without using the term racism'. Banton advocates prudence in the use of the word 'racist'. It should be used carefully, he contends, and be attached to actions rather than to people, as labelling *actions* 'racist' leaves the possibility that *people* may be capable of non-racist or anti-racist behaviour as well. Whereas calling someone – rather than something that a person did – racist, can be a political tactic, which makes no attempt to illuminate the causes of racism. Moreover, according to George Frederickson (1988: 189), the popular idea that racism comprised a set of beliefs of biological superiority, has gradually been replaced since the Second World War by 'patterns of action which serve to create or preserve unequal relationships between racial groups'. This new understanding of the term is concomitant with the development of a so-called 'new racism'. In a later chapter, we will explore this development, and argue that 'replace' might be the wrong word. However, putting the word 'racism' into the plural, to acknowledge the variety of forms it takes, might be worth considering.

The four definitions we shall use to begin the debate are the following.

I

[T]he attribution of social significance (meaning) to particular patterns of phenotypical and/or genetic difference which, along with the characteristic of additional deterministic ascription or real or supposed other characteristics to a group constituted by descent, is the defining feature of racism. (Banton, 1996: 310)

1. If we are to get to grips with racism as a sociological phenomenon, we have to address its existence in the social rather than solely the biological sphere. Banton stresses the process of attribution of social meaning to the body.

2. Racism tries to explain the social world by reference to the natural world. Nature, as we know, is in permanent flux, yet in racist social narratives, bodies and cultures are fixed and unchanging: everyone who with certain physical characteristics naturally has a tendency toward certain patterns of behaviour.

3. As a model of the natural world, 'race' functions as a set of transmitted genes: some for appearance and some for behaviour. The range of these is fixed. We can never break free, would run the argument, of our genes, because we are programmed to behave in particular ways. Determinism is the name given to the expression of this causal relationship.

II

Racism is a belief system or doctrine which postulates a hierarchy among various human races or ethnic groups. It may be based on an assumption of inherent biological differences between different ethnic groups that purport to determine cultural or individual behaviour. Racism may be described as a strong form of ethnocentrism, including traits such as xenophobia (fear and hate of foreigners), views against interracial relationships (anti-miscegenation), ethnic nationalism, and ethnic stereotypes. (Wikipedia, until April 2007)

As every undergraduate knows, Wikipedia provides information, definitions and links to further resources. While I generally try to guide students away from using it uncritically, and especially cutting and pasting its contents into essays, or even as a source of definitions in sociology (there are plenty of better ones), the definition posted until April 2007 is useful for our purposes here, if not very comprehensive.

1. It is crucial to our sociological understanding of racism that we realize it involves the expression of a power relationship. In the social reality conjured by 'race', no two 'races' are ever on an equal footing. The history of the production of 'race' as a topic and the enactment of racism as a relationship perpetually throw up hierarchies. These alter from one period to another and from one historical context to another. There is never usually a consensus about the exact intermediate positionings, but it is hard to find one in which white is not placed higher than the other racialised identities.

2. Another merit of this definition is that it suggests practical examples. It opens us up to the possibility that racism is not uniform but might contain various strands of ideas. It is therefore to be understood as a complex of ideas rather than a single monolithic one. The collapsing of ethnicity into racism is also a useful exercise ... in what not to do! Don't confuse the two! (Fenton, 2003)

III

The collective failure of an organisation to provide an appropriate and professional service to people because of their colour, culture or ethnic origin. It can be seen and detected in processes, attitudes, and behaviour which amount to discrimination through unwitting prejudice, ignorance, thoughtlessness, and racist stereotyping which disadvantage minority ethnic people. (*The Stephen Lawrence Enquiry* [MacPherson Report], 1999: para. 6.34)

The MacPherson Report (1999) was an enquiry into the (London) Metropolitan Police's handling of the investigation of Stephen Lawrence's murder in South London in 1993. The whole of section 6 of the report is worth reading because it sets out a genealogy of the term 'institutional racism' as developed in the context of what is referred to as British 'race relations'. We shall see below that this is not the only context in which the term can be understood, but it is nevertheless very significant, because the definition provided by Lord MacPherson formed the basis of a controversial shift in defining racist crime in the UK (especially England and Wales) in the early twenty-first century. It was also fundamental to an important amendment to law in Britain on racial discrimination (through the 2002 Race Relations (Amendment) Act).

1. MacPherson identifies that racism is not purely about the psychological processes of individuals dealing with each other (as most early work in the field suggested), but can be located at a broader, collective level, that is, as outcomes of an organisation's activities, rather than of one agent's activities.

2. The distinction drawn between 'processes, attitudes, and behaviour' is also helpful. It separates what people think (attitudes), from what they actually do (behaviour), and explicitly asserts that discrimination can result from long-term patterns (processes). All of these aspects can be addressed by different anti-discriminatory measures.

3. The idea that discrimination can be unintended, or 'unwitting', in Lord Scarman's terms, has proven controversial. Lord Scarman chaired an enquiry on the riots that took place in South London in 1981 (Scarman, 1986). His report suggested that actions and processes can be racist in outcome even if they are not intended to be. Because institutional racism has been developed into a legal concept which has to be proven beyond reasonable doubt in a court of law, it must also have a clear definition. Defining something by its outcome rather than by its intention, as Scarman did, and MacPherson does here, has enabled institutional racism to become a workable legal concept. The other aspect of intentionality returns us to the idea that discrimination can occur at a level beyond the individual, and as part of a set of procedures that are unfairly loaded against some groups, while favouring others. In this way, by following the set procedures of an organisation, an agent can be performing an act that has racist outcomes, even if that agent has no intention of doing so (see more on this topic in Chapter 7).

4. Racism is popularly imagined as something someone does to somebody else. However, in this definition, it is also a failure to do something positive, rather than exclusively constituting positive and detrimental acts. As a result of the police force not carrying out its functions fully and rigorously, Lawrence's family and friends were dealt with in discriminatory fashion. This type of reasoning will not be news to the many people who have waited in vain to be protected by police forces, but it is a welcome addition to the understanding of racism we are trying to explore here.

5. An overview of this definition also suggests that the phenomenon of racism is multifaceted and cumulative: a number of aspects are identified along with a timeline that extends into the past. In a nutshell, this is well worth remembering, as the rest of the book serves to underscore these dual characteristics.

IV

> Racism takes two closely related forms: individual whites acting against individual blacks, and acts by the total white community against the black community. We call these individual racism and institutional racism ... When white terrorists bomb a black church and kill black children, that is an act of individual racism, widely deplored by most segments of society. But when in that same city – Birmingham, Alabama – 500 black babies die each year because of the lack of proper food, clothing, shelter and proper medical facilities, and thousands more are destroyed or maimed physically, emotionally and intellectually because of conditions of poverty and discrimination in the black community, that is a function of institutional racism. (Carmichael and Hamilton, 1967: 6)

Carmichael and Hamilton's book emerged out of the struggles for civil rights in the 1960s. Their stance was more radical than that of the mainstream civil rights movement. Indeed, the National American Association of Colored People and the Student Non-Violent Co-ordinating Committee (the principal organising bodies of national civil rights campaigning) both condemned Carmichael's philosophy as 'black racism'. Indeed, he ended up as a leading Black Panther and changed his name to Kwame Turé. Academic Charles Hamilton was a radical political scientist who held a Professorship at Columbia University from the 1970s until he retired in the late 1990s. Together, they produced a book establishing a manifesto of black solidarity at a crucial juncture in US history.

1. Their definition is compelling, detailed and empirical. It critically links economics and racism, or class and 'race', in a vision of mutually compounding, not exclusive, sources of discrimination. In it, we find the bones of what is later referred to as 'structural' or 'systemic' racism, later explored by academics (Massey and Denton, 1994; Oliver and Shapiro, 1995; Lipsitz, 1998; Feagin, 2006), involving society-level processes and contrasting them with what is popularly thought to exclusively comprise racism, that is, verbal abuse and violent attacks. It is a common discursive strategy in early twenty-first century Western societies to distance oneself from 'genuine' racism, as perpetrated by fringe extremist movements, and find ways of criticising the idea that anything other than this is really racism at all.

2. Carmichael and Hamilton conjure up a conception of unequal and antagonistic social relationships involving two communities, the black and the white. However, implicit in their development of this concept is the idea that poverty also plays a role. Poverty is disproportionately concentrated in the African American population, although the largest proportion of poor people in the USA are white. By linking 'race' and class, they imply that racism is inextricable from class – in that people have multiple identities and locations.

Being poor in the USA would certainly lead to some of the housing and health-related problems they identify being experienced, but being poor and black would make them much more likely.

After examining these four attempts to define racism, we are a lot closer to something substantial. The point is really to demonstrate the complexity of racism. It cannot easily be reduced to a formula of the type 'racism is …'

So far, we have the following elements of what racism is:

- Distinctions have been made between the individual and the institution as sources, and between practices, attitudes and processes.

- It is a phenomenon whose roots lie in the social meanings attributed to ostensible biological difference, and has an observable history.

- It is a set of ideas organised hierarchically, and at its most abstract level, an ongoing power relationship.

The relative weights of these components can be argued about. However, we are moving to the kind of conclusion that definitions of racism are broad-ranging and numerous. Just a brief survey has highlighted this.

In his critique of the concept of racism, Robert Miles (1987) suggests that racism is primarily an 'ideology', an assertion which he and Malcolm Brown embed in their revamped second edition of *Racism* (2003: 17). It is arguable whether their definition is indeed a definition per se, but more of a five-part approach to a subject:

1. Racism is an ideology.

2. 'Race' and 'racism' as everyday concepts can be critiqued using a social science analysis of racism.

3. Racism should be flexibly defined so as to note the shifting emphases in meanings attached to it, and the constant importance in the political economy of migration.

4. The interdependence of racism and nationalism through the development of the capitalist system should be foregrounded.

5. Political and moral aspects must also be acknowledged alongside social scientific ones.

An ideology, in Miles' sense, is drawn from Marx, and can be understood as any discourse that distorts the truth about human beings and the social relationships between them. The search to avoid 'conceptual inflation' and 'conceptual deflation' that occupy two chapters in his book reminds us that too narrowly defining racism, or indeed overloading it so that *everything* is racism, lead to the rendering of the term as meaningless.

Miles' approach has been critiqued as lacking sophistication, being tied too closely to Marxism, and defining racism in too doctrinaire a fashion, as 'ideology'. These are arguments that he rebuts himself in the 2003 edition. For a student of the sociology of racism however, the work is of central importance as a critical contribution to the debate. There is rigorous attention to the specifics of the racial element that distinguishes racism from other ideologies (not necessarily a feature of much of the work in this field). Moreover, this approach is useful both in its insistence on a historical method, and in its emphasis on the intersections between bodies of ideas as being essential to understanding the way racism works *as an ideology*. Racism emerges in practice, as inextricable from, but not reducible to, class relations, gender relations and nationalism. The focus is indeed on the material contexts in which racism is enacted, and less on the cultural expressions that racist ideas may take. The overlapping of -isms may be dizzying for those seeking conceptual clarity, but it rewards the reader interested in the dynamics of inequalities.

So if we want to use a definition, we should bear in mind the contributions above, and think like Miles, of an approach that involves a minimal covering of the bases, so that we require certain elements to be present, no matter what other ones are included. The International Council on Human Rights Protection, for example, uses this strategy in an information pamphlet:

> Racism thus has three elements: (i) it is a vision of society that is composed of inherently different groups; (ii) it includes an explicit or implicit belief that these different groups are unequal by nature – often enough based on a Darwinian interpretation of history; and (iii) it shapes and manipulates these ideas into a programme of political action. Combined, these three components give racism its force. (International Council on Human Rights Protection, 2000: 4–5)

I think racism is a phenomenon manifesting itself in such a diverse spectrum of ways across time and place, that to properly anchor it theoretically, we need something of this type, which stresses foundations. Moreover, I would go as far as to suggest using the plural, racisms, to denote the variations on the main themes.[1] My contribution to definitions therefore is to assert that *whatever else* a definition has, it must include all of the following three elements:

1. **A historical power relationship** in which, over time, groups are *racialised* (that is, treated as if specific characteristics were natural and innate to each member of the group).

2. **A set of ideas** [*ideology*] in which the human race is divisible into distinct 'races', each with specific natural characteristics.

3. **Forms of discrimination** flowing from this [*practices*] ranging from denial of access to resources through to mass murder.

One element of racism is a set of ideas; the other is a set of practices, and we shall explore these in the following chapters. The gap between the social and the biological is to be emphasised. Racist ideas can be at least partly comprehended by returning to this basic adage: racism tries to explain differences in the *social* world by reference to *biological*, that is, *natural* distinctions (see Box 1.2). Social scientists would argue that differences in the social world between groups are the result of historical, cultural and economic factors, that is, that the vast majority of the poor in any society are prevented collectively from advancing through the socio-economic hierarchy by factors largely outside the control of individuals. A racist argument would state that the poor are culturally inferior and genetically ill-equipped (through intelligence) for competition in the system we live in. Increasingly, as we will argue in Chapters 8 onwards, expressions of racialised difference have used 'culture' rather than 'nature' as their main vector. In discussions of immigration and multiculturalism, for example, people's collective culture is perceived as determining their behaviour, thus rendering them compatible or incompatible with the culture of the majority.

Box 1.2 Essentialism

A key relationship to be borne in mind is the one between the social and the natural worlds. When nature is employed to account for behaviour, the idea that this behaviour is unchanging, and therefore unchangeable, accompanies it. Identities are, in this perspective, constructed around an essence which cannot change.

This is a particular source of tension: social science is about mapping and studying change and continuity, while discriminatory bodies of ideas are about fixing identity in time, and arguing that there is an essence that does not change. Some of the arguments against women receiving the franchise in the nineteenth and early twentieth centuries, for example, stated that they were naturally too emotional and irrational to be entrusted with the serious business of voting. This illustrates how unchanging and unchangeable 'essences' are advanced as part and parcel of collective identities. We refer to this kind of argument as '*essentialist*', and the practice of arguing in this way as '*essentialism*'. However, some argue that essentialism serves a purpose for the oppressed, of aligning them against a common enemy and promoting solidarity. Post-colonial critic Gayatri Spivak (Adamson, 1986) famously talked of deploying 'strategic essentialism' as a tool for liberation. Yet it is seen as having limited use. In his seminal paper 'New Ethnicities', Stuart Hall (1988) argued that essentialist constructions of blackness, and by extension other racialised identities, were ultimately deleterious for anti-racist struggles.

Armed with this definition of elements of racism, and aware of its complexities, we can now turn to a brief historical orientation.

SOME KEY MOMENTS IN THE DEVELOPMENT OF THE IDEA OF 'RACE'

The purpose of this section is to establish that the three foundational aspects of racism outlined above change over time, and from place to place. The meanings attached to 'race' and the practices it endorses are also specific to different eras and contexts. This is an important stage in the argument, because when we come to discuss configurations of racism post the Second World War, the idea that it consists of physical-based representations can be countered, and the debate moved forward. In later chapters, we shall go into some of these topics in much more detail. The three moments selected here are: the sixteenth century, the Enlightenment and classification, and racial science.

Although there were of course empires before the European expansion into the Americas, Africa, Asia and Australasia, the phase of empire that began in the late fifteenth/early sixteenth century is the key one for students of 'race'. Spanish and Portuguese involvement in establishing colonies, the slave trade and the subsequent struggle for advantage that dragged in all the European powers had immense historical consequences. In the realm of racism, this was the period which witnessed the encounter between European and native that was to frame the colonial epoch. Such an encounter was frequently violent. The Europeans held technological and military advantage, as well as pre-existing ideas about classifying groups of people by virtue of criteria such as religiosity, property ownership, communal property, government, nomadic and sedentary lifestyles, farming techniques, etc. What can be observed over the four centuries of European expansion is the construction of a set of ideas about the native/indigenous people that placed them in a position of moral and cultural inferiority. This position was either borne out by, or led to (depending on how you interpreted such events), the corresponding political, economic and military inferiority institutionalised under the various forms of colonial rule.

The sixteenth century

References to 'race' prior to the eighteenth century were much more ambiguous than we might expect. Before there were 'black' and 'white' people, there were 'Christians' and 'Heathens'. In Christian symbolism, 'white' had positive connotations (purity), while 'black' had the opposite, hence the type of negative meanings attached to the term black. The evidence suggests that ideas about explaining difference frequently focused on religion, climate and labour status, without giving the concept of 'race' the detailed content that it was to receive later.

How is this to be reconciled with the fact that the European colonial enterprises (including the conquest of Ireland) and the Atlantic slave trade had been under way for centuries before the Enlightenment? Surely ideas about superiority and inferiority revolved around physical as well as religious difference? Physical difference was explained largely with reference to religion. This can be seen as a long-term process at its clearest in the 'sons of Ham' argument put forward by the Christian churches to justify the enslavement of Africans. The argument ran that the punishment given by God to Canaan (the son of Ham) in the Book of Genesis (9:18–27) involved servitude and blackness (to denote inferiority already present in the nature of servitude).

The frame of reference for educated Europeans until the Enlightenment was one in which:

- the dominant idea about origins was that everyone was descended from Adam and Eve (*monogenesis*), and signs on the body were read as judgements of God

- the idea of separate origins (*polygenesis*) was a minority one among biblical scholars, and responded to the obvious physical diversity of the human race.

However, nowhere in Genesis does it say that all Ham's descendants were to be dark-complexioned, nor that the form of their servitude would resemble in any way the bondage of the Israelites in the Old Testament. In fact, the punishment was restricted to Canaan. The idea of the sons of Ham was added to the very broad lines in scripture in a manoeuvre by clerical scholars over centuries. For our purposes, we should note also that ideas about the inequality of classes and genders were also given justification by particular interpretations of the Bible (as well as the holy books of other religions). The logic ran: Africans could be enslaved in large numbers, therefore their slavery was natural and permitted by God. This is because they were the 'sons of Ham', designated by God to be servants.

Moreover, the military and technological power of the European states was underwritten by the unchallenged assertion that the rest of the world's land and peoples were available to be exploited. In the 1493 Treaty of Tordesillas, the Pope divided the 'New World' into two areas: one for Spain to control, the other for Portugal.

However, the most pressing problem facing sixteenth-century colonists in the Spanish New World, for example, was the requirement of workers in the labour-intensive enterprise of extracting primary materials such as gold, diamonds and silver. The debate between Spanish intellectuals Las Casas and Sepulveda over the fate of Amerindians, held in Valladolid in 1550, encapsulated early humanist thought and imperial imperatives. If Amerindians in the New World had 'redeemable' souls, they could not be used as slave labour; if they hadn't, then their labour could be passed off as penance for sinful paganism. Little of this discourse focused on what Amerindians looked like, and until the end of the sixteenth century, when Amerindian resistance had been quelled, there was certainly no consensus that their cultures were universally less developed than Europe's. Even when there was, there existed no consensus that any such developmental lag was due to an innate incapacity to become civilised. Indeed, the model of civilising by example was still a defensible (although minority) position in North America and Ireland during the British colonisations of those places into the seventeenth century.

The Enlightenment and classification

Over the decades now referred to as 'the Enlightenment' (c.1720–1820), a diffuse pattern of ideas expressed in relation to a number of disciplines including biology, philosophy, history, economics and political science, were transformed into a coherent body of thought on humankind's place in the world, containing an elaborate typology of human beings. The Enlightenment thinkers were engaged in a wide-ranging project of categorisation. Man's place in creation was the object of study, and to this end, a series of classificatory tasks were carried out, and inventories of living things (including peoples) were constructed. The Swedish biologist Linnaeus, for example, wrote an epic work, *Systems of Nature* (1735, Eze, 1997: 10), in which the physical aspects of this project appear clearly (see also Chapter 5):

> Man, the last and best of created works, formed after the image of his Maker [...] is, by his wisdom alone, able to form just conclusions from such things as present themselves to his senses, which can only consist of bodies merely natural. Hence, the first step of wisdom is to know these bodies.

In constructing the 'great chain of being', the fulcrum of Enlightenment reasoning was Linnaeus' 'bodies merely natural': that is, a set of common-sense physical markers that expressed difference.

Indeed, a causal link was made by writers such as Hume, the Comte de Buffon and Hegel, between climate, 'phenotype' (that is, physical appearance), intellectual ability, and capacity for civilisation. In this view of the world, civilisation in its highest forms emanated from the version of human beings dwelling in the temperate zones of Europe and America: they were pale in complexion as a result, and as contemporary history showed, were capable of mastering both nature and other species of man through the use of technology. The differences between the categories of human being were explicable in terms of 'race' and culture: they were two sides of the same phenomenon. Physical appearance became a marker of cultural development, not just in the present, but also an indicator of the parameters of advancement (Eze, 1997).

There is a case that the 'Atlantic Protestant' Enlightenment was more conservative than its continental counterparts. There was less polygenist argument and it was certainly less critical of the Church than the French Enlightenment, which took place against the backdrop of the pre-revolutionary period.

However, ideas about racial difference, culture and climate gained legitimacy and became part of elite ideology in the Atlantic world in the context of the commodification of human beings in the Atlantic slave trade. The conclusions arrived at by many of the Western world's most notable minds acted to justify slavery after the event. Within the Enlightenment was also an attempt to place secular rationalism above religion as the dominant explanatory model for social phenomena. It did indeed achieve predominance, and the classifications proposed were honed in the industrial and scientific nineteenth century.

Racial science in the nineteenth century

Nineteenth-century scientists built on the groundwork laid by the Enlightenment thinkers. Science began to eclipse religion as the legitimate authority for explaining phenomena in both the natural and social worlds. As the century progressed, the ideas that had been put forward linking appearance, climate and culture became the assumptions upon which new work was carried out, rather than themselves being the subject of scholarly debate. By mid-century, the idea that the causal link existed and explained behaviour was no longer debatable; it was instead the starting point for further debates about politics and inequality. If people's abilities were genetically determined and unequal, what was the point of trying to overcome these inequalities? They were natural, normal and must be the basis for the social world (see Box 1.3).

Box 1.3   The racial natural sciences

Phrenology: the study of the structure of the skull (bumps and indentations) to determine a person's character and mental capacity. Promulgated by Franz-Joseph Gall (1758–1828), it correctly suggests that different parts of the brain are responsible for different mental functions. However, phrenology is based on the idea that these can be identified from the external surface, and people's behaviour thus predicted.

(Continued)

(Continued)

Craniology: the measurement of cranial features in order to classify people according to race, criminal temperament, intelligence, etc. The underlying assumption of craniology is that skull size and shape determine brain size, which determines such things as intelligence and the capacity for moral behaviour.

Anthropometry: the study of human body measurement for use in anthropological classification and comparison. In the nineteenth and early twentieth centuries, anthropometry was a pseudo-science used mainly to classify potential criminals by facial characteristics. For example, Cesare Lombroso's *L'uomo Delinquente* (1876) claimed that murderers have prominent jaws, and pickpockets have long hands and scanty beards. From its earliest uses in identifying criminal types, anthropometry was later used specifically to research physical differences between the races (see Chapter 5).

Moreover, nineteenth-century science and pseudo-science further developed the central thesis of the Enlightenment, namely that the body is the key to culture. Sciences that flowered in the nineteenth century, such as craniology, phrenology and later anthropometry, involved the measurement of various body parts and the construction of classificatory typologies from these findings. The new 'social' sciences such as sociology, ethnology and anthropology which emerged in the second half of the century were equally influenced by the obsession with physical appearance and the meanings attributed to them by their colleagues in the physical sciences, within the contexts of colonial expansion and plantation slavery.

The texts produced by these natural science disciplines demonstrate that the notion of dispassionate and disinterested scientific endeavour held no sway over those interested in 'race': the logic underlying experiments is erroneous and the interpretations of data are so weighed down under the assumption of explicit existing hierarchies based on racial difference that the findings are not compelling. American craniologist Samuel Morton (1839), for example, filled the skulls of various 'racial' types with lead pellets to measure their capacity. He emerged with a league table showing that English skulls had the largest capacity, followed by Native Americans, and then Black Americans. His inference was that the English mind was larger, more powerful and superior. Moreover, in addition to the inability of scientists to agree upon how many 'races' there actually were, and where the dividing lines between them lay (see Box 1.4), the cross-fertilisation of ideas and conclusions meant that the enterprise of racialising the population was carried out on the basis of a relatively small, scarcely challenged and scientifically dubious corpus. Yet the ideas contained in this corpus were referred to by contemporary scientists on both sides of the Atlantic, to the point where, by the middle of the nineteenth century, according to American historian Reginald Horsman, 'the inherent inequality of races was simply accepted as a scientific fact in America' (1981: 135). This is a crucial point: where the existence of unequal races passes from the area of discussion, to the area of accepted facts upon which further discussion is premised. French sociologist Pierre Bourdieu

(1977) calls the latter *doxa*. Once an idea has become doxa, it is all the more difficult to challenge.

It was in mid-century that the crude racial hierarchies became more nuanced. Robert Knox's *The Races of Men* (1850) and Gobineau's *Essai sur l'inégalité des races humaines* (1853–55) detailed the divisions within the 'white race', dividing it into categories including Aryan, Slavic and Celtic, for example. Although Gobineau's appraisal of the various groups was not wholly negative, the elaborate nature of his treatise made it a work of reference for 'Social Darwinists' later in the century and eugenicists in the next. Indeed, he prefigured the latter group's phobia about mixing. All great civilisations, he argued, were maintained by pure 'races', and when these mixed with 'degenerate races', the result was inevitable decline and fall.

Box 1.4   How many 'races' are there?

Even among those people engaged in the process of producing knowledge about 'races' through the seventeenth to the twentieth centuries, there is no consensus about where to place the lines dividing one 'race' from another, where to place the lines dividing the sub-races within each group, how many there are, and, indeed, what they are called.

For Linnaeus (1707–78) and Samuel Morton (1799–1851), there are four races: European, Asian, American, African.

For Johann Friedrich Blumenbach (1752–1840), there are five races: 'Caucasian' or 'white race'; the 'Mongolian' or 'yellow race'; the 'Malayan' or 'brown race'; the 'Negro', 'Ethiopian' or 'black race'; and the 'American' or 'red race'.

For Charles Pickering (1805–78) in *The Races of Men* (1854), there are eleven races: two white, three brown, four blackish-brown and two black.

For Joseph Arthur Comte de Gobineau (1816–82), there are three races: white, yellow and black.

Just for comparison, the US Census 2000 provides the opportunity for the US population to self-identify as members of at least 15 'races': white, black, American Indian, Asian Indian, Chinese, Filipino, Japanese, Korean, Vietnamese, Other Asian, Native Hawaiian, Guamanian or Chamorro, Samoan, Other Pacific Islander or 'some Other race'.

Like most official attempts to capture people's racial and/or ethnic identity, this schema is open to criticisms about consistency, among others. But one thing is clear. There is no consensus about how many 'races' there are, and never has been. This should not surprise us. 'Race' is a property of the social world and not of the natural world.

CONCLUSIONS

There has been no satisfactory definition of 'race' yet offered. This is because it is a social rather than natural phenomenon. However, even though it has no basis in biology, the division of the human race into 'races' has very serious and measurable impacts on people.

Racism is a multifaceted social phenomenon, with different levels and overlapping forms. It involves attitudes, actions, processes and unequal power relations. It is based on the interpretations of the idea of 'race', hierarchical social relations and the forms of discrimination that flow from this.

Racism is not confined to extreme cases, but is present in a whole continuum of social relations.

Specific societies see and do 'race' differently, and are organised in different ways. Therefore, discussions of racism *in the abstract*, without referring to particular conditions in particular places at particular times, are quite limiting. In this book, we will use the term racism*s* to acknowledge this diversity.

Having established a working definition of racisms and that there can be no definitive one for 'race', we shall now turn to the dominant concept for understanding how 'race' becomes salient in the contemporary sociology of racism: racialisation.

NOTE

1. This is not a new idea. The term 'racisms' appears in early work such as: Husbands (1987); Satzewitch (1987); Anthias (1990); Appiah (1990).

2 Racialisation

We saw in the previous chapter that there is no consensus on the precise meaning of 'race'. This is necessarily the case because those meanings are not fixed by nature, but are instead dependent on the historical, social and political context. This creates an epistemological problem for researchers (that is, one in which the status of knowledge is at the centre). As 'race' is a social but not biological category, what exactly is the subject of our investigation? If we want to understand the social meanings attached to 'race', rather than 'race' itself, then one solution is to use 'race' with inverted commas to highlight the concept's status as contingent and contested. Another is to adopt the approach whereby the researcher uses the concept to describe what the social actors see and talk about, namely race (with no inverted commas). A third option is to look at the social process by which 'race' comes to be meaningful in a given context.

The concept of racialisation is based on the idea that the object of study should not be 'race' itself, but the process by which it becomes meaningful in a particular context. In fact, racialisation has now become one of the key ways that academics make sense of the 'meanings of race'.

As we noted in Chapter 1, Small's (1994: 30) rationale for using the concept of racialisation is illustrative of this approach. Contrary to the focus on 'race relations', he maintains, which first 'assumes that "races" exist and then seeks to understand relations between them', racialisation directs our attention to 'how groups not previously defined as "races" have come to be defined in this way and assesses the various factors involved in such processes'. In this way, it has superseded the 'race relations' paradigm in both the UK and the USA. This has entailed a transition from studies that visualize society as groups of stratified 'races' engaging in competition over various resources ('race relations'), to those that seek to chart the ways in which race is constructed and made meaningful in the context of unequal power relations (racialisation).[1] In the twenty-first century, processes can result in 'race' becoming a salient factor in the way social resources are allocated, that is, racialised.

I: DIFFERENT UNDERSTANDINGS OF RACIALISATION[2]

As noted by Barot and Bird (2001), the term 'racialisation' has a history going back to the end of the nineteenth century, and has since engendered a diversity of understandings. These range from Fanon's interpretation of it as an equivalent of dehumanisation through Banton's suggestion that it describes Europeans' response to their encounter with people from the developing world from the fifteenth century onwards (Fanon, 1967; Banton, 1977). Moreover, Miles and

Brown assert that racialisation is a 'two-way process' (2003: 102), with which I concur – with qualifications.[3] Post-colonial scholar Patrick Wolfe (2002: 58) suggests distinguishing 'not too sharply, between race as concept – which, in this case, provided White men with an alibi – and the activation of that concept in the production of racial subjects, or racialisation. *Racialisation is an exercise of power in its own right, as opposed to a commentary that enables or facilitates a prior exercise of power*' (my emphasis).

There is thus a broad agreement that racialisation is something detrimental that *is done to* others as part of a power relationship. However, it should also be borne in mind that attaching meaning to one's own group as a 'race', and instilling this meaning with positive attributes (as we shall see below) is a common practice for subordinate groups seeking to defend and assert themselves collectively (see Spivak's strategic essentialism in the previous chapter). Clearly this form of valorization and the process that Banton, Fanon and Wolfe are talking about are not equivalents. Let's begin by looking a little more closely at what Frantz Fanon argues (Box 2.1).

Box 2.1   Frantz Fanon

Frantz Fanon was born in Martinique in 1925. He joined the Free French army in 1943 and remained in France after the end of the Second World War. There he studied psychology at the University of Lyon and published *Peau Noire, Masques Blancs* (Black Skin, White Masks) in 1952. He later went to Algeria, where he became Head of the Blida-Joinville psychiatric hospital in 1953. His experiences there finally pushed him to withdraw from his relationship with the French state and he joined the Algerian independence movement as an activist. His written work was published in a variety of French-language sources in the late 1950s and early 1960s. In 1960, he was diagnosed with leukaemia and wrote *Les Damnés de la Terre* (translated as *The Wretched of the Earth*, New York, 1967) in ten months. He died in 1961 and was buried with full honours by the Algerian state. In the decade following his death, his work was translated into English. Fanon is one of the key writers influencing the development of postcolonial studies, and particularly Edward Said and Homi Bhabha.

Fanon's theory was that in the binary world of European thought, the development of which ran contemporaneously with colonisation, blackness came to embody bad and whiteness good. This process of psychological (as well as material and social) domination creates the categories 'coloniser' and 'colonised', and people who are identified (and come to identify themselves) as 'black' and 'white'. As part of this relational process, he argues, the European created the 'negro' as a category of degraded humanity: a weak, irrational barbarian, incapable of self-government. For Fanon, this psychological process, in the context of physical domination and oppression, was tantamount to dehumanising the oppressed. His understanding of racialisation was that it comprised the effects of a process instigated to relieve Europeans of guilt and to make the colonised responsible for their own oppression, because in this world view, they are too weak to rule themselves. To be racialised was thus to have been dehumanised as part of the colonial process.

Michael Banton (1977: 18–19) also links racialisation to the colonial project, although his emphasis is far from Fanon's, on abstract levels:

> There was a process, which can be called racialisation, whereby a mode of categorisation was developed, applied tentatively in European historical writing and then, more confidently to the populations of the world.

Perhaps it might be useful to step back at this point from the historical specificity that is clearly emphasised by both Fanon and Banton. Not because their ideas are misleading, but because they suppose a certain amount of historical knowledge. Going back to a different starting point, David Skinner (2006: 460), writing on science's contribution to this discourse, argues simply that: '"Racialisation" refers to the social and political processes whereby racially distinct groups are constituted'. In science's case, he stresses that this is not in the past only but in contemporary science. Indeed, it is important to stress that while historical methods are an integral component of this approach (how else can change be identified?), the process of racialisation is ongoing and multifaceted. It is very much part of the contemporary world and unfinished business.

This contemporary presence of racialisation is one of the points raised by Miles (1987), whose championing of racialisation as an alternative and improved paradigm to that of 'race relations' is one of the drivers of debate. Miles maintains that racialisation is closely bound up with labour markets: in particular with both internal and international migration of workers and the ensuing imbalance of the power relations characterising modern capitalism. Whilst phenotype is an important marker in which groups get racialised in this process, it is not the crucial feature of a population: take the Irish in nineteenth-century Britain and the Eastern European Jews in early twentieth-century England. These, for example, demonstrate the intimacy of the way in which social relations of class and 'race' intertwine to attach a specific set of racial meanings to a given group's collective behaviour. This process, for Miles, is primarily to do with material context (that is, the labour market and perceived competition between workers). As can be seen from the examples in section II (below), the term has also been deployed outside of this specific context, so it would be true to say there is no consensus either about the usefulness of racialisation, nor about its exact meaning: much like the vast majority of concepts in the social sciences, which are basically models-in-progress that help us understand different aspects of the social world, however imperfectly.

Indeed, whatever problems remain, racialisation represents an essential sociological tool because it draws attention to the *process* of making 'race' relevant to a particular situation or context, and thus requires an examination of the precise circumstances in which this occurs: who the 'agents' are; who the actors are. In other words, who does what and how? It provides us with an alternative to the binaries of racist/anti-racist. Racialisation does not necessarily include ideas of intention, but it does reintroduce ideas of 'race' and force us to look hard enough at our subject to realise that making racial identities also necessitates other forms of social identification. It restores complexity to a world of either/or. It is never 'just' racism. Ali Rattansi concludes that:

> Racialisation tells us that racism is never simply racism, but always exists in complex imbrication with nation, ethnicity, class, gender and sexuality, and therefore a dismantling of racism also requires, simultaneously as well as in the long run, a strategy to reduce relevant class inequalities, forms of masculinity, nationalisms and other social features, whereby racisms are reproduced in particular sites. (2005: 296)

RACIALISATION AS AN IDEA

Racialisation appears therefore to be a deceptively difficult idea to pinpoint. On one hand, the theoretical backing is relatively straightforward. Racialisation represents a strategic withdrawal from the position that 'race' has anything other than a social existence. The next step is to argue that 'race' becomes a meaningful element in social relations because of the existing ideological funds. It is therefore a group-level theory reliant upon a particular understanding of 'ideology' (defined as a set of ideas that distort the representation of social relations). Arguing that there is a process with identifiable outcomes that can be labelled racialisation also necessitates historical perspectives. If not, how can it be proven that there is such a *process* (by definition, a long-term phenomenon)?

My main concerns about the current balance of understandings of racialisation are, first, the degree of intentionality conveyed, and second, the implicit assumption that racialisation is *always and only* something the dominant group does to the dominated one. For the architects of apartheid, **Jim Crow**[4] or the Final Solution, which could all be categorised as 'racial projects' (Omi and Winant, 1994), the separation, exploitation and/or elimination of people categorised as racially different was clearly the paramount driving force. However, it would be an error, as suggested in the previous chapter, to imagine extreme examples of racism as constituting the only ground for study and reflection. Racism does not always end in genocide or mass murder, and racialisation is not always an intended objective. Rather, it makes more sense to think of it as an intrinsic feature of the modern State's functions of classification, biopolitics and governance (Goldberg, 2000; Foucault, 2003. We shall return to this in Chapter 4).

I understand racialisation, then, to be a process by which 'race' becomes a salient element of social relationships, frequently as a normal part of the actions of the State and its agencies regarding other social actors. However, the door should be left open to the idea that racialisation may also be a reflexive act initiated toward an emancipatory end – as a form of group solidarity. As examples, we could cite the Black Power movement and the formation of online fora aimed at, and run by, particular minority groups such as the Chinese and Asians in Britain (as Parker and Song, 2006, argue; see below). So far, so good, yet this leaves us without any concrete examples that would help us understand and further critique racialisation. In the next section, we shall attempt to do this.

II: RACIALISATION IN PRACTICE

The contributions to Murji and Solomos' (2005a) collection on racialisation demonstrate a plethora of approaches deploying an array of historical, sociological and psychological methods within the sociology of racism, analysing what is constructed as an uneven and contingent process. That it is uneven is about the only thing that emerges as a consensus. Ann Phoenix (2005), for example, shows how young white Londoners understand their racial identities in relation to those of their black counterparts through experiences of space and place. Deploying ideas from relational psychology, she observes how they theorise themselves as raceless individuals vis-à-vis raced Others. Tony Kushner (2005) argues that racialisation is the most effective tool to take into account the complexity of the responses to Jewish immigration to England at the end of the nineteenth and early twentieth centuries (by both British Jews and Gentiles). He notes how culture, the residential spatial distribution and the employment practices and experiences of new Jewish immigrants became understood as evidence of racial difference which was threatening to the English working class in particular. David Goldberg (2005), deliberately attempting to avoid using racialisation as what he calls 'an analytic', settles on the specificities of the USA, and contends that a more appropriate way to understand the topic is the 'Americanization of race'. However, it is revealing that even his critique of racialisation entails the examination of a long-term set of interacting processes involving the interplay of structures and agencies, as does racialisation. These three examples are merely to hint at the dizzying array of applications of the idea of racialisation. What we shall do now is take three themes: citizenship and belonging, immigration and the reflexive construction of minority identities, and apply racialisation to their understanding. It is, of course, not the only way to understand this process but a revealing one.

Application 1: Citizenship and belonging

Membership of a nation state is not determined by simply excluding people explicitly on the grounds of 'race'. Historically, nations might be dominated by groups who come to define themselves and others racially. Yet in the contemporary world, direct reference to race as a criterion for membership is highly unusual, and the citizenship rules for many nations now clearly state that this is not a determining factor. When legislators set the rules, they are effectively answering the questions: who is a member of the national 'family', and where are the limits of the 'imagined community' (Anderson, 1983)? In this case, racialisation works through the way in which routes to membership are regulated. In terms of broad patterns, the outcome is always to favour the access of some, while placing obstacles in the way of others.

There have broadly speaking been four principal ways to access citizenship since it became a modern phenomenon (with passports, immigration legislation, etc.). Two of these relate to Roman legal concepts: *ius soli* and *ius sanguinis* (see Box 2.2). The others are through changing citizenship through having complied with a residence qualification (naturalization), or marriage to a national, possibly followed by a residential qualifying period (post-nuptial naturalisation).

<hr>

Box 2.2   Concepts of national belonging

The two concepts governing most nations' citizenship regulations are derived from Roman law. These are *ius soli* and *ius sanguinis*.

Ius soli refers to qualification for membership through birth within a given territory. *Ius sanguinis* refers to qualification through bloodlines (that is, parents' or grandparents' nationality). While most nations combine these routes in their contemporary legislation, this was not always the case. Until the 1970s, for example, French citizenship was gained through birth within France or one of its overseas *départements* or territories, regardless of parents' nationalities (*ius soli*), while the counter-case was Germany. The concept of German nationality is relatively new, as the country was only unified in 1871, then split again after the Second World War. It relied on the idea that German nationality was in the blood and expressed through culture. This meant in effect that after Germany's reunification in 1990, people of German culture who lived outside Germany (especially in Central and Eastern Europe) were granted German nationality (*ius sanguinis*). However, the children of immigrant workers from Southern and Eastern Europe and Turkey, who had been recruited to bolster the German workforce in the post-war period, and who had been born and educated in Germany, had no way of accessing German citizenship. This only changed in 2000 when a new piece of legislation guaranteed the right of access to nationality through birth in Germany and greatly facilitated naturalisation.

<hr>

The case of the United Kingdom illustrates that there can be movement between these two poles at different times, for different reasons. Until 1948, no distinctions were made in British law other than that between British national and foreign national (or 'alien'). People born in the vast British Empire were deemed British. Only in the post-war period did large-scale migration to Britain appear as a possibility, as the economy required a larger labour supply than could be satisfied from within the country. The 1948 Act distinguished between British, Commonwealth, Irish and Other nationals, without stipulating a difference in rights accruing to members of the first three groups. At this stage, citizenship was clearly based on *ius soli*.[5]

Between 1948 and the early 1960s, discussion of the pros and cons of immigration into Britain occurred at Cabinet level, and became a political issue. A minority of parliamentarians protested against continued 'coloured' immigration (from the former colonies in the West Indies, Africa and the Indian subcontinent). By 1962, immigrants from these areas had to have a work visa, for which there was a quota – the first attempt to limit specific streams of immigration (see above). The intensity of debates on immigration and what was referred to as 'race relations' in those days peaked in the late 1960s. In February 1968, the 'Kenyan Asians' crisis occurred. Indian families resident in Kenya and their Kenyan-born children were forced to leave the country by its new leaders. Faced with the prospect of the arrival of tens of thousands of so-called 'coloured' immigrants with British passports (which was perceived to be a potential cause of hostility toward the government), the British parliament passed a new piece of legislation with unheard-of rapidity: three days for all the readings of a Bill. The 1968 Commonwealth Immigrants Act deployed the concept of people with a 'substantial connection' to Britain. This was defined as having a parent or grandparent born in the UK. Those without this connection no longer had the right to automatic entry, residence and employment. The British passport-holding 'Kenyan Asians' were, at a stroke, rendered stateless. Note that the *ius soli* criterion now applied to a much smaller territory: the UK rather than the British Empire, or the UK and its former colonies. Here too is the introduction of the idea of 'patriality', or bloodlines (*ius sanguinis*) into the qualification for rights in Britain. However, all of this, and the ensuing 1971 Immigration Act referred only to immigration and not nationality per se. It was not until 1981, after the oil crisis that had reduced levels of primary immigration in Europe (and making family reunification a significant proportion of new immigration), that a British government incorporated the developments of the previous decades into citizenship legislation. The 1981 British Nationality Act set out three broad layers of citizenship (and is the only country's legislation that splits up rights accruing to nationals) and allows for eight hierarchical layers of rights-bearing nationals. At the top of this are those who were born in the UK on or after 1 January 1983, and whose parents are UK nationals or have permanent residence in the UK. So from a situation whereby all imperial subjects and those from the UK had been equally 'British' in legal terms until the 1960s, different criteria were steadily applied to people from areas of the world where non-white people were the vast majority, thus regulating employment opportunities and residence in the UK. Finally, in 1981, the pool from which British nationals with the full range of citizens' rights were drawn was fixed in order to limit access to it by people from the former empire. Take into consideration that after 1971 it had already become more difficult for former colonial subjects to enter Britain, making it less likely that they would form part of the pool of people born in the UK or who had permanent residence rights there. The intimacy of legislation with immigration and citizenship, as well as the racialised character of both, can thus be observed from this very short summary.

As a coda, when Britain signed up to the Single European Act in 1986, it granted freedom of residence and employment to the nationals (of whom the vast majority are white) of all the other EU member states. In terms of rights, this group is now second of the nine (previously eight) levels set out in the 1981 Nationality Act. So while legislation and regulations can be talked about as though they are 'neutral' administrative categories, they do, in practice, favour some groups over others, and the reasons why they do so can be traced to political decision making at particular historical moments.

Box 2.3   Japanese nationalism

Bruce Armstrong (1989) argues that over the period from the Meiji Restoration (1868) to the 1940s, Japanese nationalist ideology became racialised in different ways. The new unitary state needed a unifying language, a project, which developed around a combination of Shinto myths and the idea of the Japanese people as a family headed by the Emperor. Japanese culture was viewed as uniquely the property of those born into this family, and contrasted with other Asian people colonised in the Japanese empire (e.g. Taiwanese and Koreans) who were not phenotypically distinguishable from the Japanese. In the late 1800s and early 1900s, prominent intellectuals explained ideas of Japanese cultural and techno- logical specificity by biological traits, as the ideas of social Darwinism developed from the European imperial enterprise were adapted to explain Japan's military domination. The rea- sons given for Japan's superiority were both genetic and cultural, and indeed Japan's des- tiny was to lead and control. This was so ingrained by the 1940s that even though direct references to 'inferior races' in the Empire were dropped, in favour of 'Japan overseas', the underlying racialised distinction remained important. Moreover, the large number of Koreans resident in Japan (due to the forced labour migration that followed Japan's annex- ation of Korea in 1909) remained distinct from the Japanese nation. Japanese citizenship is based primarily on *ius sanguinis*, although it was possible for naturalisation, conditional upon taking Japanese names (which most Koreans found unacceptable).

Armstrong's example of Japan shows interaction with global discourses of colonialism (the master race dominating others and social Darwinism); the proximity of biological and cultural forms of racialisation; and the prominence of the idea of bloodlines in forging ties as part of the nation-building process. As we shall see in Chapter 4, nationalism and racism as ideas and practices are frequently this close.

Application 2: Immigration

Immigration policies are implemented using classificatory regimes that distin- guish between nationals and foreigners, and then between different categories of foreigners. Each category is afforded a set of rights and a set of criteria for entrance and activity within the national territory. These criteria are not based on 'race' in any obvious way, but by nationality. In the early twenty-first century, for the developed economies, the more stringent conditions are, as a general rule, placed on nationals of developing countries.

So when applied to immigration policies, what can racialisation mean? Firstly, the official framing of discourse on immigration alters dramatically over time. The first immigration laws per se in the world (in Canada and the USA) in the 1880s were clearly racist, explicitly either banning or taxing only Chinese migrants. In the run-up to these pieces of legislation, Chinese immigrants had been blamed for steal- ing employment from their North American hosts, and corrupting their morals.[6] Secondly, identifying a policy as 'racialising' does not exhaust its meanings. A policy does not only have one outcome: it can combine forms of de facto exclusion – 'race', class, religion. To take an example, the UK's Aliens' Bill at the beginning of the twentieth century was directed at stemming the flow of East European Jews into

Britain, yet the final wording of the Aliens Act, 1905, stipulated that immigration officials had the right to prevent disembarkation of passengers who had paid for the cheapest class of passage and could not show proof of funds to support themselves once in the country. In practice, the implementation of the Act thus targeted poorer East European Jews, excluding them on the basis of 'race', religion and class simultaneously, but not by one of these identities alone.

However, in Europe, more than a century later, there are no outright bans on nationals of any country immigrating, nor are there exclusions of people by racial group. Indeed, all the EU nations must have equality legislation outlawing racial discrimination and providing redress to its victims. Moreover, particular visa schemes for seasonal workers, at one end, up to professionals in specific areas of employment, such as medicine, computing and civil engineering at the other end of the spectrum, target workers from outside the EU. Added to this, with the accession of the new Central and Eastern European countries to the EU in 2004, there are hundreds of thousands more white migrant workers in the West. From this starting point, I would argue that the immigration policies of European Union member states have been racialised over the last few decades.

However, we should remember that racialisation does not depend on either/or logic. They do not either exclude people completely or not exclude them at all. Immigration policies favour some categories of people over others, which means allocating differential levels of resources and rights to them once they are on national territory. Secondly, it should be noted that public policy and attitudinal responses to phenomena are neither always national nor rational. They are not purely national, because debates on immigration are affected by external events, e.g. the collapse of the Berlin Wall in 1989, the ramifications of the 9/11 attacks outside the USA, the 7/7 bombings in Britain, wars that generate large flows of asylum seekers, etc. They are not purely rational because different kinds of migrants get lumped together in popular and political debates, so that people end up not knowing the differences between asylum seekers, people with refugee status and labour migrants. Public expectations of public policy are therefore confused. Moreover, other UK research shows that for many people, belonging to a nation corresponds primarily with skin colour, and anyone who is not white might at certain times be assumed to be a foreigner.

The example I am going to use is of the way in which recent changes to the European Union's immigration policy have impacted negatively on the majority of Third World nationals. There are four relevant phases involving an EU policy. The first is the creation of the Schengen Area.

In the mid-1980s, an attempt was made to implement one of the founding aims of the European Union, that is, freedom of goods and people across internal borders. The Schengen Treaty now has the support of the majority of EU states and it means freedom of movement for EU nationals across the borders of the signatory countries. A non-EU national can obtain a Schengen Visa allowing travel within all the Schengen states for a set period (usually three months for tourists). The second element of importance is the recognition by the Treaty of Maastricht (1992) of the reciprocal rights of EU nationals in each other's countries. Greek nationals, for example, can reside and work in the UK without having to obtain a visa. After paying into the UK social security system for the same period as UK nationals have to do in order to qualify, they can receive benefits. The combined effect of these two developments is the preferential treatment afforded EU nationals in this area. The knock-on effects are that as internal borders become less important, the efforts exerted on strengthening external borders have increased. The most relevant distinction in the twenty-first century EU immigration regime is not between Germans and Italians, nor between Portuguese and Irish, but between EU nationals and non-EU nationals (or as they are called in EU jargon, 'Third Country Nationals', or **TCNs**).

It is now more difficult than it was 30 years ago for non-EU nationals to gain access to this zone, as they have to comply with the criteria for a Schengen Visa (or a UK and Ireland one). One important criterion states that in order to change status (from a tourist to migrant worker or student, for example) the visa-holder must leave the Schengen Area and return to their country of normal residence, or failing that, the nearest with diplomatic representation. Therefore, the old ties of former colonies with the metropolis which had enabled people to move relatively easily to Britain, France, the Netherlands, Belgium, Spain and Portugal for instance, under preferential conditions, have now been minimised relative to those countries' new responsibilities to *each others'* nationals.

The third important element in the equation is the phenomenon of 'managed migration', which is where a state seeks to focus on particular types of migrant by creating special visa schemes, or granting extra benefits to migrants with a particular profile, or developing a points-based system that favours migrants with particular skills. While this usually targets highly skilled workers (typically those from the health care, IT and civil engineering sectors), enabling TCNs to enter and reside within the EU, the conditions attached to these visas are usually neither particularly liberal nor conducive to settlement and integration (being short-term and granting minimal benefits and family reunion rights). The fourth element is the expansion of the EU eastwards. As increasing numbers of people from economies with lower wage levels than Western Europe enter the EU labour market, this has the effect of further reducing the chances of TCNs finding legal work outside of the highly skilled visa schemes, and also may well provide competition for those indigenous ethnic minority groups within the EU member states who are disproportionately concentrated at the lower levels of the socio-economic structure. Some countries even specify that job opportunities must be filled or at least offered to an EU national before it is offered to a non-EU national. All in all, this has meant that since the mid-1980s, EU member states have turned away from using non-European labour, and at the same time, intergovernmental action has resulted in a two-tier immigration regime (see Chapter 10 for asylum) in which EU nationals have rights very close to those of citizens. Although this has developed over a 25-year period through a number of individual, connected routes, the overall effect has been the racialisation of the EU immigration regime. White European manual workers now have a vast advantage over non-white, non-European manual workers. Even if someone from the latter category somehow found a visa scheme that allowed him/her to work legally in an EU country, that person would need to live there continuously for a certain number of years (probably 5–8 depending on the country), qualify and wait for the naturalisation process to finish (which means years of paying taxes without having rights). Remember that living continuously in an EU country is hampered by the fact that visas are often quite short-term, maybe 12–24 months, and sometimes non-renewable. Therefore, nationality and employment status count much more than other criteria towards obtaining access to labour markets. The obstacles in front of non-EU workers are much stiffer in relation to those in front of their European counterparts.

Box 2.4   Immigration regimes

Until recently, the national State had determined all the criteria used for immigration control. Exceptions to this rule were the *international* conventions on refugees (1951 Geneva Convention and the 1967 New York Protocol), which set out the criteria for deciding who was a refugee and what status could be conferred on that person. While this is substantially true now, the European Union member states have de facto abrogated part of their right to operate their own criteria in respect of other member states' nationals. All EU member-state nationals have the right of residence and employment (and having qualified, the right to access welfare) in any member state (exceptions include nationals of the **A8** everywhere except the UK, Ireland and Sweden). The context is important because international agreements then become structured around different rights enjoyed by EU nationals on the one hand, and non-EU nationals (referred to as 'Third Country Nationals' or TCNs in the EU's bureaucratic phrase) on the other. Control is exerted by placing conditions on entry, and on what rights different nationals enjoy while within national territory. The variables include whether or not the migrant has to have an entry visa; whether he/she has adequate funds; for what purpose they are entering national territory; how long they are allowed to stay; what rights they will have while in the country; who is allowed to join them; whether they are allowed to come and go without obtaining a new visa, etc. Given that these appear to be purely administrative variables, how can the process become racialised? Answer: in the placing of different conditions on people from different places, and in the practice of immigration control. The immigration regime is not a level playing field: some nationals are subject to far greater scrutiny when they apply for visas than are others. Secondly, the officials who administer the various levels of immigration control (external, border and internal) are not all trained to the same level of professionalism and some seek to be more strenuous in their application with people from outside Europe and Europeans who are not white.

In effect, this means that it becomes harder for (non-white) non-EU nationals to enter and work legally in Europe, while it becomes easier for whites. I would argue that US, Canadian, Japanese and, to some extent, Australian and New Zealand nationals do not face the same levels of scrutiny. Non-EU nationals are subject to more stringent visa regimes and immigration controls. They are required to provide higher standards of proof of identity and solvency, and since the enlargement of the EU, they compete at a structural disadvantage with new A8 migrants in Ireland, Sweden and the UK, and in the future, will compete in the other EU member-states. Administrative regulations that are bureaucratically neutral are, in practice, discriminatory. This is a local story on local labour markets, but the rules are set at inter-governmental and member-state level.

Application 3: Self-racialisation of minority identities

While it is clear that a group of people *can* be racialised by dominant groups, and thus transformed into a subordinate social category by a combination of ideological, cultural and legislative practices, inhabiting this social location can sometimes be a rallying point for solidarity, campaigns against discrimination and more. In this section, I want to give two examples of this: the Black Power movement and the online fora 'British-born Chinese'[7] represent diverse efforts to base social movements and explorations of shared identity around the idea of belonging to a 'race'.

'Black Power'

For decades after the formal ending of slavery, African Americans endured institutionalised discrimination in employment, housing and education. They were also targeted for extra-legal punishments such as lynching and beatings for transgressing, or appearing to transgress the Jim Crow legislation and wider social codes that required them to behave in particular ways, and keep away from particular places. One of the legacies of the slavery and immediate post-abolition period was the social message that white was still superior to black. One of the ways in which this was expressed was for some to physically engineer a 'whitening' process using a range of products for the skin and hair.

By the mid-1960s, however, one stream of thought in black America was aimed at re-evaluating the term 'black', which had been so negatively endowed for so long, with new positive meanings. Malcolm X recounts in his autobiography (X and Haley, 1969) how part of his conversion to Islam in prison in the 1950s involved a fellow inmate encouraging him to sit with a dictionary and read through the entries for 'white' and 'black' respectively, and to compare the meanings attributed to them. The domination of white Americans, ran the argument, involved not only physical but mental subjugation, making black Americans internalise ideas of inferiority. These expressed themselves in many ways, and one of them was by straightening natural hair and avoiding association with anything African. On the contrary, black people who were part of the Black Power movement allowed their hair to grow naturally, in Afro styles, sometimes wore clothing and took names associated with their African heritage. The phrase 'Black is Beautiful' was coined in this period, and people who identified with this project eschewed cultural identification with white culture. The movement thus focused on both cultural resistance to the American norms, to one that encompassed political action, and on economic self-sufficiency rather than integration in white society, but based on black solidarity. A range of figures such as Robert Williams (who first coined the term 'Black Power'), Stokely Carmichael/Kwame Touré,[8] Malcolm X, Amiri Baraka and Angela Davis were nationally prominent in this diverse movement, whose vanguard was provided by the Black Panther Party. A key iconic moment came at the 1964 Olympic Games, when two American medallists in the 200m, Tommy Smith and John Carlos, gave the Black Power salute (outstretched right arm and clenched fist, wearing gloves) during the playing of the national anthem, an action that provoked hostile mainstream media coverage in America, as did the Black Power movement in general.

Although the Black Panther Party, for example, was effectively closed down by the authorities, and influential figures were killed or imprisoned, many ideas attached to Black Power itself, such as self-reliance, the nourishment of collective self-esteem and the need to focus on developing institutions and economic autonomy have survived. Not that these did not exist before the 1960s. Black Power was never a homogeneous movement, and some of its critics were also black Americans, who considered it a controversial anti-white path away from the policy of slow integration into mainstream America that they had been seeking over generations, and toward unnecessary confrontation. However, this does not detract from the idea that in this movement, the negative associations of blackness were confronted and an attempt was made to reverse them, to make black beautiful, in a context where it had not been, and to fix blackness as the rallying point from which people could campaign for equality.[9]

'BBC'

BBC does not only stand for the British Broadcasting Corporation but also 'British-born Chinese'. Indeed, David Parker and Miri Song (2006) argue that British-born Chinese online fora constitute an example of 'strategic essentialism' (see Box 1.2), and this process of 'reflexive racialisation' helps a community orientate itself around shared experiences involving being racialised as Chinese in Britain. Both parts of this equation are significant. While ties with mainland China, Hong Kong and the global Chinese diaspora are acknowledged and engaged in, there is also a sense that the concerns of the contributors to the fora are specifically grounded in typical BBC experiences, such as facing verbal abuse at restaurants run by family (2006: 583), and inadequate police responses to harassment. Parker and Song contend that: 'Taken together the messages constitute a collective witness to the experience of growing up as Chinese in Britain' (Ibid.: 584).

The argument is that the complexity of racialisation is the result of the two-tier process of homogenisation (finding commonality) of BBCs, and critically examining the internal differences of the group. The ongoing discussion thus opens up the possibility of *reflexively* developing a broad identity with a racial or ethnic basis, that is, critically examining it rather than taking it at face value. Yet this construction of British-born Chineseness, if you like, is openly recognised as *not* constituting a homogenising plea for biological and cultural authenticity. Indeed, some members reacted angrily to what was interpreted as exactly such a plea from an American-based Chinese website. For Parker and Song, the 'offline' context is one of racism experienced in particular settings that are familiar to the vast majority of BBCs, and this background 'overdetermines' (2006: 584) both the content and process of racialisation.

Moreover, the website has been the nucleus of campaigning against pernicious representations of the Chinese in Britain, as in the campaign to stop scapegoating Chinese food over the Foot and Mouth health scare in April 2001, as well as responses to other negative portrayals in the media. There are also offshoots of the site in civil society, with organisations representing BBCs developing out of it and sister websites appearing. It is also a site that is used as an obvious platform for groups campaigning around issues important to the membership. So, in this case, one of racialisation 'from below', as the authors put it, demonstrates that the social process does not always have to be carried out as a direct effect of power being exerted to frame representations of a minority and/or dominated group in a negative way. It can also be a response to this minority position: an attempt to create a space in which experiences are drawn on in order to resist dominant representations and forge a positive identity that recognises plurality within a specific social location.

CONCLUSION

There is no consensus over the exact meaning or significance of racialisation, but there is broad agreement that it represents a step forward from essentialised 'race relations', and that seeing identity as a process is a useful perspective.

There are a wide variety of meanings ranging from the largely descriptive one, the increasing salience of 'race' in a given context, to something imposed as a result of unequal power relations, on one hand and, on the other, something minority groups can do, on purpose, as part of their resistance struggles. Such diversity makes racialisation of limited use beyond a certain analytical level without qualification which I hope to have suggested above. Allowing the understanding of racialisation as potentially a two-way process also moves us away from the one-way street model and toward the conclusion that racialisation is not a crude *synonym* of racism, but a means by which racism can be made functional and sustained, as well as resisted.

NOTES

1. 'Race relations' are discussed by Kushner (2005) for the UK and Jacobson (1998) for the USA. Rex (1970) is the most complete sociological exposition in my opinion.
2. After this chapter, the reader may wish to turn to the excellent introductory essay by Karim Murji and John Solomos (2005b) that introduces their collection (Murji and Solomos, 2005a), and Rattansi's (2005) critical analysis in the same volume. While some of the argument presented above is covered, theirs goes into further detail about the distinctions made by more writers than I can deal with in an introductory text.
3. See Miles and Brown, 2003: 102. Moreover, subordinate groups can make claims for representation and solidarity based on positive interpretations of 'race' – the 'Irish Race conventions' in twentieth-century urban America and the Black Power movement, for example. However, such strategies are responses to unequal power relations.
4. Jim Crow was the name given to the raft of state laws, practices that institutionalised segregation and violence against African Americans during the post-slavery period until the passage of the Civil Rights Act (1876–1964). See the *Jim Crow History* website at: www.jimcrowhistory.org/
5. Foreign Secretary Lord Palmerston's well-known speech in the House of Commons on the 'Don Pacifico' incident in 1850 encapsulates this: 'As the Roman, in days of old, held himself free from indignity when he could say "Civis Romanus Sum" [I am a Roman citizen], so also a British subject in whatever land he may be, shall feel confident that the watchful eye and the strong arm of England will protect him against injustice and wrong'.
6. See California History Online (www.californiahistoricalsociety.org/timeline/chapter7/c003.html) accessed 30 March 2009; Saxton, 1990; Chang, 2004. In the USA, the Chinese Exclusion Act 1882 followed the victory of the California Workingmen's Party in 1879. In Canada, there were three pieces of legislation placing a 'head tax' on Chinese immigrants that was not applicable to other migrants. These were the Chinese Immigration Acts of 1885, 1900 and 1904. Finally, an act banning Chinese immigration outright was passed in 1947.
7. For British-born Chinese, see www.britishchineseonline.com/ – this is probably equally true of the 'Dim Sum' site (www.dimsum.co.uk/).
8. A text of a speech made at UC Berkeley in 1966 and an audio recording can be accessed at www.americanrhetoric.com/speeches/stokelycarmichaelblackpower.html
9. See Van Deburg (1992) and Joseph (2006) for examples of analyses, as well as the foundational text by Carmichael and Hamilton (1967).

3 'Race', Class and Gender

The main thrust of this book is to suggest ways in which racism (as defined in Chapter 1) can be conceptualised, analysed and understood. None of this is possible in a model where *only* 'race' matters in the construction of identities. Nobody is 'just' an Asian, a white or a black person. They are, for example, a middle-class professional Asian woman; a working-class white man; a lower middle-class black woman. If we separate these identities out, ignore, underplay or overplay elements of them, we miss the messy combinations that make social identities and racism such complex phenomena. 'Race, class, and gender', argue Anthias and Yuval-Davis (1993: 63–6) 'are not independent variables that can be tacked onto each other or separated at will … They are concrete social relations … enmeshed in each other'.

Around this simple and compelling argument lie the investments of scholars in vast corpuses that focus on class, or gender or 'race', or sometimes combinations of two of these. A smaller group have been committed to the theory of 'intersectionality', which combines class, gender and 'race'. In this chapter, we will look at some very basic outlines of class and gender. Then we will introduce the idea of *intersecting* identities and forms of discrimination (class, 'race' and gender), before examining some case studies drawn from scholars' work on these sources of identity. This will illustrate what is useful about understanding social relationships through the prism of multiple identities (used here to mean taking class, gender and 'race' into account as a normal practice).

CLASS AND GENDER

Both class and gender are, at the abstract level, hierarchical systems of global power relations with national, regional and more local configurations. However, there is a great deal of contestation about their relative significance. There is, for example, a corpus of writing on social class in the Marxist tradition, going back to the nineteenth century, whose focus has been on the over-riding salience of class as a system produced by the capitalist market economy in its various guises. In relation to *that* global set of relations, gender would appear as having limited significance, as its main role is to play a part in ordering the composition of the workforce and its reproduction (through accomplishing the domestic work that enables families and workers to continue their productive lives). However, the critique that has developed of academic work on class is based on the conditions of that work's production. The male-dominated academy, it is argued, prioritises class over gender, not necessarily because there is intrinsic merit in doing so, but because men hold relatively privileged position in what is termed a patriarchal society. The production of knowledge is a reflection of the existing power relations. In reference to women, Donna Haraway (1988: 578) comments that Marxist sociology has been impotent 'in historicizing anything women did that didn't qualify for a wage'. Indeed, one of the principal critiques of Marxist sociology is its relative neglect of areas of life outside the workplace. It is unsurprising then that some of the first attempts to demarcate territory in feminist studies included a focus on the home (as an unpaid workplace) in which housework is accomplished on a gendered basis (Oakley, 1974; Davis, 2001).

For scholars of racism, such as Omi and Winant, this over-emphasis on work has had the effect of turning racism into a secondary effect of class domination, or an 'epiphenomenon of other supposedly more fundamental categories of socio-political identity' (1994: 66). Engagements with racism from the Marxist tradition go back to the 1940s (Cox, 1948), through to Robinson's (1983) attempt to draw the two together in the American context. In relation to the UK, there is also Miles' (1982) reformulation of racialisation as the key concept to use, and the way he embeds it in the labour process, particularly migrant labour, from the nineteenth century onwards. San Juan (2001) notes that the left-wing line was always that racism is functional to capitalism because it hides and confuses the oppressive social relations of capitalism, turning worker against worker to the benefit of the capitalist class. The solution to racism is therefore the end of capitalist relations per se. Indeed, the problem for progressive sociologists studying racism is that most of the available models are either the very deterministic orthodox Marxist view (which reduces all other struggles ultimately to class), and those postmodern cultural-based explanations that have very limited historical specificity or relation to the material world. 'Race' can be deconstructed effectively in the world of ideas, but it still remains embedded in the material social relations of twenty-first century capitalism. In the Marxist tradition, the labour process and class relations are everything, and in the cultural turn, they account for virtually nothing.[1] The space in between these poles has been filled by attempts to set out 'race' as the primary organising principle in American life, in 'racial formation' (Omi and Winant, 1994) and 'critical race theory' (Delgado and Stefancic, 1995, 1997),[2] and by an absence of a particular unifying school in the UK. On the other side of the Atlantic, Charles Mills' work (2003) is the most recent engagement with Marxism from a 'critical race theory' scholar. He sets out very clear arguments (2003: 156–60) for 'race', rather than class, to be considered the key social division in the USA. His claim is that, among other things, 'race' is 'the stable reference for identifying the "them" and "us" which override all other "thems" and "us's"' (ibid.: 157). Gender is not the most acute contradiction because the majority of American women benefit from the family structures of whiteness, and in terms of gender relations, 'sleep with the enemy'. Whiteness provides a cognitive and experiental shell protecting white people against knowing about discrimination due to the largely segregated living patterns in the USA. The radical European political tradition, he maintains, was forged in a context where 'race' was about the interface with the colonial world, and is thus not equipped to deal with the New World context of the Americas, constructed upon the collective theft of land, slavery and a racialised system of white supremacy. I am expecting that these terms and ways of talking about the topic will be difficult to accept for some of the American readers, which in fact underscores Mills' allied assertion that the 'dominant categories' of the 'white cognitive universe … block apprehension of the centrality of race' (ibid.).[3] Mills' provocative claims continue with his argument that there is no universal rule of symmetry between different forms of oppression (class, gender and race). Using the example of Nazi Germany, he contends that in *that* case, racial oppression was worse than the other two. 'So the point is', he contends,'that the relative badness of oppressions in a given country is an empirical matter to be settled by looking at its structure' (ibid.: 166). The causal relationships and genealogical roots of forms of oppression do not determine 'continuing causal preeminence' (ibid.: 164), so although it could be argued that capitalism brought racism into being, this does not mean that in every place at every moment, class is the most potent form of oppression. Moreover, Mills has continued his attempt to theorise the institutional exclusion and deprioritisation of racism within academia and American political discourse by collaboration with key political theorist Carole Pateman (Mills and Pateman, 2007) who has pursued a similar line of argument in relation to gender, with the *Sexual Contract* (1988). Their arguments derive from the understanding that the formal Enlightenment social democratic contract of rights was empirically rather than theoretically exclusive. It was based on a rigidly hierarchical set of norms in which both all women and all black people were chattel. One of their insights is that not only does the ensuing normative exclusion impact on society in a way that produces disadvantage for the marginalised groups, but it also generates advantages for the dominant group, whether individuals are in support of it or not. In other words, white people benefit from racism even if they disagree with it because the way society functions at a collective level is not affected by their personal beliefs: there are different levels of action. All men benefit from sexism in the same way. The amount by which people benefit depends on other factors, but this principle is a challenge to the theories of racism and sexism as merely forms of individual prejudice. The second challenge is to the way gender and 'race' are discounted in mainstream models of social theory, particularly that of dealing with rights, which seem to suppose that both racism and sexism are relics of the past. Indeed, it is the critique of mainstream models of social sciences that brings us to the connected sets of arguments about the status of the concept 'woman'.

THE CRITIQUE OF 'WESTERN' FEMINISM

The 1970s saw the rise of 'women's studies' and 'gender studies', both as courses at universities and as corpuses of academic theory. The feminist critique of mainstream sociology was that it ignored women's experiences, and focused on areas of male dominance such as employment. A feminist perspective developed, whose minimum parameters were, according to Ann Denis (2008), that:

- women are legitimate subjects of study
- their identities, like those of men, are socially constructed rather than biologically determined

- as a social category, they have been subordinated (at least since private property as a concept came into existence)

- there is a commitment to social change aimed at the elimination of women's subordination.

The point for feminist sociologists was to examine social phenomena from a feminist 'standpoint' (a methodological stance that relies on the position of the researcher as having experienced social relations from a particular, relevant perspective (Haraway, 1988; Harding, 1991)). This recognises that all positions are partial, rather than one being impartial and objective. The experience of living out social inequalities means that standpoints differ from one person to another, with a pattern of experiences shaping particular positions, such as 'woman'. Standpoint feminism then is aimed at injecting knowledge of women's experiences into research problematics, rather than imagining that it will make research less objective to incorporate their points of view.

By the late 1970s, however (Combahee River Collective, 1977/1982), the various streams of feminism (e.g. liberal, radical, Marxist) were being criticised in a similar way to that in which mainstream sociology had been critiqued. In other words, it represented the experiences and priorities of the dominant minority, in this case, white, middle-class (straight and able-bodied) women.

Alongside this raised profile, however, flowed a stream of criticism from scholars and activists within the feminist movement in its broadest sense. These concerns were voiced by women 'of color' in the USA and 'black' women in the UK (with the broader meaning of black in use at that time, covering all minority groups). The critique identified a discrepancy between the priorities of 'Western' feminism and those of minority groups. Historically, the feminist movement had campaigned for a set of rights: freedom from chattel status, to own property, reproductive rights, access to higher education, employment, etc. Because of the hierarchical way in which these societies were structured, the priorities of minority women were different, geared toward combating racism; freedom from slavery, from low-paid work, from sexual abuse by employers; and in the developing world, freedom and justice, bread and peace.

Box 3.1   Background to the split in the US women's suffrage movement

The women's suffrage movement officially began in 1849 at the Seneca Falls (NY) congress on the abolition of slavery. The campaign for the vote for women (woman suffrage) thus developed out of the movement to abolish slavery. Indeed, some people were part of both organisations, and the social background of activists in both was often similar: professional, wealthy and with religious leanings. In 1865, after the Civil War, with the abolitionists' objective achieved, women's rights campaigners expected to resume where they had left off, with the added support of the former abolitionists. However, the Fourteenth Amendment then led to a split within the women's rights movement. Section 2 of the Fourteenth Amendment proposed full voting rights for all males (not just whites). Women's rights activists were therefore split between opposing the amendment in order to argue for votes for women, or supporting it, and placing white women behind African American men in the pecking order of voting rights. Campaigners such as Julia Ward Howe, Frederick Douglass and Lucy Stone backed the Fourteenth Amendment, while others like Susan B. Anthony and Elizabeth Cady Stanton led the opposition. After it had been ratified, they unsuccessfully pressed for an amendment introducing universal suffrage.

Supporters of each side of the argument viewed the others as having betrayed a principle of equality (either racial or gender equality) and the split remained for decades. This tension, argue critics like bell hooks (1982), Patricia Giddings (1984) and Angela Davis (2001), characterised the women's movement well into the contemporary period.

Moreover, not only was this discrepancy the subject of debate, but the social relations of the world outside the feminist movement were, in the eyes of the critics, being reproduced within it. bell hooks' (1982) historical study of the American feminist organisation (which was referred to as 'woman suffrage' – see Box 3.1) excluded black women (although it fêted high-profile black men, such as Frederick Douglass). The two simultaneously functioning hierarchies were those of gender and 'race', and hooks argues that American feminists opted for the solidarity of 'race' over that of gender. Women workers in the same industries and workplaces as black women segregated the latter; the priorities of the mainstream movement catered for white middle-class women who formed the core of the movement; yet, ideologically, the movement projected the image of a bloc of homogeneous sisterhood. For hooks, this homogeneity is based on white being the norm. She illustrates this by reference to a book on women in the Southern States (hooks, 1982: 137–8) – Julia Cherry Spruill's *Women's Life and Work in the Southern Colonies* (1938). As she finds no reference to black women in the book, hooks contends that the title should begin with the word 'white', rather than assume that white women's experiences are the only or most important set. However, hooks observes that if an author had written a book focusing only on black women (as opposed to only white women), the publisher would have insisted on a title beginning with 'Black'.

The American feminist movement failed to manage the tension between the hierarchies of 'race' and gender (as well as class). It was imperative for the strategic purposes of the feminist movement for it to be recognised as respectable (which meant middle class): 'Negative attitudes toward black women were the result of prevailing racist-sexist stereotypes that portrayed black women as morally impure. Many white women felt that their status as ladies would be undermined were they to associate with black women' (hooks, 1982: 130). Indeed, the theme of the critiques that hooks so concisely summarises is the ongoing gap between lip-service paid to equality for all women and the practical sidelining of women of colour within the movement. 'The women's rights movement', she concludes, 'had not drawn black and white women close together. Instead, it exposed the fact that white women were not willing to relinquish their support of white supremacy to support the interests of all women' (ibid.: 136).

In Britain, similar notes of frustration are sounded by Carby (1982) and Amos and Parmar (1984). The latter point to the family, sexuality and the women's peace movement in the early 1980s as three arenas illustrating the mismatch of priorities and the underlying racist assumptions of mainstream feminism – what they call 'the "imperial" nature of feminist thought and practice' (Amos and Parmar, 1984: 10). They contend that black and Asian families are constructed as deviant (through the figures of dominant single mothers and submissive women in arranged marriages respectively). In terms of sexuality and reproduction, it is noted that white British feminism (like the American version) has been complicit with eugenics and imperialism, through support for population control and of uncritically accepting ideas of blackness as sexual threat (from men and women). The Women's Peace movement, which was significant in the first half of the 1980s, is seen as nationalist and parochial, reliant on defending 'our country', in which minority women have to struggle to justify their presence, and not being interested in wider global offshoots of the nuclear industry with its impacts on developing world nations.

Along the same lines, in what is now one of the key texts of postcolonial studies, Mohanty (1988) argues forcefully that the construction of third-world women in the Western academy is of people 'outside history'. They appear as a pre-constituted product of backward culture. The reference point is Western women (usually middle class), against whose norms putative distance is measured. One of the key points Mohanty makes is that Western feminism is often stuck in a binary set of understandings that fail to grasp the complexity of the social realities experienced by women from the developing world. She critiques the practice of understanding things as signs that can only be read in one way (such as wearing the veil, which is only ever interpreted as a sign of oppression – see Delphy (2006) and Chapter 11) and the practice of universalising social relations by understanding them from a white European women's perspective and assuming homogeneity.

However, by the mid-1990s, we find Avtar Brah (1996) still arguing against the homogenisation of women and especially that of developing-world women. She uses the 1991 Gulf War as an example of how gendered experience is also raced and how women are not a unitary subject. She contrasts European ex-patriates who lose property in Kuwait with immigrant Asian women forced into the Kuwaiti desert, and then out of employment. This has an important impact on remittances, etc., thus worsening the economic position of those women's families in the country of origin.

She goes on to make two sets of distinctions about how 'difference' is conceptualised. First, she separates social relations from social position. Even though black and white women are nurses in Britain, for example, and thus linked by occupation and income, their experiences of exploitation (status) are different. Second, there is what she calls 'experiential diversity', that is, the distinctiveness of collective experience contrasted with personal experience, which may exemplify or contradict the collective experience, depending on other factors. Cultural difference, she contends, is open to both positive and negative uses. It is more usefully conceptualised as a process than a static set of artefacts. There can be opposition to various forms of cultural practice from within the culture. To illustrate this, she gives the example that you can be against *suttee* without being 'positioned within those colonial and postcolonial discourses which represent such practices as symbols of inherent barbarism of Indian cultures' (Brah, 1996: 92). So, just as feminists had once argued that male standpoints had become the invisible norm, and were partial, these contesting voices have been raising questions about the standpoints of the female protagonists in debates about what it means to resist sexism. One epistemological solution to the problem of standpoint is that of the approach called 'intersectionality'.

Intersectionality: Theory and methods

The term 'intersectionality', coined by Kimberlé Crenshaw in her essay, *Mapping the Margins* (1991),[4] addresses the articulation of class, gender, language and immigration status. Over the decades since this term was first deployed, there has been an uneven take-up of the methods internationally (Denis, 2008) with American, then UK and Canadian and more recently French scholars trying to adopt its tenets. These, put very briefly, state that focusing on one of 'race' (or ethnicity), class or gender alone cannot capture the diversity of women's experiences. This perspective was adopted most readily by African American academics, indeed Angela Davis' pioneering *Women, Race and Class* (2001) prefigures this without using the term 'intersectionality' itself.

Although theoretical studies and discussions of intersectionality are a growing corpus, there is relatively little critical attention paid to methodology within that strand. Leslie McCall's (2005) systematic analysis of the strands of intersectional theory is worth looking at in order to help us gain purchase on this area. Her analysis can be loosely broken down into the two principal 'complex' methodologies she identifies. These are 'anti-categorical' and 'intra-categorical'.

'Anti-categorical complexity' is aimed at *deconstructing* the abstract analytical categories used in discussions of discrimination and identity such as 'gender', 'masculinity', 'femininity', etc. The constructed nature of categories can be demonstrated with the various methods drawn from the disciplines such as anthropology and sociology. This involves a degree of reflexivity about representing people as being part of categories at all. The idea is to leave open the question of what the categories mean, and not to take them for granted as social realities.

However, argues McCall, the beginnings of intersectionality came with 'intra-categorical complexity'. This method 'interrogates the boundary-making and boundary-defining process itself', and focuses on 'particular social groups at neglected points of intersection' (McCall, 2005: 1773–4). Examples of these are the works of Davis, Crenshaw and Hill-Collins cited below. The intersection is often explored from the perspective of an individual, which is then used to illustrate the broader collective experience of this particular set of intersections. There may also be comparative work comparing classed experiences of 'race' or 'raced' experiences of gender. However, there is also a recognition that categories might be restrictive and oppressive in their own right. 'The point is not to deny the importance – both material and discursive – of categories, but to focus on the process by which they are produced, experienced, reproduced, and resisted in everyday life' (ibid.: 1783).

McCall then goes on to advocate the 'inter-categorical' approach, which is based on a strategic use of analytical categories. This is a quantitative method, and unlike the other two approaches, it deploys a statistical analysis to compare a variety of groups. It analyses the full range of dimensions of multiple categories rather than one location at a specific intersection. The point of this is to determine whether at local levels (as this analysis is done in terms of particular cities (McCall, 2001a, 2001b)), there is actual economic advantage, and to find out which groups are specifically advantaged and disadvantaged vis-à-vis each other. She argues that using this method enables us to see that different cities demonstrate different patterns of inequalities; some more class-based, some more gender-based, etc. McCall's reliance on statistical data, however, is unrepresentative of intersectional work, which on the whole, tends to be more qualitative and theoretical.

Patricia Hill-Collins (1990) sets out the three propositions that underpin what she terms 'black feminist thought', which can be seen as one version of intersectionality:

- The forms of oppression experienced as 'race', class, gender, sexuality and nation are linked to each other.

- Negative definitions of black womanhood imposed from outside have acted as obstacles to black women's development.

- The world views created by black women have been generated out of the need for self-definition, and with the aim of working toward social justice.

Hill-Collins argues, with reason, that this constitutes 'a fundamental paradigmatic shift in how we think about oppression' (1990: 221). Where it gets challenging for people involved in progressive struggles, however, is when she talks about people's multiple positioning within different frames of domination:

> Although most individuals have little difficulty identifying their own victimization within some major system of oppression – whether it be by race, social class, religion, physical ability, sexual orientation, ethnicity, age or gender – they typically fail to see how their thoughts and actions uphold someone else's subordination ... In essence, each group identifies the oppression with which it feels most comfortable as being fundamental and classifies all others as being of lesser importance. Oppression is filled with such contradictions because these approaches fail to recognize that a matrix of domination contains few pure victims or oppressors. Each individual derives varying amounts of penalty and privilege from the multiple systems of oppression which frame everyone's lives. (ibid.: 230)

Moreover, a different way of thinking about forms of oppression is required because they not only all function simultaneously, but are mutually dependent. This is why Hill-Collins advocates thinking in terms of 'both/and', rather than the dichotomous 'either/or' model. 'No one group has a clear angle of vision', she contends. 'No one group possesses the theory or methodology that allows it to discover the absolute "truth" or, worse yet, proclaim its theories and methodologies as the universal norm evaluating other groups' experiences' (ibid.: 237)

This set of interlocking oppressions (a 'matrix') then alters the paradigm in which 'race', class and gender, for example, are understood to operate *independently*. The emphasis on reflexivity pushes actors to identify themselves as oppressing as well as oppressed on different lines, and explicitly calls for dialogue and empathy: a radical shift. How does this play out? We can see by looking at Crenshaw's original (1991) essay.

Crenshaw discusses domestic violence as inscribed in the matrix described above. 'The problem with identity politics', she contends, 'is not that it fails to transcend difference, as some critics charge, but rather the opposite – that it frequently conflates or ignores intra-group differences. In the context of violence against women, this elision of difference is problematic, fundamentally because the violence that many women experience is often shaped by other dimensions of their identities, such as race and class' (1991: 1242) Crenshaw illustrates this in the second half of the article, by recounting the story of an immigrant Latina woman who was unable to find a place in a domestic violence shelter (ibid.: 1262–4). The shelter refused to take non-Anglophone clients, and she wanted to bring her young son, who would translate for her. However, it was against the shelter's policy of not allowing clients to be isolated by language difficulties.

Moreover, her immigration status compounded the position of powerlessness she was in. The woman was obliged to stay married in order to be able to apply for US citizenship. The 1990 amendments to the marriage fraud provisions of the Immigration and Nationality Act meant: 'a person who immigrated to the United States to marry a United States citizen or permanent resident had to remain "properly" married for two years before applying for permanent resident status, at which time applications for the immigrant's permanent status were required by both spouses. Predictably, under these circumstances, many immigrant women were reluctant to leave even the most abusive of partners for fear of being deported. When faced with the choice between protection from their batterers and protection against deportation, many immigrant women chose the latter' (ibid.: 1247).

Eventually, the woman did not call back to the shelter about being housed and nothing more was heard of her. She had previously reported living on the street and being mugged, so the shelter had failed in its mission to protect her. In this case, the complexity of gender, class, language group and immigration status meant there were fewer choices available to her, and these had more detrimental outcomes.

Intersectional analyses: from domestic work to the global sex trade

As we have seen, part of critical feminist epistemology involves stressing that employment is not the only starting point for studies of oppression. Yet focusing squarely on employment however can be just as revealing about class, 'race' and gender. My argument is not either/or, but both/and. Angela Davis' chapter on black women's employment in the post-abolition period (2001: 87–98) demonstrates the enduring power of categories developed under one structure (the slave mode of production) to influence people's lives even after that structure has been dismantled. Often, the abolition of slavery in various countries is simply understood as a point where everything changed for the better in terms of the formerly enslaved people's life chances. The reality was very different. In the British Caribbean, the sugar plantation owners attempted to keep the former slaves dependent on the plantation system for an income by making it difficult for them to create a viable peasantry. In the USA, similar strategies were deployed, all aimed at making former slaves into dependent and often indebted peasant farmers reliant on their relationship to land. Moreover, the practice of arresting black people on spurious charges and renting them out as convict labour (the 'convict lease system') was widespread in the post-abolition Southern States. In this context, as people left the land to work in cities, what were the employment options available for black Americans? Of the 2.7 million black women over 10 years of age counted in the 1890 Census, more than a million were in paid employment. Their distribution is presented in Table 3.1.

Table 3.1 **Percentage of African American women in various forms of employment at the 1890 Census**

Agriculture	Household domestic service	Laundries	Manufacturing	Others
38.7	30.8	15.6	2.8	12.1

Davis argues that the main types of work that African American women did was similar to the work they had carried out under slavery: agricultural and domestic. Also, they were often subject to sexual advances from the white men for whom they worked. This cultural aspect, in which white men could force themselves on black women with impunity, is another continuation of slavery-period relations. She cites a domestic worker from Georgia in 1912:

> I believe nearly all white men take, and expect to take, liberties with their colored female servants – not only the fathers but in many cases the sons also. Those servants who rebel against such familiarity must either leave or expect a mighty hard time, if they stay. (Aptheker, 1946: 49, cited by A. Davis, 2001: 92)

By 1890, domestic service was the largest single occupation for black men and women in 32 of the 48 states of the USA, while an 1899 study of Pennsylvania found that 60 per cent of black workers in total (and 91 per cent of women) were employed in some kind of domestic service. These women worked long hours in an unregulated, virtually non-unionised sector, in which the only competition was newly arrived European immigrant women, the only other group who would perform this kind of low-status labour. The obstacles before women seeking better-paid work in other industries were formidable. Over the 1890–1940 period, the figures show that there was little mobility. The 1940 Census shows that 59.5 per cent of black women were still in domestic service with another 10.5 per cent in other service occupations. While the Second World War altered the conditions of entry and movement within the labour force for all women, the pattern was not completely broken. As late as 1960, more than one-third of black women were in domestic service and another 20 per cent were in other forms of service employment (A. Davis, 2001: 97–8). Davis maintains that this concentration of black women in domestic and other forms of service demonstrated that genuine emancipation was far from being achieved, as women were still tied into slavery-period social relations, and blackness was still synonymous with 'servant'.

Intersectionality is not only about women, of course. Gendered roles and structural positions belong to men and women. Lois Weis' work analyses the transition from the types of masculine identities derived from being the breadwinner in a single income family in the post-war period (because of the prevalence of jobs for life in heavy industry), to those available for men in the post-industrial landscape of service-sector and casualised employment. She argues (2006) that the re-making of this segment of the working class is accomplished through ongoing changes in gender relations. Comparing the ideas about gender roles from her interviewees in 1985 (then aged 15–16) and in 2001 (aged 30–31), she concludes that the gender regime has been transformed. The dominant model of the mid-1980s involved a continuation of the heavy industry job, the family constructed around male employment, and for younger men, a certain lack of accountability and responsibilities. By the beginning of the twenty-first century, men in 'settled' jobs are those who no longer correspond to the hard-living stereotype of the 1980s, but those employed in 'feminised' areas (hospital work) or whose work is based on going back to adult education to learn new skills. They also share childcare with a partner in similarly paid work. Talking of one of her two exemplary case studies, she concludes that 'John's "stable" or "settled" new working-class existence, which he values highly, is wholly dependent upon his breaking away from hegemonically-constructed white male masculinity' (Weis, 2006: 268).

This is contrasted with the traditional male breadwinner's guarantee of his sacrifice made for provision (of food, clothes, cleaning, etc.). There are no men in Weis' sample who think gender roles have stayed the same, yet a few cling to the construction of self that is based on strength and unaccountability. The example in her article is 'Clint', who has failed to engage either with the world of work, or a stable emotional life. He lives between parents' and girlfriend's homes, has a tenuous relation to the labour market, and is not accountable to anyone. He recounts how he spent $15,000 on a motorbike instead of on a house, as his girlfriend had suggested, and predicts the imminent demise of his relationship with her. This is a minority position, however, with most men negotiating childcare and work roles with a partner in an equal position. Weis writes: 'Ironically … while the old industrial order rested upon a stable gender regime, it is the unsteady fulcrum of gender (roles, definitions, and hierarchy) that lies at the very heart of reconstituted white working-class life' (ibid.: 271).

Indeed, working-class identities can also be viewed using an intersectional frame that seeks to identify their gendered dimension. This project might not always be as easy to accomplish, given the dominance of frameworks that reject class as a useful point of focus, as in the UK since the late 1980s. Beverley Skeggs' work with young working-class women in the north-west of England shows that the fraught relationship of gender to class is characterised by rejection and dis-identification, as the women realise that they are being judged by standards they feel are unfeasible (1997). They rarely embrace working-class identity unequivo-cally. However, Skeggs goes on to argue (2005) that in the 1990s and 2000s, the place that class used to occupy has been usurped by other discourses covering ostensibly the same object, but which are to do mainly with culture (especially visual and popular culture). In this domain, class values are represented in the middle-class norms from which judgements are made about working-class bodies and habits. The term 'Chav' embodies this switch to culture, and for Haywood and Yar (2006: 16), it is 'a term of intense class-based abhorrence'. For Skeggs and Wood (2008), this process is particularly visible in contemporary real-ity television show formats in which working-class subjects are made to reflect upon their behaviour and 'improve' it in order to attain middle-class norms of restraint and femininity. The drama for the audience is the struggle of the working-class body to shake off its association with working-class culture, and the fre-quent inability to accomplish this goal. This is presented as a personal failure, and the social world of economics and material obstacles remains cut off from the personal 'journey' in which the participants of the shows engage. Skeggs' argument is that in early twenty-first century Britain, the focus on culture is a proxy for class.

This substitution of culture for class emerges strongly from Imogen Tyler's study of the use of the term 'Chav' as a way to say 'underclass' in contemporary Britain (2008). She demonstrates the gendered nature of the process of division, and how it intersects with racialisation. The subjects of this discourse are white working-class British people. In this context, the term 'underclass' has been used relatively little in public and academic discourse since the mid-1990s. The use of 'Chav' and its regional variations since the early twenty-first century has now become, for Tyler, 'a ubiquitous term of abuse for white working-class subjects' (2008: 17). She argues that the Chav has become a representative 'figure' of clas-sification accumulating power through repetition. The disgust that is a central feature of class relations (Ahmed, 2004; Lawler, 2005) is attached to bodies through talking about culture. Laughter and disgust create a community of non-Chavs, distinguished by not sharing the excessive and tasteless consumption of Chavs, that is white poor people who are not normal, but rendered abnormal in the constant repetition of the themes that 'make' the Chav. They are instead 'hypervisible "filthy whites"' (ibid.: 25). Moreover, the bodies of Chavettes (female Chavs) are most explicitly objects of disgust. The figure of the Chavette begins to absorb a number of 'disgusting' practices: wearing garish and excessive clothes, revealing too much flesh, being overly sexualised, having children out of wedlock and frequent 'race' mixing. Tyler suggests that one reading is also that the Chavette's extra-fecund and sexualised body is read as a mirror of middle-class, middle-aged and possibly infertile women who have put their careers first:

> Indeed, the disgust for and fascinated obsession with the Chav mum's 'easy fertility' is bound up with a set of social angst about infertility amongst middle-class women, a group continually chastised for 'putting career over motherhood' and 'leaving it too late' to have children. The figure of the Chav mum not only mocks poor white teenage mothers but also challenges middle-class women to face their 'reproductive responsibilities'. (ibid.: 30)

This eugenicist theme, of the 'wrong' people reproducing and the 'right' people not, is taken up again in both Chapters 4 and 5. What Tyler seems to be indicating is that the term 'Chav', and the many negative practices associated with it, now occupy a space in which to express overtly racist comments that is now shut off elsewhere in public discourse.

So intersectional analyses, whether explicitly inserting themselves into the 'matrix of domination' paradigm or not, can reveal plenty about the ways that discrimination compounds 'race', gender and class. Our last two examples move the frame of analysis from the national to the global.

Joanne Nagel (2003) locates the intersection of global inequalities, gender, racialised identities and class squarely within the domain of US military imperialism in the latter part of the twentieth century. The US military in Asia, she asserts, has generated an extensive sex trade. Off base becomes an arena for the enactment of masculinities. Moreover, the 'military-sexual complex' (2003: 177) spreads this dimension of the sex trade to the USA because of relationships with women who are brought back. Moon (1997) estimates that at least 100,000 women came to the USA as brides of servicemen in the decades between the 1950s and the early 1990s. When relationships fail (or because they were marriages of convenience to start with), the women's poor language skills and low educational achievements give them few labour market options. The US bases in Asia, Europe and Central America since the Second World War have spawned a dependent industry of sexual services catering to servicemen. The long-standing images of Asian women as docile, mysterious, exotic and subservient serve as the backdrop to this for US servicemen:

> the sexual recreation areas that surround US military bases, especially in Asia, are ethnosexual sites where Western fantasies of Asian female sexuality meet material manifestations of Asian women and where the marriage of geopolitics and racial cosmologies is consummated nightly. (Nagel, 2003: 179)

Moreover, the growth of sex tourism in Asia is linked to the US military presence, as the post-conflict relations are constructed on the economic foundations built for the 'Rest and Recreation' (R&R) programme of the US military. The most obvious example to put forward in this respect is Thailand. Bishop and Robinson (1998) argue that in 1971, World Bank President Robert McNamara, who had been Defense Secretary when a contract was signed with the Thai government to provide R&R services to US troops in 1967, 'went to Bangkok to arrange for the bank's experts to produce a study of Thailand's post-war tourism prospects' (Bishop and Robinson, 1998: 9). The Thais took the advice of the World Bank experts and developed the tourist industry – but on the basis of the go-go bars and brothels that had been created to service the US military. In this relationship then, Thai (and the other poor, young Asian) women who become sex workers in Thailand's major cities and resorts are placed in a position of subjugation by Thai men who economically exploit them and foreigners who sexually exploit them. This has not been a historical accident but an outcome of US military presence, just as Japanese men's use of Asian sex workers both in Japan and abroad is, for Watanabe (1995: 506), a continuation of the war-time activities engaged in by the Imperial Japanese army from the 1930s, whereby women from occupied countries (from China to Burma (Myanmar)) would be taken and forced into prostitution to service Japanese troops.

In the rapidly expanding Irish economy of the early twenty-first century, Ronit Lentin (Lentin and McVeigh, 2006) explores the position of developing-world women.[5] Her study demonstrates not only the interconnectedness of gender, 'race' and class, but of the first and developing worlds in how these are articulated. She starts with the murder of Paiche Onyemaechi, a Malawian woman (and mother of two Irish citizens) to highlight some of these relations. Onyemaechi was a sex worker and former asylum seeker and was constructed in media coverage as a bad 'm/other' to use Lentin's formulation, against which white married Catholic women can be contrasted as good mothers.

The movement of women in global migratory flows – into low-paid work, as domestics, nannies and sex workers (Ehrenreich and Hochschild, 2003) – is reaching places that had not previously been destinations for mass migration. The Republic of Ireland is one of these (Garner, 2004).

Until 2005, any child born on the island of Ireland became an Irish citizen regardless of the nationality of his/her parents. For Lentin, Irish women are seen as representing the nation (through Erin, Hibernia, etc.), and reproducing the nation through giving birth. Yet foreign women's bodies in twenty-first century Ireland mark a crisis for Irish identity. They are seen as transgressive, threatening the integrity of Irish nationality through unnaturally giving birth to Irish nationals (through their non-national bodies). These women are accused of putting strain on Irish maternity care provision, and unfairly getting access to resources through residence and citizenship (Lentin, 2004; Luibhéid, 2004; Garner, 2007c). Their giving birth is also portrayed by politicians and the media as a threat to the integrity of the Irish citizenship system. The bodies for whom the residence rights acquired through mothering an Irish national is a worthwhile asset are from outside the EU (specifically Africa, Asia, Latin America, Middle East and Eastern Europe) so, primarily, this means women of colour. Responses go as far as people spitting at them, abusing them and perpetrating physical violence on them.

In the end, the 2004 Citizenship Referendum closed off the avenue of birth right for Irish children with foreign parents, as 80 per cent of the voters accorded the Minister of Justice the right to exclude children born to foreign nationals the right to access Irish citizenship (unless a condition of three years' residence prior to the birth, not including time spent as an asylum seeker, was satisfied).

Ireland has a history of regulating women's bodies (unmarried mothers, women seeking abortions, etc.), and the focus on sexuality of foreign women in the discourse of impurity continues the process of displacing problems onto external sources, and in thus removing responsibility from the nationals. Absent from the exposure given to female migrants is the fact that the Irish sex industry is sustained by mainly Irish men paying to have sex with mainly foreign sex workers, many of whom are trafficked. Ireland's expanding economy 'needs' highly mobile low-paid workers, women like Paiche Onyemaechi, to continue to grow, and allow white Irish women to forge careers:

> the globalisation of domestic work brings ambitious and independent career-oriented western women and striving women from the Third World together, though not as sisters, rather as mistresses and maids. (Lentin and McVeigh, 2006: 105)

This reminder that power relations suffuse social relationships that may seem ostensibly relatively equal ends our brief introduction to intersectional analysis.

CONCLUSIONS

These small slivers of much more complex and dense work, along with the much more bountiful theoretical discussions on intersectionality, bring into view the idea of a multiplicity of axes of domination. This is not understood as an additive approach, in which people add each element of their identity onto others like layers of a cake, but as a three-dimensional relationship, a matrix, in which all these identities are constituents of the others, and create specific experiences and oppressions.

Intersectionality is therefore not a mechanical reading of what the actors will think and do, but of the *structural conditions* they are likely to have faced, and therefore the sometimes pitiful options available the lower down the local scale of status the actor(s) may be.

Intersectionality is the product of tension between the (white male) epistemologies of mainstream academia and feminist research in its broadest sense. At the heart of the critiques of feminism, racism is seen not as an aberration from the humanist post-Enlightenment tradition of liberalism, but as an intrinsic dimension of how capitalism functions at all times. The types of historical and local specificities thrown up by such research seem to me to make the search for a general Marxist theory of racism rather a wild goose chase. The principles are that these forms of exploitation cannot be readily distinguished in practice: they are *in articulation* with each other. Class is, to borrow Stuart Hall's formulation, the 'modality through which' 'race' is lived, and 'race', the modality through which class is lived. Moreover, 'race' is not just for people not racialised as white, nor is it only for men, as we will see more closely in Chapter 8.

NOTES

1. For a general critique of the cultural turn's impact on sociology, see Rojek and Turner (2001). More specifically on racism, try Mac an Ghàill (1999).
2. See Ladson-Billings and Tate (1995). In the UK context, the attempts to integrate CRT into British theory by Gillborn (2005) and Hylton (2005) are also worth consulting, with multidisciplinary interventions from law, philosophy and cultural studies.

3. The objection might be that if you do not accept the centrality of the assertion that there is a separate racialised 'cognitive universe', then none of the rest follows. However, the statistical basis of differential outcomes (income, wealth, educational achievement, segregation, life expectancy, etc.) for people in different racialised groups in the USA is surely by now incontestable. Denial that this matters is proof in Mills' term of inhabiting a separate cognitive universe.
4. Crenshaw had used the concept of intersectionality in a previous article (Crenshaw, 1989).
5. See Chapter 6: Black Bodies and Headless Hookers: Women and Alternative Narratives of Globalisation, pp. 97–111.

4 'Race', Nation, State

There is a distinction between the nation, nationalism and the nation state, and in this chapter we are focusing on the latter and its relationship with 'race'. Nation states are a product of what sociologists refer to as 'modernity', the period of global changes starting from around the turn of the sixteenth century and ending in the late twentieth, a period which includes processes such as secularisation, industrialisation, urbanisation, democratisation, and the division of the world into the nation state system. Regardless of the extent to which people in various nations argue over how long their nation has existed, and what the roots of nationalism are, the nation state as we know it today itself dates to the French Revolution. The nation state is a political entity that claims legitimacy to control and represent a territory full of people who owe allegiance to that state, and who share aspects of culture, language and history. The nation state makes sense now as one unit of many in a world of nation states: the nation state system. Indeed, reference to this system of states is a widespread practice in locating oneself individually in the contemporary world ('I'm English', 'I'm French', 'I'm 'American', 'I'm Chinese', etc.). We shall first look at how we talk about membership of nations and how we arrive at the conclusions that we do in fact belong to them, before moving on to the study of how nation states shape our understandings of 'race', and play a role in the generation of racist practices and ideas.

NATION

Belonging to a nation has been conceptualised by academics in different disciplines in a number of ways. For nineteenth-century political scientist Ernest Renan (1992 [1882]) a nation is 'a daily plebiscite' in that people elect to remain part of the nation by not challenging this format or replacing it with something else. This formulation raises the question that scholars have been trying to answer ever since: what keeps all these people together, when objectively there are all kinds of potential lines of division such as wealth, class, region, ethnicity, gender, political viewpoint, religion, language and cultural orientation? For Renan again, this is a secondary issue:

> What makes a nation is not speaking the same language or belonging to the same ethnographic group, it is having done great things together in the past and wanting to do more great things in the future. (1992 [1882]: 54)

So being part of a nation requires a collective act of imagination and an emotional investment in belonging. Nation states are constructed by people and are not natural units into which groups of people fall without being pushed. Convincing people that they legitimately belong to a community so large that they will never know all its other members, but to which most have a strong allegiance, and for which many are prepared to die, requires a variety of methods. Looking backwards and forwards in time involves placing oneself among people who are either already dead or not yet born, and allying oneself with them all. Clearly, this is a potent set of emotional investments. The language of the nation is all about this emotional response, whereas that of the State is more about interests. Indeed, the nation state and people's multiple bonds and allegiances to it are terrain on which the ideas that are crucial to that of 'race' are embedded. Nations are often talked about as biologically 'natural' units, whether this is in relation to the world of plants or people. German historian Herder argued that:

> The most natural state ... is one nation, with one national character ... a nation is as much a natural plant as a family. Only with more branches. Nothing therefore appears so directly opposite to the end of government as the unnatural enlargement of states. The wild mixture of races and nations under one sceptre ... . (1784–91: 249–50)

Nascent concerns with the problems allegedly posed by multilingual and multicultural populations within the territory of a nation state are foreshadowed in Herder's comments. Language is also a key factor in one of the most often quoted commentaries on nationhood, Benedict Anderson's 'imagined community' (1983). Anderson, a historian of South East Asia, studied Indonesian nationalism and focused on the way that the nationalist activist managed to create a shared language, using the printed word, from a set of cultures with a multitude of languages. 'Indonesian-ness', if you like, had on one level to be invented in order for all Indonesians in their various parts of what is a huge territory, to feel as though they belonged to one unit. Indeed, the role of invention in this process is underscored by the historians Eric Hobsbawm and Terence Ranger, in their famous collection of essays, *The Invention of Tradition* (1983) containing case studies drawn from the British Isles, Continental Europe, and colonial India and Africa. They argue that it is a function of the nation state to create national traditions rather than merely observe existing ones, and that this is part of the process of constituting nationhood and inculcating the idea among its people that nations stretch back in time, thus legitimising the present situation.

Box 4.1   Nations and nation states

The nation is a self-defining cultural and social community. One of the most dominant, normative ideologies is that which sets out that the natural unit for groups of populations is the nation. In theory, the members of a given 'nation' share a common identity of some kind. The idea of a nation stretches across time to include the dead and the as yet unborn in a continuous narrative of belonging. Thus, the use of 'we' and 'our' to describe history, heritage, armies, victories, etc. is a normal part of this idea. Although the term 'nation' is informally used as a synonym for a *state*, there is a distinction between the two.

A **nation state** is the political and legal structure of a state that has jurisdiction over a particular nation. Nation states therefore differ from previous forms of governed entity such as city states. Although the nation states defined themselves as relatively homogeneous cultural groups, this was never the exclusive model. Moreover, since the European expansion into the developing world, and the accelerated movement of migratory flows, I would argue that the multicultural nation (as a *description*) is now the norm. Every nation (group of people) is associated with its own specific territory, the national homeland, although some territories may be part of other nation states, e.g. Kurds, and Jews prior to the foundation of Israel. There might also be arguments over the legitimacy of particular territories, e.g. Israel/Palestine, Northern Ireland. A nation state's nationality and citizenship laws determine who is a member and under what conditions membership is allowed. This is usually a combination of bloodlines, residence periods and/or marriage.

Craig Calhoun, taking a concept from Foucault, calls the nation a 'discursive formation', 'a way of speaking that shapes our consciousness' (1997: 3). This does not have to do necessarily with using the term 'nation', but to do with:

> whether participants use a rhetoric, a way of speaking, a kind of language that carries with it connections to other events and actions, that enables or disables certain other ways of speaking or acting, or that is recognised by others as entailing certain consequences. (1997: 3–4)

So the nation is an implicit presence in how we frame our talk about identity and social problems, for example. What I am trying to get at is the quality of taken-for-grantedness that the nation state now assumes in our talk and actions. Greek sociologist Alexandria Halkias (2003) finds, in her interviews with women about the low birth-rate crisis (*demografiko*), that:

> The need to have at least one child in order to be considered a good Greek woman, which is implicitly underscored in the official public sphere's articulations of the *demografiko*, is never challenged by the women interviewed. (ibid.: 224)

So while they talk about their careers, the problems of bringing up children in an expensive place, etc., the supposed role of women as 'reproducing the nation' (Anthias and Yuval-Davis, 1993) is not questioned.

While in terms of people, the language of nation is shot through with references to family, community, kinship, bloodlines, homogeneity, and purity. The language of essentialism (Box 1.2) and the natural world to understand the social world are key elements of 'race', and we find them both in the discourse on the nation. We have, from this perspective, a series of undeniable bonds with the other members of the nation, as an extended family, with whom we face other nations, equally constituted, in the global competition of nation states. As part of that bond, we owe allegiance to the State, which 'protects' borders against incomers, and provides us with signs and symbols of membership, such as passports. How have we arrived at the point where this all seems natural and the only way the world could be?

NATION STATES

French political philosopher, Etienne Balibar, argues that the link between 'race' and nation is actively made by the State (Balibar and Wallerstein, 1991). Nations are constructed as 'natural' entities, as we have seen above, in which the human race can be broken down into homogeneous groups. The nation is at once a territory, a special space protected and managed by a state, and a people who owe solidarity to each other and allegiance to that state. Thus, blood (genealogy) and soil (territory) combine to make nationals who 'belong' in that place to that group. However, this process does not happen on its own. Instead, through its institutions, particularly the legal and education systems, the state 'produces' both 'nationals' and 'non-nationals' (ibid., 1991). This happens by socialising them into the idea that people in a given nation are intrinsically different from those of other nations, and that any internal divisions are less important than this principal one. This idea is approached from a different direction by social psychologist Michael Billig (1995), who argues that nationalism is not all about wars, national heroes and flag-waving, but also the innumerable ways in which the idea of belonging to the nation state is transmitted and picked up by the nation's population on a daily basis, through maps, oaths, school curricula, language, official procedures, the use of 'we' to talk about the nation, etc. He terms this 'banal nationalism'. What both he and Balibar underline is that nations are necessarily *exclusive*, established as they are in permanent opposition to all other nations. In saying 'we', the nation simultaneously says 'they'. It is to where this line lies, and what it means for students of the idea of 'race', that we shall now turn.

SCHOLARSHIP ON 'RACE' AND THE STATE

The bodies of academic writing on racism and the State seldom overlapped before the late twentieth century. We will look at some exceptions to that rule before focusing on Omi and Winant (1994) and Goldberg's (2000) explicit attempts to flesh out the racialisation of the State in modernity. Racism in the Western view is still popularly seen as an aberration, something that marks *individuals* as deviant. In short, racism is viewed as a marginal and undesirable outcome that the State now strives to combat. When it is talked about seriously in social terms, it is frequently described as an illness, a cancer maybe that has infected society from within. However, I am going to argue in this section that 'race' has been an important part of how Western society governs itself *normally* for centuries, and that racism is, as Bauman (1989) suggests, politically inseparable from the project of modernity due to the imbedded process of categorisation undertaken in the Enlightenment.

In this chapter, we shall examine the ideas put forward that suggest that the State is a key actor in the process of racialisation, and an integral part of contemporary forms that racism has assumed. Part of this is the idea that racialisation is an integral element of modernity. It is the period in which the racialisation of the world's population occurs (Banton, 1977). If we want to begin to understand racism in the contemporary period, it is essential to get to grips with two ideas. Firstly, although racism is a historical process, it is an ongoing one and cannot be located wholly in the past. Secondly, the State is not a neutral arbiter in the way that 'race' becomes pertinent in various fields, but a significant player in defining membership of the nation. It does so using concepts deriving from essentialism and attaching these ideas to bodies deemed different, both physically and culturally.

The idea that the State plays a role in racialisation was first explored explicitly by the German political theorist Erich Voegelin, publishing in the 1930s and 1940s (Voegelin, 1933 [2000], 1940). American writer W.E.B Du Bois, in his history of the decades following the American Civil War (1998 [1935]), also addressed this issue. A refugee from the Nazis, Voegelin sought to understand the process of state formation, and, unlike any other political theorist before him, concluded that racialisation was crucial to this. Nations, he argued, have to put themselves forward as unique entities, natural groupings of people each different from the other nations. The idea of 'race', with its spurious scientific basis, provides ideal fuel for such ideological labour. So by making the idea that the nation represents a racial group, what Lentin and Lentin (2006: 3–4) call 'the theoretical glue' binding people to each other, and to the otherwise abstract State, is provided. 'Race' therefore emerges as one of the principal factors underlying the legitimisation of nation states as the accepted, appropriate and 'normal' way to organise societies.

Zygmunt Bauman (1989) has suggested that the act of classification is a crucial element of modernity, and especially of the Enlightenment, which itself is a crucial phase in the idea of 'race'. One of the activities engaged in by the Enlightenment thinkers was the hierarchical classification of all forms of life. The incarnation of this desire to order and list was Linnaeus' taxonomy of people based on skin colour, humour and geographical location (see Chapters 1 and 5).

The context of this is very important. By the time that the Enlightenment was in full swing on both sides of the Atlantic, in the last quarter of the eighteenth century, the Triangular Trade of slaves, raw materials and finished products that linked Europe, Africa and North America, was at its most profitable juncture, and the United States had already written its constitution. The United States' economy was based upon the slave mode of production, and this was recognised as intrinsic to the country's form of governance. Senator Henry Wise, in the debates on anti-slavery in the 1830s, argued that: 'they [our northern brethren] cannot attack the system of slavery without attacking the institutions of our country, our safety and our welfare' (Nye, 1949: 34, cited by Feagin, 2006: 12). Indeed, 10 presidents between 1790 and 1869 had been slaveholders at some point in their lives (Feagin, 2006: 12). Although the constitution holds the 'truths to be self-evident', all men were not created equal in terms of their right to live in the absence of servitude. Moreover, the annexation of territory that the first 13 states of the Union would later claim for itself, to the north and the west of the initial colonies, involved violently usurping Native Americans from their ancestral lands. Elsewhere, other imperial powers, acting first through private companies, then through state powers covering colonial possessions, were involved in similar activities of mineral extraction and the creation of economies serving Europe under armed rule. As the beginnings of what we recognise as modern nation states with varying degrees of democratic participation began to emerge across the West, the ideas incorporating 'the people' as citizens with rights excluded the poorer, the female and enslaved members of those societies, and cast the colonial subject as the opposite of the rights-bearing citizen. Summarising this process, Lentin and Lentin write:

> Because the idea of universal humanity was constructed in the image of the white European, against the non-European, the blacks in the colonies and the internal others, the application of the essence of humanity, as it was defined by European thinkers, to all men and women was impossible from the outset. It is simply not possible for those who do not comply with a definition of humanity – rationality, individuality, white aesthetics – to be considered (fully) human. (2006: 6)

This is the context of the instigation of the modern nation-state system, and it is important to take this fact into account because the very invisibility of these groups in the original vision of the citizen is the basis for the 'racial state' described by Omi and Winant (1994) and Goldberg (2000), and explored further in Lentin and Lentin (2006).

The State's role is to control its population, and as Foucault's merciless expression runs, to 'make live' and 'let die' (2003). Bauman had earlier captured this necessary cruelty in his metaphor of the 'gardening state'. Here, the State represents rationality and order. To maintain the garden's order against chaos, the gardener must weed out 'every self-invited plant which interferes with his plan and vision of order and harmony' (Bauman, 1989: 57). What this means in terms of 'race' and the State, is that the former comprises the plants and grass, while those seen as weak or alien constitute the weeds. The procedure and mechanisms for deciding who is an insider, and subsequently sorting insiders from outsiders, is the work of this gardening state. This operates on the basis of a racialised vision of the nation, whose population is bound together by a shared destiny and heritage.

Yet even within the nation, there are people who are 'weeds in the garden', preventing the superior plants from flourishing. It is clear from historical work on 'race' in the Victorian era, for example, that in nineteenth-century Britain and America, very similar ways of talking about the working classes and slaves or colonial subjects were in use. These are essentialising discourses, identifying reasons for the existing status quo (the weakness of one group and the strength of another, measured in terms of industriousness and moral codes), and thus fixing working-class bodies to a culture that represents the opposite of middle-class virtue, restraint and dynamism. John Hartigan's study of the racialisation of the American working classes (2005) demonstrates very clear parallels. There, a discourse that explained fecklessness and moral turpitude by reference to environmental factors of socialisation and heredity, was grafted onto an anti-immigrant ideology in the works of the well-funded and communicative eugenics lobby, and writers such as Madison Grant (1915) and Winthrop Stoddard (1922) which placed the Anglo-Saxon at the summit of the racial hierarchy and warned against degeneration by breeding with other 'races' and with the weaker elements of the Anglo-Saxon 'race'. We shall see how the 1924 US Immigration Act was influenced by such ideas, in Chapter 5, on science.

In the contemporary period, scholars have grappled with the concept of the State influencing the struggle for power between groups that organise around the basis of 'race', in order to obtain social justice for those groups. Michael Omi and Howard Winant's pioneering thesis (1994 [1986]) situated the US federal state as an active player in the racialisation of its population in different ways. They first provide a working definition of what they mean by the State:

> The State is composed of institutions, the policies they carry out, the conditions and rules which support and justify them, and the social relationships in which they are imbedded. (Omi and Winant, 1994: 83)

This definition is interesting in that it moves away from the strictly material to encompass the ideological, and for us, interested in the ways in which states encourage people to think about social relationships in terms of closed and natural groups, is a very appropriate one.

Much of what the authors describe focuses, as their book's sub-title suggests, on the period from the 1960s to the 1980s, the civil rights and backlash period. However, in order to understand their claims, we have to go back to their historical model, in which they deploy Antonio Gramsci's (1971) concepts: 'war of manoeuvre' and 'war of position'. In the former, the civil society actors have no legitimate outlet because they are excluded from the democratic community. The mission there is to establish spaces and counter-cultures in which their own group can be valorised, and in which oppositional ideology can be developed. In the 'war of position', however, they are enabled to influence the democratic process from within. This allows political and ideological projects to be developed. These are aimed at contesting the dominance (or 'hegemony', to use Gramsci's term) of the most powerful group and the ideology it uses to justify its dominance. In terms of American history, the authors see the period before civil rights as that of the 'war of manoeuvre', whereas the 1960s usher in the 'war of position', which the authors maintain is ongoing.

In the model that Omi and Winant establish, 'race' is never stable and indeed 'racial formation' is crucial to understanding it as an unfinished process. The process of attaching meaning to 'race' is engaged in by the State in the form of legislation, Census, immigration and citizenship rules. Social movements generally focus on the State as an entity from which to extract concessions in a struggle for equality and the politics of recognition. So instead of starting and finishing with group identities that are set in stone, social movements engage the State and other civil society actors in a struggle over meanings that result in steps forward and backwards being made at different moments. Progressive social movements may influence the State to the point where the very idiom in which they are conducting the war of manoeuvre is appropriated and used for non-progressive ends (such as a blanket opposition to any affirmative action-derived programme on the grounds that they constitute 'reverse racism'). Conservative social movements may also have 'racial projects', and can use the language of previous progressive campaigns for their own ends. The widely held view that affirmative action (fought for during the 1960s to compensate for generations of discrimination) constitutes 'reverse discrimination' against white Americans, and the attempts to eliminate quotas through state legislation and the courts since the 1970s, are examples of this process.

While Omi and Winant raise interesting questions about contemporary America (1994), David Goldberg (2000) is concerned to trace a historic trajectory of the State in the West, and how it has addressed 'race' as a central part of its existence, rather than as a marginal and specific activity. From a complex, dense piece of work, there are a number of useful points, three of which are summarised below.

First, Goldberg's starting point is that the normal ways in which Western states function sustain the idea of 'race', even in the official ideology of racelessness. So the 'racial state' is the norm. However, most political and academic focus under the heading 'racism' has been on states where 'race' has been made into an explicit rather than implicit tool of governance. So, 'racial' states can become 'racist' states, as did Nazi Germany, Apartheid South Africa and the Jim Crow states of the USA.

Second, he conceptualises a distinction in the racialised attribution of difference from the Enlightenment era onwards, between 'naturalist' and 'historicist' racism. 'Naturalist' racism views peoples as naturally and unbridgeably different, and structured into a hierarchy of civilised and not-so-civilised states. Those at the bottom of the pile can never attain the sophistication of those at the top. 'Historicist' racism, on the other hand, uses the same hierarchical template, but understands 'race' as a relative developmental time lag: the less civilised may catch up, given time. He argues that while each was dominant at different moments, they are both still used to explain the state of the world.

Third, the difference between civilised and less civilised, which has been an intrinsic part of the way in which people in imperial countries are socialised to see themselves, is now a condition for the contemporary scenario. For the modern Western state, the aspiration is for a 'raceless' society in which the past divisions no longer have an impact (cf. classlessness). To attain this aspiration, states have education, public information and special equality legislation aimed at squeezing out the residual racism in each nation state. In this model, argues Goldberg (2000), the State places itself outside the field of racism, unconnected to it except in its interventions aimed at ridding society of this 'disease'. The only way that states and people can arrive at such conclusions, suggests Goldberg (ibid.), is from uncritical acceptance of the dominant paradigms of 'white' thought in the face of evidence that the State plays important roles in structuring the terrain on which nationality, citizenship and immigration statuses are defined, how Censuses are designed, etc. These roles have developed over centuries of European and North American domination of military, financial and technological arenas, and are based on the Enlightenment's project of creating 'universal man'. In the context of that project (Eze, 1997), only whiteness can be racially neutral, and therefore universal in this view: everyone else is 'ethnic', and the only residual racism is caused by the aberrant individuals of social psychology.

Western states now aim to be 'raceless', that is, where 'race' plays no role in the allocation of social positions, which ideally, are all down to the capacities of the individual. This ideology of the raceless society, pursued to different degrees in different places, denotes the triumph of Western liberal thought, and there is little recognition of the contradiction between official state objectives in this regard and the work carried out by the State in the fields of immigration, citizenship and now, increasingly, security. However racism is defined by Western states, it excludes consideration of citizenship laws that include genealogical criteria; immigration regimes that place obstacles in front of developing-world nationals but which are not placed in front of other people and/or apply different laws to people who have asylum-seeker or migrant statuses; and security regimes that use racial profiling.

Goldberg's work (2000) makes it impossible to claim that the state is a neutral arbiter in the field of racial politics. He presents us with a timeline, a qualified commentary about what ideas have been dominant at which time, and how this helps us make sense of the contemporary world.

THE GENDERED NATION AND 'BIOPOLITICS'

Theses such as those of Goldberg (2000), and Omi and Winant (1994), break new territory in terms of attaching a major role to the State in racialising their populations across time and place. However, there are other dimensions of this process neglected in their work, such as the importance of gender. Nira Yuval-Davis (1997: 26–38) makes an important contribution to plugging that gap. She focuses on 'the intersections between women's reproductive roles and the constructions of nations' (ibid.: 26). The international market for, and technology surrounding, egg donation has developed at a furious pace since Yuval-Davis published this book, and their ramifications for membership of national collectivities have become evermore complex (Nahman, 2008). Here, I will simply draw out the distinctions she makes between varying forms of natalist policies that states impose on women, who comprise the 'natural', physical borders of the nation.

First, she notes that some states have tried to encourage higher birth rates at different moments in order to strengthen the nation. Examples of this are Israel, France (Camiscioli, 2001) and Australia. Often the political rivalry over territory is engaged in through exhortations to maintain or increase a birth rate, as in Lebanon, Bulgaria and the former Yugoslavia. This can be to increase one racialised group in the face of perceived growth in another, as identified by Angela Davis in early twentieth-century USA (2001). President Theodore Roosevelt, whose 1906 State of the Union speech she quotes, blamed white middle-class women exercising reproductive choices for endangering the USA by practising 'race suicide':

> ... wilful sterility is, from the standpoint of the nation, from the standpoint of the human race, the one sin for which the penalty is national death, race death; a sin for which there is no atonement. (Roosevelt, 1906)

Second, Yuval-Davis identifies the 'eugenicist discourse', which is aimed at improving the quality of the population (see Chapter 5). Typically, this takes two forms: positive and negative eugenics. In positive eugenics, groups seen as more valuable in terms of genes (typically wealthy, able-bodied, better-educated) are encouraged to have more children. In 'negative eugenics', the focus is on preventing groups considered less valuable (typically, poorer, maybe with disabilities, ethnic minorities) from having children. The State's role in this is to construct a legal framework in which particular actions are given legitimised rationales and carried out through the courts, from compulsory sterilisations to cash incentives. Underlying this idea is the connection made between culture, values and genes. The association in eugenics practice is for these things to be naturalised as a trinity.

The third point, which overlaps with negative eugenics, is the idea of population excess. This fear of overstretching existing resources provokes a set of policy responses based on the objective of reducing or at least stabilising population through birth control. The fear of a mismatch of resources and population is drawn from the ideas of English clergyman and economist, Thomas Malthus (1798), who argued at the end of the eighteenth century that population increased at a much faster rate than food supplies. Only natural disasters and wars, he maintained, would control population growth. Yuval-Davis (1997) points to China and India as key Malthusian states in this respect, and highlights the fact that Western governments, as well as multinational companies, have long provided the wherewithal for population-control policies.

Fears over resource consumption in the West aimed at developing countries neglect the fact that the majority of resources have been consumed in the West (with the exclusion of Japan and the small but dynamic 'tiger' economies of South East Asia) for centuries. It is only at the start of the twenty-first century, with the economic growth of China and India as future super-powers, that the pattern of consumption is changing.

The other salient point to note is that women have become key 'combatants' in recent civil wars because of their role as reproducers of the nation. In both the former Yugoslavia and Rwanda, women have been targeted for mass rape (sometimes with AIDS attached). The rationale for this is to destroy the nation's border, populate the nation with non-nationals, and bring shame on the women, and by extension shame on 'their' men for not defending them properly. This functions within a masculine world view where women are the cultural property of men and of the nation. To acknowledge this tactic and the context in which it was being used, the International Criminal Court made rape a 'crime constituent of genocide' in 1997.

Box 4.2   Michel Foucault

Foucault (1926–84) was a French philosopher, much quoted in sociological and political theory because of his groundbreaking work on the social construction of key concepts in history such as discipline, sexuality and madness, and his theorisation of power. For Foucault, this ties new forms of power into the emergence of the modern nation state, and he coined the term 'bio-power' to explain this.

Biopower is a 'technology' (or mechanism) of power, that is, a means of managing an entire population. For Foucault, the phenomenon he labels 'bio-power' emerges in the seventeenth century. There are two elements: scientific categories of human beings, and 'disciplinary power'. The categories are based on gender, sexuality, nationality, etc., while 'disciplinary power' is targeted on regulating bodies (a process he analyses in *Discipline and Punish*, 1977). Traditional types of power, he maintains, were derived from a sovereign's power to kill his/her subjects. However, in a period after feudalism, where there has to be a rationale for the exercise of power beyond divine right, biopower is utilised by emphasising the protection of life instead of the threat of death. Foucault summarises this alternative as the passage from 'let live and make die', to 'make live and let die'. When the State is so heavily involved in protecting the lives of 'its' people, it can use this to justify anything. Biopower is therefore an essential characteristic of modern nation states, and ties in neatly with eugenics. Groups viewed as threats to the life of the nation can be eliminated with impunity. This idea is explored most fully in Foucault's lecture on 17 March 1976, reproduced in *Society Must Be Defended* (2003), in which he analyses what he terms 'race struggle' and the modern state.

Michel Foucault's lectures at the Collège de France in 1976 contained a series around the development of the State's power to control its population, and how this had evolved from feudal times when a lord or king had the right and power to 'let live and make die'. The striking change brought about, argues Foucault, is that by the nineteenth century, the State had accrued the power and right to 'make live and let die'. Who fell into which category and why is really the subject of this chapter, and indeed of all the work on 'race' and the State. An important element of Foucault's way of discussing the topic of the State is that he has developed a set of concepts to refer to the process he identifies, most importantly 'biopolitics' (see Box 4.2). Moreover, his use of the word 'race' is primarily drawn from the European context, holding within it the older connotations of 'stock' and 'people', and he explicitly notes that he is not using racism to refer to the kind of social relationships between the European powers and colonial people. This is an important qualification to make, but one that enables us to focus on a significant part of the equation that we will see anchoring the concept of 'new racism': the way biological difference is made cultural and vice versa. Indeed, Foucault sees 'race' as one of a number of 'technologies' (or mechanisms) enabling the State to control populations and their behaviour:

> It (race) is primarily a way of introducing a break into the domain of life that is under power's control: the break between what must live and what must die. The appearance within the biological continuum of the human race of races, the distinction among races, the hierarchy of races, the fact that certain races are described as good and that others, in contrast, are described as inferior: all this is a way of fragmenting the field of the biological that power controls. (Foucault, 2003: 255)

So the biological and cultural distinctions between human beings are used in Foucault's theory as ways of first establishing, then justifying, control over the population of nation states. At one end of the spectrum of state powers lies the protection of the good (defined racially, that is biologically and culturally), yet this contains its opposite, the genocidal dream of eliminating the bad, whether through the very rare opportunity to actually kill the membership of an out-group, or more likely, to prevent them from reproducing, or stopping them living as a distinct cultural group. 'In the biopower system', he contends:

> in other words, killing or the imperative to kill is acceptable only if it results not in a victory of political adversaries, but in the elimination of the biological threat to and the improvement of the species or the race. There is a direct connection between the two. In a normalizing society, race or racism is the precondition that makes killing acceptable. (ibid.: 256)

He could quite easily be talking about social class as 'race' in the European nineteenth-century context, but Foucault has carefully selected 'race' because of its capacity to melt the biological into the social and the cultural, and throw up hierarchies that are both partly embedded in and partly independent of class.

So much for the theories. How do these processes actually work? We will look at three examples: the classification of populations, legislation on equality and citizenship policies.

Orders: classification, census

How do states 'make race'? How do they introduce 'a break into the domain of life that is under power's control', to use Foucault's terminology? Census categories are not a neutral reflection of a country's population. They are simultaneously a political response to social pressures, and a means of exerting one strand of Foucault's biopower. If such categories were merely a reflection of the natural world, we would expect them to be universal, their boundaries to be uncontroversial, and their substantive content and naming easy to rationalise.

Instead, categories differ from one country to the next, so that a person categorised in one way in one country falls into a different category in another (e.g. a UK national whose parents were Nigerian might tick the box saying 'Black African' in the British Census, but in Nigeria, they would more likely select a religious grouping and/or cultural or ethnic affiliation). Second, where the line between different groups falls is also open to debate, the most obvious example being people whose parentage lies in more than one of these categories. The idea of somebody not fitting clearly into a category usually disturbs the hierarchical construction of racial groups in a given society. Responses can range from attentive detail to neglect. In the colonial Americas, we find absurdly detailed language to cover every possible combination of European, Amerindian and African origins. In the contemporary USA, there has been a political campaign to have the category 'bi-racial' included on the Census (see Chapter 6). In the 1980 UK Census, there was originally a catch-all box labelled 'Other', which in 1991 became 'Mixed' with no specification, and by 2001, people could choose from a small number of combinations of mixedness. In apartheid South Africa

(1948–94), people in this category might have ended up in any of the major official categories used: 'Black', 'White', 'Coloured' or 'Indian'. The consequences of being in one rather than another seriously impacted on people's life chances, their treatment by authorities, their access to healthcare, employment and education, and their freedom to move around. The latest US Census invites people identifying culturally as 'Hispanic' to also identify 'racially'. The ethnic group Hispanic (which itself appears only at the 1981 Census) is thus comprised of people whose origins lay anywhere between Tierra del Fuego, Puerto Rico and the Mexican border, and is overlaid by the racial categories of 'African', 'Caucasian', 'Asian', 'White' and 'Bi-racial' among others. The question of what it actually means to identify oneself with any of these categories cannot be captured here, but the point remains that the State uses categories that have varying degrees of relevance to how the people it enumerates live their lives, and the social processes in which they are agents.

Finally, the categories themselves are not arbitrary, but attempts to enclose something that might not be enclosable. Or the substantive groups may not be meaningful in themselves, or may not make sense in the context of the other categories. Take 'Indian' in the UK Census, which is put forward as an ethnic group to choose as an option. In India, there are around 80 linguistic groups, all the major world religions plus a number of smaller ones. Even this small amount of information seems to make the idea that 'Indian' is a relatively homogeneous ethnic group somewhat implausible. It is more of a nationality than an ethnic group. When in the same Census (1981) another option is 'White', it can be argued that 'Indian' and 'White' are not of an equivalent order. One is a nationality, the other a racial group. Moreover, the headline category 'Asian' does not include 'Chinese', which geographically belongs to Asia. There is, clearly, even at this fundamental level, something illogical about the breakdown of the British Census that should alert us – in looking at other Censuses – that they are social interpretations of given societies rather than incontestable versions of social reality reflecting nature.

When we step back and look at the Census categories, we ought to ask, what assumptions are such categories based upon? The assumptions are that such ethno-racial distinctions are socially meaningful, and that the data collected aids in a State-led process of amelioration of particular problems associated with the social divisions that are put forward as meaningful. In other words, if there was no associated or potential social division attached to the categories, why collect demographic data in this way? The Census is an ongoing outcome of a historical process that has national distinctiveness, reflecting struggles over experiences of racialisation. The State, through its Census, introduces ways of thinking about the social world that are made meaningful in official policy-making circles and upon which services, employment and the legal system are based. Most of it is ostensibly driven by social policy on equality, which we shall address below. However, there are also political stakes in being made an ethnic category if you live in a nation state where some form of multicultural governance is operated, as political-community power-related projects can be embarked on with legitimacy. The case of the Irish in the UK in the 1980s (O'Keeffe, 2007), and the Travellers in the Republic of Ireland and Northern Ireland at the turn of the twenty-first century, illustrate the way in which access to resources via the State are considered motivation for a targeted campaign in which the ethnic group is put forward as authentic and deserving of recognition.

Social policies on equality

Nation states provide minimum resources through welfare and social security programmes, services and employment (through the provision of such services). They also intervene in varieties of ways, one of which is that of formal pro-equality work, a relatively recent area. As we will see in Chapter 7, the introduction of legislation aimed at providing equal access to employment, services and other resources dates back only to the 1960s in the USA and the mid-1970s in some European countries.

In order to enact and implement such policies, there has to be, firstly, a consensus that there is structural discrimination (or institutional racism) to overcome, and a division of the population into ethno-racialised groups through the Census. This is because the data from the Census is used to establish the parameters for policy. If the object is to make the workforce approximately reflect the national population, for example, then the targets for the employment of minorities would be set at around the national levels or possibly at local levels. All the collection of data by Human Resources departments or external monitoring organisations is based on the Census categories. Moreover, with statutory bodies being obliged to collect data on their workforces and clients in order to establish that they are carrying out such a duty, the importance of ethno-racial categories starts to overtake the social realities they are supposed to cover. As the focus is on the quantitative and statistical production of records, the other questions lose importance: they become to a certain degree 'fetishised' (pursued as if they were real and distinct entities rather than outcomes of other processes). This is not to say that formal anti-discrimination legislation and practice do not achieve some of their goals, but that there are also unintended consequences. From our viewpoint as critical sociologists, we also have to be aware of them, and be interested in them.

One significant outcome is the way that equalities legislation has drawn up the field of the social into particular sub-fields of inequality. Currently, the EU directive of November 2000 (European Union, 2000) has encouraged this pattern, and there are between seven and nine grounds currently used by national semi-state agencies responsible for enforcing equality legislation. None of them, anywhere in the world, include social class. This is significant for two reasons: first, it demonstrates that one of the most obvious sources of inequality (and possibly the most ubiquitous) is not considered feasible ground for remedial action. Second, for us, interested in 'race', it reveals the liberal democratic framework of the Western democracies that we are primarily studying here in this book. The orthodox thinking is that ameliorative measures carried out by redistributing resources through taxation, social security welfare, education systems, etc. are all valid actions for government, but the redress of collective inequalities by individual cases does not fit the model. In the majority of cases, equalities legislation is about individuals proving cases of discrimination.

Immigration/nationality/citizenship policies

Two of the clearest areas for following the trail of the State's input into racialisation are in the official constructions of national identity – through laws on citizenship, nationality and immigration.

There is a set of ways to socialise people into feeling that they belong to the nation which is completely different from that encouraged by citizenship laws. We have already been introduced to Etienne Balibar's idea (Balibar and Wallerstein, 1991) that the State 'produces' nationals, and therefore non-nationals, through its education system, and that there are myriad forms of everyday or 'banal nationalism' (Billig, 1995). People can often see this happening and either join in approvingly because they identify with the symbols or the people embodied in the symbols, like Maria Kefalas' working-class Chicagoans (2003) who participate in military remembrance events. Sociologists carrying out fieldwork also identify people's complicated relationships with the nation. Whether people feel comfortable or uncomfortable (Condor, 2000) with belonging to their nation state at a given moment, they seldom, if ever, query the existence of the nation state, as the example of Greek women (above) shows. However, here we are concerned only with the formal regulation of belonging: citizenship.

Since the nation state began to extend privileges to its members in the form of passports and different forms of protection, it has laid down rules for membership. There are four principal rules for being part of the formal national community related to bloodlines, birthplace, residence and marriage. At the beginning of the twenty-first century, most nations used combinations of these. However, for a long time, blood and birthplace were the two most important. On the spectrum where bloodlines constitute one pole and birthplace the other, some nations have historically tended toward one end. The French Republic based its citizenship laws until the 1970s on the idea that anyone born on French territory, regardless of the parents' origins, was French. This civic community can be placed against the classic German conception of nation in which only those who could trace bloodlines to other Germans are included. In practice, these two nations now have laws that are much more similar. However, the two ideas – either being joined to people by historic genealogy, or by shared relations to a place – are the founding ones for today's nationality laws. Added to this come other ways to qualify as members, even though you are originally a national of another country: residence and post-nuptial citizenship. This means that either you qualify by residing in the nation for a set period of time, and then applying for nationality, or you marry someone who is already a national and you qualify through that person's nationality.

So what we are describing here appears on the face of it to be a series of administrative procedures based on neutral decisions about how to frame the nation. However, closer critical attention demonstrates something more revealing in terms of the racialisation of citizenship and its historical timing. The example of the United Kingdom shows a shift from a very broad-based civic to a more exclusive racial emphasis. In the period until the early 1960s, British nationality was extended to anyone from a colony as well as the British Isles. In response to post-war migration from former colonies, and the social issues raised by the reactions of the British public and politicians, there then followed a number of adjustments to the rules. The concept of patriality (bloodlines) was introduced to distinguish people who could trace their parentage back two generations to the UK from those who could not. The latter group thus found it more difficult to become UK nationals, especially when partiality was enshrined in the 1971 Immigration Act. By 1981, the new Nationality and Citizenship act introduced a very complicated set of layers of nationality (a concept that is unique to the British legislation) which sought to make it impossible for people in the bottom two layers to automatically reside, work and enjoy benefits in the UK. At the same time, increasingly strict immigration rules have made it more difficult for people from outside the European Union to access the British labour market, and therefore accrue residence which qualifies people for nationality. In effect, this means that the path to British nationality has become, in general, more difficult to negotiate for people whose origins lie outside Britain or the 'white dominions' of Australia, Canada and New Zealand (territories to which more white UK nationals had traditionally emigrated). The outcomes of the combined changes in immigration and citizenship laws in Britain since the 1960s are racialised: of the people for whom they primarily if not exclusively operate negatively, the majority are not white. It could be argued, for example, that this outcome was not intentional, and that it affected all the Commonwealth countries rather more so than the non-white majority countries. I would counter that, in practice, these changes turned British citizenship into a resource accessible more easily by Whites, than by any other racialised group. Moreover, this trend has been exacerbated by immigration policies over the last three decades because the European Union (EU) has become the key context for European national immigration laws. All EU member states (which have predominantly white populations) must allow each other's nationals to reside in them and have access to their labour markets without visas. One knock-on effect of this has been for the external borders to become more tightly controlled, and the conditions applying to all but the most highly skilled workers from outside the EU have become more onerous (Garner, 2007b).

LIMITS

While the State seems from the arguments set out above to be extremely powerful, it also has its limits. These are to do mostly with supra-national governance and privatisation. As we will see in the chapter on whiteness, the European Union advocates integration and equality while making it increasingly difficult for non-EU nationals to enter, move around and access resources within the EU. There is no official EU immigration and asylum policy, but decisions taken and implemented by joint action at inter-governmental level acts as a de facto EU policy. Indeed, tourist visas issued by one nation can be used in any other EU nation. This type of policy overrides national ones in terms of the core principle, which is that EU nationals get preferential treatment over non-EU nationals in terms of rights of movement, residence, employment, etc. So countries that had colonial relationships and reflected these in their immigration regimes (by giving preference to nationals of colonies and former colonies), such as the UK, France, Belgium, the Netherlands, Portugal and Spain, had to alter their rules to reflect the more simple relationship between the EU member states, all of which are majority white countries. This constitutes a sea change in the way nations construct the idea of who belongs to their national communities. It is not a natural and obvious, taken-for-granted process: it is a practice based on political decisions taken about the social world.

The second limit on the State's intervention is an ideological one. One of the consequences of the increasing trend toward neo-liberal philosophies in the West since the early 1980s is the idea that services have to be evaluated by market-oriented criteria and can be provided more efficiently by private companies than by the State (central or local). In terms of immigration, this has not been quite so simple to implement because control of borders is one of the remaining sovereign powers of the State, rather like security and military matters, and so privatisation is deemed inappropriate for much of the work. However, aspects of the work can be shifted onto private individuals, officials working for private companies and, only sometimes, private companies engaged in specific functions such as transporting people to and from holding centres, removing people from the country and actually managing detention centres. The new Immigration Act (1996) made it obligatory for various levels of administration to check people's immigration status in the realms of benefits, employment and educations, for example. In the British Commission for Racial Equality's research (1998) into the implementation of the 1996 Act, it found that an array of untrained staff in private and state bodies were now responsible for checking immigration status and deciding on what implications the status had for people's access to resources. Unsurprisingly, a lot of errors had been made, exclusively to do with the rights of minority ethnic people in the UK, even some who were already British nationals! This is not to say that when it is only trained state officials who make decisions, there is no deviance from the letter of the law (Jordan et al., 2003). This type of procedure, where the State divests itself of a number of immigration-related functions is also seen in continental Europe, and is expressed most fully in the move toward handing over responsibility for the processing of asylum claims and the handling of individuals expelled for breaching immigration rules to non-EU countries on the peripheries of Europe, but we shall see that more closely in relation to asylum (Chapter 10).

CONCLUSIONS

The nation, nationalism and the nation state are topics that have fascinated scholars from a wide range of disciplines for a long time. However, only since the mid-twentieth century has attention been paid to the idea that there might be a link between expressions of nationalism and racism, or between the construction of national and racial identities. Moreover, this has been a relatively late and minority interest among sociologists. Despite the long-standing neglect of the role of the State in generating racialisation, there is a lineage of work on this topic going back to the 1930s. The main contention in this corpus is that the State influences racial identities through setting the rules of engagement, legislation on membership of the nation and access to various resources that can be either explicitly or implicitly constructed along racialised lines. This is backed with the authority and legitimacy derived from the exercise of power within a democratic electoral system. The growing number of case studies regarding different nations illustrate points of similarity, and indicate that contemporary areas of interest to sociologists are the State's treatment of the immigration and asylum policy areas, as these reflect racial underpinnings. However, we should also be aware that the sovereignty and power of the nation state in the twenty-first century are diminished in some areas due to the increasingly evident global nature of economic change, and the shared sovereignty implied in international bodies such as the United Nations, NAFTA and the European Union. One particularly sensitive area is the nation state's capacity to defend itself militarily and define laws for entry into, and movement and access to resources within, the State.

5 Science

In Chapter 1, we briefly looked at some examples of how the natural sciences gave support to racial theory in the late eighteenth and early nineteenth centuries. In this chapter, we shall examine in more depth the role that the natural sciences have played in racialising the world's population. At first glance, science might seem an unlikely place to investigate 'race'. Aren't the natural sciences a set of arenas in which the objective truth is more important than the social inequalities and political ideologies of the world we look at elsewhere in the book? Many practitioners of the natural sciences would argue that their work is concerned only with facts and the quest for knowledge, that their 'knowledge and the assumptions that guide knowledge production, now, as never before, transcend the times' (Duster, 2006: 487). However, here we are going to question that assumption by looking at a series of fields and episodes in which 'race' is effectively made by and through science in particular contexts. We shall return to the period of 'race science' in the late eighteenth and early nineteenth centuries and ask what contribution scientists of the day made to establishing 'race' as a fact in the natural and therefore social world. Then we shall consider the role of eugenics, particularly in the first decades of the twentieth century, and its relationship with the political ideology of social Darwinism, followed by a section dealing with medicine's relationship to 'race'. Finally, we will look at cosmetic surgery and suggest that part of what that does is recast people's bodies racially to more closely resemble the somatic norms of the dominant racialised group. It is worth pointing out before we begin that although 'race' has been designated a social reality rather than a biological one by most social scientists and many natural scientists, it is still used as a variable in contemporary scientific research in a way that suggests that it has biological validity. People are frequently asked to self-report their 'race'/ethnicity in relation to medical treatment, for example, so, in the practice of science, the social often overlaps with the natural. In the examples below, we will try to unpick some of this confusion.

'RACE' SCIENCE

The fields of science that can be encompassed by this term stretch from the pseudo-sciences of craniology and phrenology (the study of skull shapes and bumps) through biology, and the origins of anthropology, sociology and ethnography, which developed in the middle of the nineteenth century. Here we shall use two examples: a classificatory system still used today, and some particular applications of the very broad science called anthropometry which involved measuring body parts and extrapolating social conclusions from them. This is a clue to why science is important to the student of racism. In the nineteenth century, science overtook religion as the legitimate source of authority in explaining natural and, by extension, social phenomena in the Western world. For something to be established by scientists henceforth meant that it had entered into the set of assumptions that people held about their world and which they used to decipher it.

Box 5.1   Linnaeus (1707–78) from *The System of Nature* (1735)

'Man, the last and best of created works, formed after the image of his Maker, endowed with a portion of intellectual divinity, the governor and subjugator of all other beings, is, by his wisdom alone, able to form just conclusions from such things as present themselves to his senses, which can only consist of bodies merely natural. Hence, the first step of wisdom is to know these bodies; and be able, by those marks imprinted on them by nature, to distinguish them from one another, and to affix to every object its proper name …

Mammalia
Order 1: Primates

HOMO
Sapiens. Diurnal; varying by education and situation

1. Four-footed, mute, hairy. *Wild man.*
2. Copper-coloured, choleric, erect. *American.*
   Hair black, straight, thick; *nostrils* wide; *face* harsh; *beard* scanty; obstinate, content, free. *Paints* himself with fine red lines. *Regulated* by customs.
3. Fair, sanguine, brawny. *European.*
   Hair yellow, brown, flowing; *eyes* blue; gentle, acute, inventive. *Covered* with close vestments. *Governed* by laws.
4. Sooty, melancholy, rigid.
   Hair black; *eyes* dark; *fever,* haughty, covetous. *Covered* with loose garments. *Governed* by opinions.
5. Black, phlegmatic, relaxed.
   Hair black, frizzled; *skin* silky; *nose* flat; *lips* tumid; crafty, indolent, negligent. *Anoints* himself with grease. *Governed* by caprice.'

Eze (1997:10)

Linnaeus' classification schema is still used in biology. It uses a binomial system (two words: one denoting genus and one a specific title), plus it is arranged hierarchically. Prior to Linnean classification, animals were categorised according to their method of movement. So what he is doing here, logically for an Enlightenment scientist, is classifying people in the same way as plants, fish and animals. In this schema, however, we see the rationale: there is a typology of phenotype informed by innate characteristics, which then enables an appropriate level of governance. The hierarchy runs from rational to capricious. The 'bodies merely natural' can be read as mediations of capacity for civilisation. A causal relationship between these things has developed and been locked into place. The legitimacy and authority of science is crucial to this understanding becoming accepted. Once this relationship is deemed a natural fact, there can be no changing it, and no rational argument against it.

Box 5.2   Comte de Buffon (Georges-Louis Leclerc) (1707–88) from *A Natural History, General and Particular* (1748–1804)

'The most temperate climate lies between the 40th and 50th degrees of latitude, and produces the most handsome and beautiful men. It is from this climate that the ideas of the genuine colour of mankind, and of the various degrees of beauty ought to be derived. The two extremes are equally remote from truth and from beauty. The civilised countries situated under this zone are Georgia, Circassia, the Ukraine, Turkey in Europe, Hungary, the south of Germany, Italy, Switzerland, France and the northern part of Spain. The natives of these territories are the most handsome and most beautiful people in the world. The climate may be regarded as the chief cause of the different colours of men. But food, though it has less influence upon colour, greatly affects the form of our bodies.'

Eze (1997:17)

Buffon links climate with appearance and capacity for civilisation, locating the apex of the latter in the temperate zone of southern to central Europe. We can see here a version of Linnaeus' ideas, and what is noteworthy is not just the assertion of causal links between observable differences in climate and physical appearance, but the process of reiteration. Scientists, philosophers, economists and historians of this period read each other's work and framed their own through it. By force of repetition, assertions enter into the realm of indisputable facts. Here also we have a standard of authenticity: the 'genuine colour of mankind', and of beauty proposed as part of the ideological domination of the West over the presumably inauthentic and ugly others. European and North American elites read the work of the Enlightenment thinkers, and this formed the basis of consensus about what 'race' meant in terms of the social world. If you could successfully argue that some types of people were naturally inferior to others, and this was marked on their bodies, then what could mankind do but respect this divine pattern? The baton is picked up by the social Darwinists later in the century.

ANTHROPOMETRY

Anthropometry is the study of human body measurement for use in anthropological classification and comparison. It has a number of benign uses to do with monitoring health and development, for example. However, it also had another strand that was aimed at producing empirical evidence for the establishment of hierarchical typologies of people. One of the best known is the 'criminal types' typology constructed by Italian physiognomist Cesare Lombroso (1876) that links physical traits (nose shape, length of chin, ear size, distance between eyes, etc.) to different criminal tendencies. Lombroso believed that people were born criminals and that if the types of physical feature were analysed, then criminals could be identified before they reached the stage of actually committing crimes. His understanding was an evolutionary one: human beings were evolving and criminals were a throwback, degenerating and therefore the bearers of physical deformities that betrayed their inner natures. Lombroso's socio-biological interpretations of crime were part of a much wider set of assumptions held by scientists about the link between civilisation and appearance.

Scientists constructed bodies as the clue to meaning about whole groups of people. How could they be read? What 'social sense' could be made of them? In Australia, as late as the 1920s and 1930s, the effort to understand who and what the Aboriginal Australians were entailed an intensive anthropometrical effort described by Warwick Anderson (2006). The various understandings of them – childlike savages, Caucasian throwbacks, people who die out when confronted with civilisation, people who die out when confronted with disease (especially from contact with 'immunologically incompetent' poor white males (ibid.: 221) – were put to the test by researchers from the Adelaide Institute. They measured, weighed, photographed and took samples from hundreds of people. While there was a concentration of the rare type B blood (like Northern Europeans), intelligence tests showed 'childlike levels' of achievement. These findings were significant because they were taken on board by policy makers, who then understood Aboriginals as Caucasians, who were therefore redeemable, rather than irredeemable savages genetically incapable of attaining civilisation. Particularly interesting to these scientists was the discovery and analysis of what they termed the 'half-caste', people with one white European and one Aboriginal parent. An entire project was constructed around this exploration and involved researchers from Harvard as well as Adelaide University in 1938–9. As a result, the anthropologists involved recommended that absorption, rather than isolation, of the native Australians was the way forward. Their conclusion about what studying 'half-castes' could tell us was that it was not particularly revealing. However, once it had been scientifically established that Aboriginals were racially close to Europeans, the path of absorption was taken across Australia. The policy developed aimed at civilising them by separating 'full-bloods' from 'half-castes' in the form of wide-scale adoption to bring them up in all-white environments, and reservations to protect the 'full-bloods' from civilisation. In an uneven process across the states, around 100,000 Aborginal children were removed from their own families and brought up by white families up until the early 1970s (the 'Stolen Generations'). The debate about this is ongoing. A national report, *Bring them Home*, was published in 1997 (Australian Human Rights Commission, 1997). A South Australian won the first compensation from the Federal Government in 2007, and in February 2008, Prime Minister Kevin Rudd gave an official apology to the Aboriginal and Torres Strait Islanders. We thus arrive at the 'Stolen Generations' via 'race' science.[1] Regardless of the intentions of any researcher involved in the data-gathering process, the ultimate consequences of their work were catastrophic for large numbers of Aboriginals. Yet within the context of their profession, these scientists were not deviant but mainstream practitioners, probably even located toward the more progressive end of the scale. They did, however, share the general assumption that 'race' was a matter of blood, bodies and genes, and that this was an accurate predictor of civilisation and development. The Australian case clearly demonstrates the power relations of racial science: the dominant measure the dominated, not the other way around. The production of knowledge flows in one direction, and feeds into policy in which the dominated have no voice. This conclusion sets us up for the next example, that of eugenics.

EUGENICS

Eugenics is the idea that the State can and should intervene in demographic development by encouraging some groups to breed and/or preventing other groups from doing so. It also extends into the domain of euthanasia, where such a policy can be defended, like the previous ones, through claims to protect the national interest. Although eugenics per se is now seen as a historical phenomenon, there are still existing national eugenics societies, a small but vocal pro-eugenics lobby (examples can be found on www.eugenics.net) and a legacy of the ideas put forward and made central to policy in the twentieth century. The origins of eugenics lie in the last quarter of the nineteenth century, when the ideology now called social Darwinism was dominant. Darwin's ideas about evolution, competition and adaptation in the natural world, as published and popularised from the 1860s, were extrapolated into an ideology applicable to the human world.[2] This kind of 'social' interpretation of Darwinism claimed that existing hierarchies (class, gender, 'race') were the result of the natural tendency for the strong and adaptable to dominate the weak and inflexible. War and conflict were seen as ideal mechanisms for accelerating the process of sorting the strong from the weak, which fitted perfectly with the strand of imperialism that was blooming. This idea was deployed to rationalise massacres of colonised people and even their extermination: the last native Tasmanian died in 1868, for example, and some commentators argued that this merely demonstrated the workings of Darwin's model in the human world. Those unable to adapt run to extinction. The development of social Darwinism, however, should really be more associated with the work of the pioneering sociologist and philosopher Herbert Spencer, whose work (prior to and contemporaneous with Darwin's) popularised similar ideas. Spencer sold nearly 400,000 copies of his books in the USA and in the UK, which would mean perhaps a million sales worldwide. In the nineteenth century, that represents astounding sales, and indicates the extent of his appeal. Spencer, for example, used Darwin's phrase 'survival of the fittest' in *Principles of Biology* (1864) a number of times to refer to the social struggle for survival, whereas Darwin used it as a metaphor for 'natural selection'. Spencer understood society through natural frames, organic relationships, struggle and development by means of this struggle.

Against such an ideological background, the application of similar principles through state policy would receive a sympathetic hearing. The word 'eugenics' was coined by Francis Galton in 1883 (Pearson, 1930: 348). Galton's idea of eugenics, as expressed to the Royal Anthropological Society, was the following: 'Eugenics is the study of agencies under social control that may improve or impair the racial qualities of future generations, whether physically or mentally'. Galton and his growing group of supporters, which included people from across the political spectrum of the day, from right-wing imperialists through to Fabian socialists, worked hard to popularise the idea of eugenics as public policy, but found the going difficult. Two decades later, Galton was still talking hypothetically, arguing that it should be 'first an academic matter, then a practical policy', and finally, 'it must be introduced into the national consciousness like a new religion' (Galton, 1905: 50).

The basis of the eugenic standpoint was twofold. First, there was a belief in the State's powers to improve society, and second, an understanding of social hierarchies as deriving from the reflection of nature: the professional classes were seen as the fittest, most competitive and able section of society, with neither the indolence nor the weakness of the poor, nor the vices and lack of dynamism of the aristocrat. Yet this group's birth rate was diminishing, while that of the lower classes was increasing. The eugenics response was couched in terms of the positive and negative. 'Positive eugenics' consisted of measures aimed at promoting higher birth rates among the middle classes, and 'negative eugenics' entailed measures aimed at reducing it among the poor and those with serious congenital problems. While the British eugenicists were unable to move these ideas into the arena of public policy, their counterparts elsewhere were more successful.

The extent of eugenic practice reached from Scandinavia (Broberg and Roll-Hansen, 2005) through Germany across the Atlantic to North and South America in the period 1910–40 especially. It took a variety of forms on a continuum: with increased European immigration and educational programmes at one end (Latin America), through mass sterilisation (USA) to genocide (Nazi Germany) at the other. The Latin American republics such as Mexico, Argentina, Brazil and Uruguay, for example, saw the problem of governance in different ways, but shared the general assumption that European genes were stronger and more desirable than indigenous and African ones. Educational policies aimed at civilising the working classes were deployed alongside immigration policies targeted at Europeans in order to demographically whiten the nation (Stepan, 1991; Dávila, 2003; Appelbaum et al., 2003).

Eugenics in the USA

The case of the USA is interesting in that it preceded the Nazis and provided models that were later acknowledged by German scientists. The success of the American eugenicists is owed to the funding and organisation provided through, firstly, the Carnegie Institute, and then, after 1910, through the New York-based Eugenics Records Office.[3] The director, Charles Davenport and his deputy Harry Laughlin were dedicated lobbyists with a message that people were willing to hear. The work of the ERO was focused on three areas: population control, anti-miscegenation legislation, and immigration control.

Population control

The ERO was concerned to put in place measures to stop people it considered a public menace from having more children. The groups targeted were those with anti-social and/or immoral habits and genetically transmittable illnesses.

Since the mid-nineteenth century, a body of work had been growing that sought to locate the source of America's ills in the family environment and bad genes of its poor (Hartigan, 2005; Wray, 2006). Moreover, alcoholism was in those days considered an immoral behaviour rather than an illness, and conditions such as 'feeble-mindedness', which were later dropped by medical practitioners as being without substance, were still in circulation. The Commonwealth of Virginia was the most eager state to take on board the ERO's arguments, and in the landmark Buck vs Bell case in 1927 (an appeal to the Supreme Court by Buck), the state government was granted its right to compulsorily sterilise a young woman called Carrie Buck. She had been raped by a family member, and her child, Vivian, had been 'tested' at seven months by a child psychologist who argued that she was 'feeble-minded', like her mother and grandmother. The case revolved around the Commonwealth's duty to act in the public interest by preventing the Bucks from continuing to produce mentally ill children, and it had modelled its statute on Laughlin's draft in 1924. In the Supreme Court, judge Oliver Wendell Holmes' summary was that: 'Three generations of imbeciles are enough'. The case set a precedent for state powers of compulsory sterilisation, and by the next decade, more than half the states in the USA were following Virginia's lead. The compulsory sterilisation procedures were carried out disproportionately on African American, Native American, Hispanic and on white working-class women (A. Davis, 2001). This practice went on into the 1970s before it was recognised as being inappropriate. The Head of the Federal government's Department of Health, Education and Welfare admitted in 1974 that between 100,000 and 200,000 sterilisations had been performed in 1972 alone (A. Davis, 2001: 218). From the various inquiries into forced sterilisation, it appears that the proportions of Native American, Black and Latina women sterilised by the mid-1970s lay at upwards of 20 per cent (ibid).

The Nazis also ran sterilisation and euthanasia programmes (Burleigh, 2001) aimed at people with disabilities and alcoholism, etc. in Germany in the 1930s. Indeed, the so-called 'Final Solution' can be read as a eugenics project: aimed at eliminating the unwanted 'races' and sub-humans from Europe. The shared understanding among eugenicists and the policy makers they influenced was of a natural genetic order of things that shapes the social world. This period (the 1920s to the 1940s) seems to have been the one in which federal and local authorities felt they had the authority to act according to that order. What distinguishes it from the earlier period is not so much the ideological underpinning, but the target populations. Prior to the 1920s, colonial powers or their agents had either allowed high death tolls because the natural and social order suggested the colonised groups were expendable, or inflicted mass killings for the same reasons. This can be seen, for example, in the responses to nineteenth-century famines in Ireland and Bengal for the former (M. Davis, 2001), and the Philippines (1899), the Congo Free State (1902–10) and German South-West Africa (1904–7) for the latter. The movement of eugenics into policy *at home* shaped a remarkable three decades of state terrorism against elements of its own population, and it was based on racial logic: first, that people are genetically different (superior and inferior) and second, that the superior have the right to impose policies including execution on those it deems inferior.

Miscegenation

'Miscegenation' was a term invented by two political journalists in the 1860s to talk about 'race mixing', specifically between black and white, in order to exacerbate white anxieties over the abolition of slavery (see Chapter 6). The ERO was interested in protecting what it saw as the white gene pool, both from defective Whites (like Carrie Buck) and from non-Whites. Mixing was held to lead to degenerate individuals more susceptible to illness and the supposed flaws of the inferior partner's 'race'. The important eugenics theorist and activist, Madison Grant, argued in his *The Passing of the Great Race* (1915) that great races were undone by not protecting their gene pools. Although Davenport (1911) found that by 1913, 29 states already had anti-miscegenation laws on their books, he offered support for tightening them and extending them to other states. Again, the Commonwealth of Virginia was first to benefit from this expert advice, and its Virginia Integrity Act (1924) banned marriage between a white person and anyone 'with a trace of blood other than Caucasian'. All the country's anti-miscegenation laws were abolished in 1967, and in 2001, the Commonwealth of Virginia publicly renounced its role in American eugenics.

Immigration

Davenport stated early in the ERO's existence that the organisation was concerned about the future shape of American demographics. In a 1911 publication, *Heredity in Relation to Eugenics*, he argued that:

> the population of the United States will, on account of the great influx of blood from South-eastern Europe, rapidly become darker in pigmentation, smaller in stature, more mercurial, more attached to music and art, [and] more given to crimes of larceny, kidnapping, assault, murder, rape and sex-immorality. (Davenport, 1911: 219)

To understand this statement, we must look at the changing character of immigration into the USA after 1890. Increasing proportions of Southern Europeans (Italians, Greeks, Yugoslavs) and Eastern Europeans (Poles, Lithuanians and Russians, especially Jewish Russians) were immigrating to America at that time due to the poor economic conditions in Europe and the phase of labour-intensive expansion experienced by the US economy. The ERO, with its eye for putative natural/genetic distinctions that would play out in cultural terms, found it dangerous that so many poor Catholic and Jewish Europeans from the east and south were outnumbering the northern and western, mainly protestant stock. Harry Laughlin's role in the formulation of the US 1924 Immigration Act is extraordinary. The ERO was contacted in 1911 by the Immigration Restriction League and successfully lobbied the government to take such bio-cultural consequences into account when setting quotas. The ERO had powerful allies: the Public Health Service (whose officials dealt with incoming immigrants at Ellis Island), and labour organisations fearing a drop in working conditions for their members. Laughlin carried out research on the mentally ill and prison population with a view to arguing that the immigrant population were causing the degeneration of American standards, and in 1920 he appeared before the US Congressional Committee on Immigration and Naturalization, where he gave evidence suggesting that the US gene pool was being polluted by defective genes. He was appointed as an expert by the Committee, and for the next decade had his research funded by the tax payer. He was instrumental in determining the 1924 Act's content. The result was that the 1924 Immigration Act granted quotas to the various countries based on the levels of the US population as of 1890. This date was deliberately chosen because it preceded the peaking wave of Catholic, Slavic and Jewish European immigration from 1890 onwards, and therefore established quotas for such sources of labour at very low levels. That Act remained in place until 1965.

The interpretations of genetic diversity made by eugenicists were backed up by seemingly scientific analyses and impressive amounts of statistical research. However, their understanding of what constituted a 'race' is far from consistent, even from one researcher to another. Moreover, as part of the ERO's work, entire nationalities became prone to particular types of crime; a clear line was established between worthwhile and useless members of society, and into the latter category fell people with physical and mental disabilities, as well as pseudo-categories such as the 'feeble-minded'. Deciding that a given group is worth less than another, based on a medical condition (for reasons of money/ collective security), is saturated with assumptions that must be to do with racialised thinking (blood determines culture, and cultures are arranged in a hierarchical order), whatever else they are also about. The main thrust of eugenics discourse is to argue for the common good, for the improvement of society. However, in practice, it is the relatively powerless who are the victims, so the questions that must always be asked about eugenics are: 'improvements for whom?' and 'who will lose out in the improvement process?'

RACIALISED BODIES AND MEDICINE

Early racial science sought to measure, and thus interpret, the meaning and value of bodies through a framework of a division of the world into civilised and savage cultures and people. According to the prevailing logic, the people who were members of the inferior cultures, had, by extension, physical and intellectual capacity inferior to those of others. This made their bodies interesting to anthropometrists and anthropologists, as we have seen above, and also to medical practitioners. Once you begin with the assumption that some generic types of phenotype are vehicles for a different and distinct biology (within the body and not just its surface), then other things also become possible, such as the placing of thresholds of deviancy and normality in places where it might now, with the benefit of centuries' more scientific research and social change, be thought very odd. One example of this 'medicalization of deviance' is given by Troy Duster (2006). In an article setting out the links between the legal profession, science and medicine, he points to the invention of a new mental illness, *drapetomania*, coined by prominent American surgeon Samuel Cartwright. It represented Cartwright's assertion that slaves' repeated attempts to escape the plantations constituted a mental health condition whose source was a particular deviant psychological state. While it might appear perverse to characterise such behaviour as anything other than normal, it has to be understood that the diagnosis stemmed from a particular interpretation of the social world. In this view, black men were naturally prone to violence, against their own women and children (Duster, 2006: 490–91), and had to be treated with a balance of familiarity and discipline, but not too much of either. Imbalance in either direction could create the conditions for 'drapetomanic' behaviour:

> The cause, in most cases that induces the negro to run away from service is as much a disease of the mind as any other species of mental alienation, and much more curable, as a general rule. With the advantages of proper medical advice, strictly followed, this troublesome practice that many negroes have of running away can be entirely prevented … (Cartwright, 1860: 707)

This only makes sense if black people are understood to be biologically and psychologically inferior to white people and to require governance that only disciplinarian Whites can provide; if the violence inflicted by white slave-owners and their staff does not therefore count as violence; and if this is a natural state. Why else would the quest for freedom from slavery be viewed as unnatural? Indeed, the inferiority of black people is made a material reality in the US Constitution of 1790 that categorises them as chattel rather than people, and the equation of black personhood with the 1787 'Three Fifths Compromise'[4] which went unchallenged until the 1856 *Dred Scott* Supreme Court ruling upheld the principle.

Further examples of scientific practice predicated on the idea that European and African Americans have such different physiognomies as to allow differential pathologies, can be seen in the 'Tuskegee Syphilis Experiment', where controlled experiments were carried out on black subjects, and in the recent developments in pharmaceuticals such as BiDil, the so-called 'ethnic drug' (– see Box 5.3).

The 'Tuskegee Syphilis Experiment'

The experiment, whose full title is the 'Tuskegee Study of Untreated Syphilis in the Black Man', is notorious: President Clinton publicly apologised in 1997. Its notoriety derives from both its assumptions and its conduct. The experiment was aimed at studying the effects of syphilis and its remedies on the human body. A number of studies have been written (Jones, 1993). However, the African American sample group were not told about any treatments that developed during the lifetime of the trials, and were used de facto as a control group without their consent. This contradicts the ethical responsibility to inform patients, and not to do them harm, which is part of the Hippocratic Oath taken by medical practitioners.

The experiment, funded by the Public Health Service (PHS), was run from the University of Tuskegee in Alabama, and began in 1932. The nearly 400-strong African American sample consisted of peasant farmers from the surrounding area (Macon County) who were suffering from syphilis. They were observed and tested at various intervals over a 40-year period. However, they were not told what illness they had, merely that they had 'bad blood'. At the outset, they were given very small amounts of the contemporary remedies such as bizmuth and mercury. Yet these were soon replaced with aspirin. Moreover, even when some of the men joined the armed forces in the Second World War and were required to have treatment, the PHS obtained an exemption from treatment for them. When penicillin became the standard remedy for syphilis in 1947, the men were not informed, and were allowed to go untreated for the purposes of the experiment. Scientific papers on the men were presented and published throughout the experiment, but the sample were mainly illiterate and in any case not likely to read the specialist medical journals in which the papers were published. Basically, the real data could only be retrieved once the person had died and his body could be inspected in a post-mortem, to gauge the effects of untreated syphilis on the body. The medical interest in them therefore began after death, and so it was actually in the researchers' interests for them to die! Eventually, details of the experiment's conduct were leaked to the media by concerned public health workers, but by the time the experiment ended in 1972, 28 of the men had died directly of syphilis, and 100 had died of related complications. Forty of their wives had been infected, and 19 children had been born with congenital syphilis. In 1973, the National Association for the Advancement of Colored People (NAACP) won a $9-million settlement in a 'class-action' lawsuit. Free healthcare was extended to the remaining sample, and to infected wives, widows and children.

The Tuskegee experiment changed the way research ethics were conceptualised and controlled. Its legacy was serious distrust of the government among African Americans over any area relating to public health (Freimuth et al., 2001). There are also complicating factors in this story. Tuskegee University was a black college founded by Booker T. Washington. It lent the PHS access to its laboratories and amenities without question, and a senior black nurse was one of the project's key staff throughout. This does not change the assumptions behind the research, or its overall functioning, but raises troubling questions about Tuskegee's institutional involvement. If we compare the Tuskegee Experiment with the policies implemented in response to the work of the American eugenicists, the power relations are evident. The powerful research the powerless and, in this case, virtually wield power of life and death.

Box 5.3   BiDil: an ethnic drug?

One of the rationales put forward for continuing to do race-based medical research is to target illnesses specific to different racial groups. The marketing of the drug BiDil (isosorbide dinitrate/hydralazine hydrochloride), approved by the US Food and Drugs Agency (FDA) in 2005 as a drug specifically for African Americans, is a case where commercial practices,

(Continued)

(Continued)

scientific reasoning and research methods, and concepts of 'race' intersect. BiDil was not a new drug but a combination of two old ones. However, the marketing plan, run by NitroMed, Inc., was new: it exclusively targeted African Americans.

The new marketing plan was based on a clinical trial in 2004 that used only African Americans in the sample group. As there was no control population (for comparison), there is nothing to sustain the company's claim that 'race' is a useful variable. Moreover, if the principle is to market a drug by a group who it is tested on, all other drugs would have to be marketed as 'white drugs'. Jonathan Kahn (2006: 3) explains that: 'NitroMed holds at least two patents to BiDil. One is not race-specific, but it expires in 2007. The other is race-specific; it does not expire until 2020. With its race-specific patent in hand, NitroMed can even block the marketing of the generic components of BiDil specifically to treat heart failure. NitroMed therefore has a vested interest in framing BiDil as a race-specific drug – regardless of the limitations imposed by the actual evidence'.

The use of figures in convincing customers comprises a sleight of hand. The company quotes a higher ratio of overall African American to white deaths from heart failure than is the case. However, the age cohort in relation to which the ratio is actually true (45–64), accounts for only a maximum of 6 per cent of all heart attacks. The vast majority (94 per cent) occur at age 65 and over. In that older age group, there is virtually no difference in mortality rates between whites and African Americans.

Moreover, lots of factors other than what scientists call 'race' or ethnicity affect the body's responses to drugs. It would be possible to arrive at a technical profile of these factors. However, a drug cannot readily be marketed to a technically defined group, only a social group. Therefore, the marketing of BiDil is part of a commercial rather than medical and research-driven agenda. Even if the set of markers that people have traditionally considered 'racial' were clear and unequivocal (which they are not), there is no consensus among scientists about the response rates to drugs being only to do with those markers.

The BiDil episode demonstrates how science naturalises 'race' by passing it off as being reflected in nature (it thus racialises nature). Could this type of marketing usher in a trend? Kahn (2007a: 387) thinks this is possible.

Figures show that 65 patents have claimed a racial basis since 2001. There were zero in the 1976–97 period, and 12 between 1998 and 2005 (Kahn, 2007b). Kahn's conclusion about science, marketing and 'race' in the twenty-first century is troubling: 'In the context of gene patents, genetic race is becoming a commodity as race-specific patents allow biotechnology corporations to raise venture capital and develop marketing strategies that present a reified conception of race as genetic to doctors, regulators, and the public at large' (Kahn, 2007a: 416).

The racialisation of pharmaceuticals therefore appears to be emerging as a strategy for marketing medicines, and this is not based on rigorous science. Indeed, as an editorial in the science journal *Nature Biotechnology* puts it: 'Race is simply a poor proxy for the environmental and genetic causes of disease or drug response ... Pooling people in race silos is akin to zoologists grouping raccoons, tigers and okapis on the basis that they are all stripey' (*Nature Biotechnology*, 23: 903, 2005).

COSMETIC INTERVENTIONS

In the video for Michael Jackson's 'Black or White' (1991), people morph into different 'racial' bodies, as he sings 'I don't want to spend my life being a colour'. Indeed, with cosmetic surgery increasingly lucrative and popular, Jackson's own problematic relationship with the racialisation of his body seems to be an increasingly mainstream concern. The video-enhanced morphing has become, in a way, a reality for some people ready to make the financial commitment required. However, the contention in this section is that a specific set of cosmetic procedures are not really about refining features toward a neutral universal version of what a beautiful face and/or body should look like, but a heavily racialised reproduction of dominant culture. Cosmetic surgery can be a project of whiteness for those who recognise the cost of it and are prepared to make an investment to profit from it. It can be seen as an advantage in employment, in business, in the marketplace for partners and as a way of avoiding some of the obstacles that are placed in front of people who are not white.

Skin-whitening creams have been available as products at least since the late nineteenth century. By 1930, over 230 brands of skin lightener were available (Peiss, 1999: 149). At the outset, these were mainly marketed at white women in America through magazines but this does not mean that they were the only people to use these products. The creams usually contained either hydroquinine or mercury or derivatives of the former (Box 5.4). They function by suppressing the production of melanin in the basal layer of the skin. These creams have been used to lighten skin shade in Africa and Asia, and latterly also Europe. As Amina Mire (2005) points out, skin-whitening creams are an integral part of a global cosmetics trade, earning large multinationals such as L'Oréal, Ponds and Garnier billions of dollars annually. She calls the emerging skin-whitening industry 'a lucrative globalized economic enterprise with profound social and political implications'.[5] Just as an indicator, estimates suggest that as of 2001, the Japanese skin-whitening market was estimated to be worth $5.6 billion, and China's market (the fastest growing) was estimated to be worth over $1.3 billion. India is another huge market for such products. By 2007, skin lighteners were worth around $318 million, a rise of 43 per cent since 2001. Melwani (2008) reports that the country manager for L'Oréal India told *The Times* that half of this market was accounted for by skin-whitening creams, and that 60–65 per cent of Indian women were daily users of these products.

There are two parts to this market. One is for cheaper products, often containing excessive amounts of the two main constituents, which are sold to less well-off customers. The other is a 'high end' market aimed at the affluent. The creams are marketed to white women as 'anti-ageing' products, and to non-white women as a means to make themselves radiant, attractive and Western. Considerable argument has occurred within African American circles about the use of skin-lightening products, and they are now marketed as ways to even out skin tone (by removing blotches) and to slow the ageing process rather than directly as skin whiteners. The link in Asian and American cultures between whiteness and success is used as a ploy to draw in more customers (mainly women, although there is a growing market for men).

Box 5.4   How skin-lightening products work

There are two chemicals found in skin-lightening products:

- hydroquinone ($C_6H_6O_2$) – a highly toxic chemical used in photo processing, rubber manufacture and hair dyes
- mercury – in the form of mercury chloride and ammoniated mercury, which is carcinogenic.

Both appear on the list of toxic substances that can only be purchased via pharmacies with prescribed labels of toxicity. Both products perform a similar process. In the short term, they will initially cause the skin to lighten by inhibiting the production of melanin. Many contemporary forms of skin lightener use derivatives of hydroquinine or compounds with a similar structure. If the products contain too high a proportion of either hydroquinine or mercury, they cannot legally be sold in many countries. In the 1930s, US products contained around 10 per cent mercury. It is now illegal for products to contain more than 2 per cent. Amina Mire (2005) reports that in developing world countries and ethnic grocery stores in North America and Europe, many of the creams are cheap and toxic, exceeding the toxin thresholds set out by the US federal government, for example.

Although there are criticisms of how advertising marks whiteness as the aspiration and darker skin as something to get rid of, this has not stopped advertisers from blatantly promoting their whitening products as a way to attract the opposite sex and to gain financial success. A series of mini films used to market the subtly titled Pond's 'White Beauty' cream in India in 2008 attracted a lot of controversy. In it, a trio of prominent Bollywood actors (Saif Ali Khan, Priyanka Chopra and Neha Dhupia) perform. The story is that the darker-skinned Chopra splits up with Khan, who years later becomes famous and goes out with the pale-skinned Dhupia. Chopra uses Pond's product to make herself more attractive, that is, whiter, and wins Khan back. A film with a virtually identical storyline (Pond's 'Flawless White') was also used in the Japanese market. Another advert, for men's cream this time, was also the subject of controversy in India months prior to this. Bollywood actor Sharukh Khan appears in an advert for Emami's 'Fair and Handsome' product (all these clips can be accessed through YouTube). Other Asian countries are experiencing similar cosmetic bonanzas. Fuller (2006) claims that 40 per cent of women in Hong Kong, Malaysia, the Philippines, South Korea and Taiwan use a whitening cream, according to market research company Synovate, and that more than 60 'new skin-whitening products were introduced in supermarkets or pharmacies across the Asia-Pacific region' in 2005, which is an increase on the average of 56 new products introduced annually since 2000. While there are different explanations within each culture as to exactly why a lighter complexion is so desirable that people use toxic chemicals to achieve this goal, the main role must go to the legacy of Western domination of the rest of the world for centuries. Regardless of existing social stratifications such as caste in India, and the negative associations attached to darker complexions elsewhere, possibly partly to do with class (as in Europe until the mid-twentieth century, outdoor work activities meant a darker complexion), the European practices and ideas of 'race' connected with and altered them, so that the available ways of understanding colour as a social marker are a combination of local and imported systems. In the USA and other plantation societies, the social correspondence between fairer skin and social prestige led to increased differentiation between darker and not so dark-skinned people, both on plantations and off them, as small 'coloured' or 'Mulatto' middle classes developed (Lacy, 2007). The profound legacy of vilification of blackness in the Americas, which grew out of the slave system and has long outlived it, cannot be ignored – the hierarchical social relations in which lighter skin is afforded more value, known as 'colorism', are still pertinent (Morrison, 1970; Yancy, 2001; Hunter, 2007). Although the civil rights movement and its message of Black Power marked a cultural shift in the way African Americans could evaluate themselves culturally and physically in the public arena, that legacy has not disappeared.

It is not only skin-whitening creams but also cosmetic surgery that enables people to change their appearance racially. I am not claiming that every surgical operation such as reconstruction after injury or illness, or tummy tucks or breast enlargement/reduction, is solely to do with expressing a desire to be whiter. I am concerned here only with surgeries undergone by minorities (including Jews) that are aimed at changing the body shape or features in a way that makes them appear closer to Western norms. This is not merely taking place in larger numbers in the two centres of world plastic surgery, the west and the east coasts of the USA, but also in a number of Asian countries, where new racial surgeries are being improvised (Box 5.5)

The number of surgeries in Asia, for example, is also increasing, and they are clearly focused on approximating to the white ideal, of larger breasts, a different appearance of the eyes, paler skin and longer, thinner legs, as the example of Korea (Box 5.5) demonstrates.

Box 5.5   Special surgical procedures for Asian women

'Just as Asian faces require unique procedures, their bodies demand innovative operations to achieve the leggy, skinny, busty Western ideal that has become increasingly universal. Dr Suh In Seock, a surgeon in Seoul, has struggled to find the best way to fix an affliction the Koreans call *muu-dari* and the Japanese call *daikon-ashi*: radish-shaped calves. Liposuction, so effective on the legs of plump Westerners, doesn't work on Asians since muscle, not fat, accounts for the bulk. Suh says earlier attempts to carve the muscle were painful and made walking difficult. "Finally, I discovered that by severing a nerve behind the knee, the muscle would atrophy," says Suh, "thereby reducing its size up to 40 per cent." Suh has performed over 600 of the operations since 1996. He disappears for a minute and returns with a bottle of fluid containing what looks like chopped up bits of ramen noodles. He has preserved his patients' excised nerves in alcohol. "And that's just since November," he says proudly'. (from 'Nip and Tuck', a special feature in *Time* Magazine, Asia section, 2006, www.time.com/time/asia/covers/1101020805/story.html)

Table 5.1   **Percentage of cosmetic surgery patients, by ethnicity, 1999, 2003 and 2008**

Ethnic group	1999	2003	2008
Caucasian	85	80	73
Hispanic	6	8	10
African American	4	6	8
Asian American	3	4	7
Other	1	2	2

Source : American Society for Aesthetic Plastic Surgery (1999:3) and (2003:2); American Society of Plastic Surgeons (2009)

Table 5.2   **The three most commonly requested surgical procedures for 'ethnic' patients, 2007**

African American	Asian American	Hispanic
1 Nose reshaping	1 Nose reshaping	1 Breast augmentation
2 Liposuction	2 Breast augmentation	2 Nose reshaping
3 Breast reduction	3 Eyelid surgery	3 Liposuction

Source : American Society of Plastic Surgeons (2009)

Meanwhile, back in the USA, the numbers from the American Plastic Surgeons Association are revealing a growing trend among minorities for cosmetic procedures since the turn of the century.

In the period 1999–2008, the overall number of cosmetic surgeries increased massively, from 4.6 to 12.1 million. Of this, the ethnic minority customer share rose from 15 per cent to 27 per cent (Table 5.1). This seems to reflect increasing affluence on one hand but also a pattern of surgeries (Table 5.2) reflecting a desire to move toward a 'Caucasian' standard (especially nose reshaping for all and eyelid surgery and breast augmentation for Asian Americans).

We should not be surprised, however, that the origin of cosmetic surgery is a wish to change one's appearance to something closer to the dominant phenotype. The 'nose job', or rhinoplasty, to give it its medical term, was invented in India in the sixth century as a reconstructive procedure. However, rhinoplasty as a *cosmetic* surgery was pioneered by German Jewish surgeon Jacques Joseph in Berlin in the 1890s. Many of his operations were responses to Jewish patients' experiences of anti-Semitism (Gilman, 1991). The 'Jewish nose' was seen as an ethnic giveaway by German Jews of the day, and Joseph became aware that it was as much in the minds of some of his patients as an observable fact. The surgery seemed to serve psychologically reassuring ends, although it was no guarantee against further anti-Semitic violence. Joseph's textbooks on cosmetic surgery that were published in the 1930s became landmark medical texts.[6] The rhinoplasty went on to become the stock cosmetic surgery until other procedures, such as liposuction and breast enlargement, became more popular from the 1990s. A point of comparison is the blepharoplasty: a procedure developed to alter the appearance of Asian eyes by inserting a permanent crease in the eyelids. It is the most popular procedure in Asian clinics, which, buoyed by the increasing amount of work they received, began attracting Western customers in the twenty-first century in a phenomenon referred to as 'surgery tourism', where people plan a vacation around having relatively cheap surgery in a private clinic in Thailand or Indonesia, for example.

So the procedures chosen by many minority women (for they still comprise the vast majority of cosmetic surgery patients) are not, on the whole, mainstream surgeries but those which make the patient's body approximate more closely to a white norm than their starting point. So what does this tell us about standards of beauty, individual agency and collective understandings of beauty? I think that whatever else cosmetic surgery is about, such as the search for the self (Elliott, 2008), it can also be about racialisation and white supremacy. Mire's conclusion about the skin-whitening industry is just as apt in relation to the cosmetic surgery one, albeit with a more complex dynamic. It is, as she argues, 'part and parcel of our old enemy, the "civilising mission"; the violent moral prerogative to cleanse and purify the mind and bodies of the "dark/dirt/savage"'. The added complexity of skin-lightening and specific cosmetic surgeries is that they are part of the postcolonial internalisation of this civilising mission, among those whose ancestors were the original objects of the mission. Is the object to approximate to whiteness, or to stave off blackness and Asianness? The fact that people risk their health and spend considerable amounts of money on cosmetic products and services, indicates that there is something significant at stake.

NOTES

1. See the Australian Indigenous Stolen Generation resource centre at Trinity College, Western Australia's site: www.trinity.wa.edu.au/plduffyrc/indig/stolen.htm
2. The two major works are *On the Origin of Species* (1859) and *The Descent of Man* (1871).
3. See a superb online collection relating to the ERO at: www.eugenicsarchive.org
4. At the 1787 Constitutional Convention, an argument between the Northern and Southern delegates took place over whether to count slaves as property or people. The reason was that they were discussing each state's representation to the US Congress. The greater the population, the greater the relative representation and therefore power that a state could wield. The delegates from the non-slave-owning Northern states wanted slaves not to count, and the Southern delegates held the opposite view. James Madison's compromise meant that each slave would count as 3/5ths of a man, that is, 15 slaves would be counted as 9 voters. The obvious irony is that slaves could not vote anyway.
5. See also Glenn (2008).
6. For further information on Joseph, see www.jacques-joseph.de/

6 Mixed-ness

One of the most noticeable phenomena in terms of demographic trends in the West is the increase in the proportion of people identifying themselves as 'mixed race' or 'bi-racial' or the equivalent. While this pattern is far from news in many countries outside Europe and North America (and I suggest not really new there either), it is a point that poses two interesting questions for students of racism. The first is the challenge to existing racial categories in which the State, groups and individuals invest politically and emotionally. The idea of people belonging simultaneously to more than one group, or not, depending on the context, undermines the racialised boundaries that most people now recognise. What are the implications of 'bi-racial' becoming a bloc in itself, or what are the implications of those individuals consistently finding themselves marginalised by the mainstream groups? Secondly, what does a growing mixed-race population tell us about today's patterns of sociability and about tomorrow's national identities? Is there a classic postmodernist blizzard of hybridity and options, or is it more a case of people strategically juggling and choosing identities on a political basis? While I was writing this chapter, the Unites States elected its first non-white President, and some of the early public responses questioned whether he was 'black' or 'mixed/bi-racial', which, I suggest, is a false dichotomy. We shall look at what is at stake in these types of debates in more detail in the later sections of this chapter.

We are going to begin at a relatively abstract level and move on to some case studies from fieldwork. Throughout this section, readers should bear in mind that the discussions about multiraciality/bi-raciality/'mixed race' in the UK and the USA are derived from some quite different social realities and dynamics, which will be explained as we go along. For the purposes of this chapter, I am going to use the terms 'mixed-ness' and 'mixed race' in inverted commas, which reflects my British habitus, and the lack of really good alternatives. This is an area of contestation in the literature, with some preferring the use of other terms (bi-racial, multiracial, mulatto, métisse, etc.). However, as important as this might be, there are other equally important elements to this field that need contextualising and attention. The starting point will be historical and comparative.

Jane Ifekwunigwe has worked on international comparisons of the phenomenon of 'mixed race', and in her reader (2004), she puts forward two overarching frameworks. The first is that there are 'four pillars' of international comparative studies, and 'three phases' of attention paid to mixed-ness, each characterised by a different understanding of it. Figures 6.1 and 6.2 represent my interpretation of these frameworks in a tabular format.

I am going to use Ifekwunigwe's historical and thematic framing in this chapter because they represent a theoretical intervention that enables us to approach this

Figure 6.1 **The four pillars of international comparative work on mixed race**

Pillar	Function	Details
European expansion, settler colonisation and imperialisms	Political power-producing	Since 1500. Settler colonization, in some cases displaced and subordinated indigenous peoples.
Slavery		The process of importing a labour force from Africa to the New World. This led to the economic development of Europe and North America, and the underdevelopment of continental Africa.
'Race'/colour hierarchies	Structural/status-defining	White superiority and non-white inferiority assumed and bolstered by racial science in the nineteenth century. Local social conditions determined whether mixed population would be assimilated or cultivated as a 'buffer' group between Europeans and Natives.
Gender hierarchies		White men, then White women, then non-white men, then non-white women. This hierarchy led to the production of a 'mixed-race' population through the sexual exploitation of non-white women by white men.

Source: Ifekwunigwe (2004: 7)

Figure 6.2 **The three 'ages' of 'mixed-race' studies**

The age of …	Themes	Questions
Pathology	Miscegenation and moral degeneracy	What does 'race-mixing' mean for individuals and societies? Should 'race-mixing' be regulated or legislated?
Celebration	Contingency of identifications: 'actor-centred' approaches; social constructionism	What do 'mixed-race' identities look like from the perspectives of the actors? What options for identity construction are open, where, when and why?
Critique	'Multiraciality'; the politics of identification	What are the political implications of counting 'mixed race' in the Census? What is the future of 'mixed-race' studies?

Source: Ifekwunigwe (2004: 8–9; 137; 201)

very diverse set of writings and perspectives from a position of cohesion and awareness of the comparative dimension. Although there are British and American-based essays in some of the edited volumes (Parker and Song, 2001), much of the writing in the latter two 'ages' is extremely focused on the national conditions of the USA, as in the sub-field of 'whiteness'. Using an internationally and historically comparative perspective therefore will provide a starting point.

THE IDEA OF MIXED RACE IN HISTORY

It is in the colonial contexts of the New World that the idea of 'race' became salient as a way of dividing up people by status and employment. This is not the same thing as saying that prior to the sixteenth century there were no people who were what might now be described as 'mixed race'. Indeed, as 'race' is about *political and social interpretations* of bodies and culture, it is these that form the focus of this section. This is why the expansion of Europe into the Americas, Asia, Africa and Australasia is the key moment. In the Spanish New World, for example, the social hierarchies were imported. The feudal nobility of bloodlines, represented in the ideal of *limpieza de sangre* (biological and cultural purity) could be extended to cover 'race' as well as class. However, the practical impossibility of keeping Spaniard, Native and African from producing children with each other (a gender and power relations framework) meant that the authorities responded by constructing a complicated human typology, using terms such as *mestizo, castizo, mulatto, quadroon* and *zambo* to describe various mixtures. This status typology (in which the paler complexion was afforded higher status) signifies the entry of such phenotypical groups into public life. Soon, factors other than bloodlines also began to enter into the social equation, such as occupation, wealth, religion and education. In particular areas of labour shortage, 'mixed race' people were afforded marginally better status than others who lived where there was no such shortage. 'Mixed race' people could, as Ann Twinam (2006) demonstrates, also petition the authorities for the right to be officially designated white, which gave access to more lucrative opportunities for employment and higher status.

In North America, there was no shortage of labour in the seventeenth century due to the indentureship of poor white Europeans and the growing trade in enslaved Africans. The mixed population grew through the planter and his staff's access to African women. At this time, children born to an enslaved woman were the property of the slave-owner, so there was even an economic interest in this type of forced and imposed race mixing. At the same time, fugitive Africans frequently mixed with Native Americans across the Americas. However, laws against having children across the colour line were introduced at the end of the seventeenth century in the slave states. This was primarily aimed at black men and white women, as the opposite combination continued to generate children until the abolition of slavery. Indeed, this was the case wherever there were plantation societies. Ifekwunigwe points out (2004: 16–17) that in a BBC documentary, *Motherland* (2002), that focused on tracing mitochondrial (m-DNA), that is, female DNA, and Y chromosomes (male), a very strong pattern emerged. The sample was 228 American and British people whose grandparents and parents were all Afro-Caribbean. Only 2 per cent of British Afro-Caribbeans have m-DNA that can be traced to Europe rather than Africa, while 25 per cent have a Y chromosome that can be traced to Europe rather than Africa. For Ifekwunigwe, this demonstrates 'the particular gendered, economic and erotic politics of the transatlantic slavery enterprise' (ibid.: 17).

So laws against black men marrying white women were attempts to mark out a gendered and racialised limit to race mixing, and as with *limpieza de sangre*, suggest the basis of such legislation was the fear of threats to white purity. From this perspective, whiteness can be made impure by mixing with others, whereas the other identities cannot be.

As the era of 'race' science blossomed in the mid-1800s, those theorists interested in 'race' concurred (with very few exceptions) that 'mixed race' people were degenerate and more prone to the supposed racial characteristics of the darker partner. Although the idea that mixing between the human races produced infertile offspring was quickly disproved, it was argued that whole civilisations were doomed to cultural as well as physical degeneracy if they allowed such mixing. This was a constant theme in writing on 'race', from de Gobineau in the 1850s, to H.S. Chamberlain in the late 1890s, to Madison Grant in the twentieth century.

The idea of degeneracy is combined, according to Robert Young (1995), with the desire for exotic difference. His thesis is that the development of the concepts of 'hybridity' and 'sexuality' in Victorian England and America were essential to the development of the Western world's image of itself as all-conquering and civilising at that moment in the nineteenth century. While these were elements supporting the push for English cultural domination, they simultaneously fuelled a desire for interracial sex. So the paradox, claims Young, is that Victorian disgust with sexuality and the inferior alien 'Other' is constantly in tension with the profound desire for interracial sex, as played out in the Empire. This tension then 'destabilises' the stable idea of Englishness derived from the avowed disdain for dirt and impurity.

By the time of the American Civil War (1861), the word 'amalgamation', borrowed from metallurgy, was in use as a general term for ethnic and racial intermixing. It would be superseded by the new term, 'miscegenation', around the 1864 presidential election. Two pro-Democratic Party journalists, David Goodman Croly (managing editor of the *New York World*), and George Wakeman, a *World* reporter, produced a hoax pamphlet called, 'Miscegenation: The Theory of the Blending of the Races, Applied to the American White Man and Negro'. The pamphlet was aimed at scaring voters away from the pro-Abolition Republican Party (led by Abraham Lincoln) by suggesting that race mixing was a Republican policy. In the climate of the day, with tension between pro- and anti-abolition forces, and with even anti-slavery supporters unlikely to see 'miscegenation' as a good thing, such a piece of propaganda was highly inflammatory. Of course, it focused only on black men having children with white women: the other groups were omitted from the account. Ifekwunigwe's 'four pillars' are thus demonstrated here: European expansion brought Europeans to the Americas; slavery was instituted as a device for supplying and controlling labour; within the society, a colour hierarchy developed in which white was at the summit and black at the bottom; and within this hierarchy was a gendered one – white men's relationships with black women were neither legislated against nor socially policed, whereas as much was emotionally invested in preventing relationships between white women and black men. It is in this context that the function of the rule of hypodescent (see Box 6.1) can be understood as an attempt to protect the line that was white women.

Box 6.1 Hypodescent and national frameworks

Hypodescent is the social and legal idea that fixes whiteness as a pure identity that cannot be claimed by anyone with an ancestor who is not white. Also referred to as the 'one-drop rule', this was the dominant practice in the USA, where a variety of terms came into use to describe people with varying amounts of what was called 'negro' blood: mulatto (one non-white parent), quadroon (one non-white grandparent), octoroon (one non-white great grandparent) etc. This was bolstered by 'anti-miscegenation' laws, passed in many US states in the inter-war years which made it illegal for white people to marry anyone who was not white (a set of laws not overturned until the *Loving* vs *Virginia Supreme Court* case in 1967). As there were no laws against non-white people marrying each other, it can be concluded that these laws were aimed at protecting the purity of whiteness.

F. James Davis, in his 1991 book, *Who is Black? One Nation's Definition*, argues that while the one-drop rule may be the dominant one in mainland USA (thus consigning children of 'interracial' unions to the social status of the non-white parent), it is not so in other places. Davis produced a typology of statuses for the children of such unions, which he updated for David Brunsma's (2006) edited collection on Mixed-ness (Davis, 2006). The seven status positions are:

1. Hypodescent – the dominant frame for the USA, except Louisiana.
2. In between both parents – this is to do with the reclassification of mixed-race people, e.g. under South Africa's apartheid laws (1948–94), and the creation of mixed groups as buffer groups under colonial rule.
3. Bottom of the ladder – this is true when a previously 'in-between' status group suffers economic dislocation, like the Métis in Canada, or where there is strong cultural antipathy toward mixed-ness, as is the case for the descendants of US servicemen in Korea and Vietnam.
4. Top of the ladder – in some colour-conscious majority black societies, a lighter complexion confers high social status which then gives access to greater resources so that after a while, lighter-complexioned people are the economically and politically dominant group. This is the case for Haiti, Liberia and Namibia.
5. Highly variable – this status depends on other contextual factors (such as education and wealth), but is found in Latin American and Caribbean societies. Davis makes a distinction between former Spanish and Portuguese colonies, where he argues there is more mixing between whites and mixed race people, and the former British, French and Dutch colonies, where there is less fluidity.
6. Egalitarian pluralism – the special history of Hawaii, where there have been frequent and successive waves of migration from Asia and Europe, as well as internal migration from mainland USA, meaning that there is no ethnic majority. Moreover, there is a higher proportion of *hapa* (people of mixed origins) than elsewhere in the USA. The status

afforded to people of mixed origins is no different from that of white, black, Asian or indigenous Hawaiians.

7. An assimilating minority – this status is for people with mixed descent (with no black component), often with one non-white grandparent. The person becomes (in the terminology of the one-drop rule) three-quarters white in the second generation, and is treated as an honorary White.

I am not sure that the line between Spanish and Portuguese colonies and British and French ones is as stark as Davis maintains. In the latter, I would place mixed-race people (with white as part of the mix) in the 'in-between' status, and possibly, if their complexion and features are European, in position number 4. However, Davis' typology demonstrates the social, geographical and historical contingency of mixed-ness, which is very easy to lose sight of in the relentlessly parochial American discourse.

Therefore, if we can understand race mixing as representing a threat to white purity and supremacy, it becomes more comprehensible why black–white mixing was socially problematic. Simply put, little was challenged in either the idea of people of colour mixing with each other, or of white men exercising patriarchal rights. The penalty for even being perceived as threatening the gender and 'race' hierarchy could be extrajudicial killings, which of course was the case in the USA, especially in the post-Civil War era. A frequent pretext for lynching African Americans was the protection of white women from their rapists, potential rapists, or occasionally their husbands (Wells, 1893). Moreover, riots in the UK ports of Cardiff, Liverpool and South Shields in 1919 are also partly explicable through reference to this fear, as well as demobbed soldiers' and unemployed workers' concerns about scarce employment and competition.

'WON'T SOMEBODY PLEASE THINK OF THE CHILDREN?'[1]

This kind of comment about mixed relationships, suggesting they should not result in children because the latter would be unable to integrate into society, is still heard in British and American culture (Childs, 2005; Sims, 2007). We might, in the light of the preceding development on the gendered and structured nature of social hierarchies, read this as a mechanism for reiterating racial boundaries, in the same way as the Spanish administrators' attempts to classify and rationalise the extended legacies of the newly settled territories: by recreating and reasserting the boundaries between groups as something natural, with social outcomes. Trangressive behaviour has a penalty. European and North American white women may lose their racial privileges by having mixed children (they and their children can be insulted in the street). Black women with light-skinned mixed children (Ifekwunigwe, 2001) may also lose their place as mother when they are seen together. Obviously, this is all in the eyes of other people: such ruptures are social and psychological. By falling outside the established order, people are identified as deviant and then 'corrected' by being fitted into an 'either/or' category. The marginality of 'mixed-race' children and adults (which is one step further along from their degeneracy and infertility) was developed in the inter-war period. Rich (1990) relates the story of the 1930s Liverpool enquiry into mixed-ness that concluded that mixed-race people were prone to childishness and psychological weakness. A similar theory was being worked on across the Atlantic by the Chicago School sociologist, Everett Stonequist (1937). His position was that people can become stuck between two cultures, are therefore marginal and consequently suffer identity problems that are expressed psychologically. There are three stages to this process of marginality. First is a lack of awareness of difference, followed by some crisis in which the person is rejected and comes to know their real place. The pain this causes then leads to a third stage in which they choose to adopt one or other of the identities open to them. As Tizard and Phoenix (2002: 44–5) note, this 'plot' heavily echoes those of stereotypical American novels about mixed-race people from the late nineteenth-century onwards, in which the central protagonist goes through these traumatic stages. Often in the academic literature this scenario is referred to as the 'tragic mulatta' figure (Raimon, 2004): a key work is the film *Imitation of Life* (1934) starring Fredi Washington as a mixed-race woman 'passing for white'.[2] Stonequist's framework of in-built marginality is applied not only to 'race' but to other scenarios as well. The point is that this marginality is the result of a dual set of identifications that divides the self, rather than a lack of identification that would cast the person adrift. In any case, the pathologisation of people due to their mixed ancestry is the most salient characteristic of academic attention paid to the experience of mixing. Even in Latin American states where *mestizaje* is officially the national philosophy, the reality is closer to a search for whiteness, which acknowledges white supremacy and regards mixing as impurification (Garner, 2007a).

TERMINOLOGY, CONTINGENCY AND IDENTIFICATION

We will now look at some fieldwork after a brief examination of the terminology. There is no consensus on what term to use for people who are variously labelled 'mixed race', 'bi-racial', 'multiracial' or 'of dual heritage' in English (as well as a host of other place and time-specific terms). We noted in Chapter 1 that the study of 'race' is inherently paradoxical in that the focus is always something that is both simultaneously real (in the social world) and not real (biologically speaking). One of the many consequences of this central fact is that any effort to name a state, process or product that emerges from crossing or mixing reflects what the origins of the 'mix' are. In other words, the source is individuals from different (mixed) 'races'; two distinct 'races' (bi-racial); more than two distinct 'races' (multiracial); two separate 'heritages' (dual heritage); more than two 'heritages', and so on and so forth. Some American writers note the use of the term *hapa* drawn from Hawaii, or *haafu* from Japanese, in specific contexts. However, both these words approximate to the meaning of 'half'. The lexicon of French, Spanish and Portuguese terms (*mulatto, zambo, mestizo, griffe, sang-mêlé*, etc.) deployed in the Americas also refer to breeding, animals and fractions. Ifekwunigwe's flirtation with the French term *métisse* (1999) ended two years later. Indeed, Mengel summarises the terminological bind:

> all of these terms perpetuate notions of blood division that can be quantified in fractional terms, and, in a race-conscious society, serve to reinforce the ideology that the mixed race individual is somehow less than a whole person. (2001: 100–1)

While the fact of mixed-ness challenges the boundary between racialised groups, there is no discursive escape from the treachery of the 'r' word or its synonyms. I have opted in this book to use 'mixed race' in inverted commas, not because I think it is an especially appropriate term to use, but because there are none that strike me as any less tainted by the illogicality of deconstructing 'race' through a concept rooted in the fetishisation of 'race', or what Paul Gilroy (2000) calls 'raciology'. Talking about the social identifications made in a racialised world without using the concepts upon which that process is built presents a significant challenge.

The picture that emerges from fieldwork on the social and personal identities of people classifying as mixed race/bi-racial/multiracial/of dual heritage, etc. is far from that which could have been expected from the 'marginal man'. We will look at two sets of qualitative fieldwork, one based in Britain and the other in the USA.

Barbara Tizard and Ann Phoenix's (2002) updated study of young people in London reveals some thought-provoking and counter-intuitive patterns. They interviewed 58 young people in London with one black and one white parent. Their findings contradicted the prevailing assumption in social work practice, according to which mixed children had to be brought up by black parents in order to feel properly black. Very few of those they spoke to felt marginalised or wanted to consider themselves white. Just under half considered themselves 'black', while just over 40 per cent felt 'both', 'brown' or 'mixed'. This is contrasted with how they are viewed by the black and the white samples. Only 30 per cent of the former and 16 per cent of the latter saw the mixed-parentage people as 'black' (ibid.: 220). The children's identities were analysed using responses to a number of questions about how they identified with different people and groups. In their search for causal relationships, it emerged that one predictive factor for having a strong black identity was a politicised background within the home, where racism was a topic for discussion. This was a better indicator than just having at least one black parent per se. Having a problematic identity though seems to be related to a variety of factors, from the racial composition of the child's school through to the quality of the relationship with one or other of the parents.

Indeed, the contrast between the young people's personal image of themselves and those of others was an important theme, with as much racism experienced by mixed as by black interviewees. The distinguishing feature is that mixed-parentage young people report encountering prejudice from *both* white and black people. Moreover, there are distinctly classed and gendered patterns to the experiences. Many people with a black parent in this sample were in private schools, so benefited from class privilege. Moreover, boys and working-class students report more frequent experiences of name-calling and other forms of racist behaviour than do middle-class students and girls. The authors thus conclude from the stories told that the experience of being of mixed parentage is more difficult for working-class boys than middle-class girls.

The gendered nature of mixed-race experiences in the USA also comes to the fore in the work of Kerry Ann Rockquemore and her colleagues (Rockquemore, 2002; Rockquemore and Arend, 2002; Rockquemore and Laszloffy, 2005). They note that in the USA, there are constraining factors on the identity of mixed-parentage individuals:

> Because the one-drop rule operated as an unquestioned assumption held by researchers, racial identity was not understood as a negotiable reality, nor was it an area where individuals had options. Because anyone with black ancestry was assumed to be black, black identity models were used to assess the racial identity development of mixed-race people. In this context, mixed-race people who resisted categorization as exclusively black were often seen as 'confused' and were patholo-gized by researchers. (Rockquemore and Laszloffy, 2005: 2)

They put forward a model that reflects the attempts to struggle against the dichotomies of ascriptive identities: either black or white, by stressing the diversity of self-identifications they encountered in the five years of research carried out since the late 1990s. Their model is called Continuum of Biracial Identifications (COBI) (ibid.: 5) and is basically a line running from black to white. People position themselves at any point along the line, they argue, but the majority are somewhere in the middle. The position might alter at different times in the respondents' lives. The model also reflects the interaction between social responses to the individual's appearance and the self-image that person has. Rejection and validation play a part in how individuals then see themselves. The authors use the case study of the light-skinned bi-racial woman 'Kathy' (ibid.: 11–13), who began by identifying as bi-racial, but leaning toward the white end of the scale, and ended up bi-racial leaning toward the black end. Her acceptance and rejection among the students at the three education institutions as a teenager and young adult had been quite different. The experiences began at a public school (50 per cent black, 50 per cent white), in which she had identified as bi-racial but was not accepted by the black students. In her next school, a private Catholic one, there were a small number of black and bi-racial students with whom she bonded. They validated her identification as bi-racial rather than black or white. Prior to her attending college, she went to a black student's induction course and made friends with a number of her future black and bi-racial peers. She was encouraged by this experience to explore her black side more and ended up identifying more with that element of her heritage. The acceptance of her choice as bi-racial had differed – from its interpretation as being hostile to black people (in her first school), to a normal one (Catholic school), and finally to one in which her blackness could be further explored. The COBI model enables a resistance to be developed against the dichotomy of black vs white, not through rejection of these two identities per se, but through the negotiation of the spaces in between as spaces in their own right, not just a gap between the only two options.

Moreover, in her interviewing work, Rockquemore notes the gendered way in which bi-raciality is experienced. The appearance of women seems to be focused on more acutely than that of men, particularly hair, skin, eyes and mouth (the racial giveaways, if you like). The visual compartmentalisation processes of which these women are often subject has effects on their view of themselves and their relationship to blackness and whiteness:

> In experiencing the gendered nature of racial identity development, female respondents reported feeling the awkwardness of not being accepted by Black women yet being routinely categorized as Black by whites in their daily environment. This explains why some biracial men and women develop a Black identity, and yet that process is more fraught with psychological distress for women who feel less group acceptance. (Rockquemore, 2002: 495)

Either/or, or both/and?

All of this fieldwork raises questions about binary oppositions in the way identity is usually understood, and which are confounded by the stories people tell about their own lives, and the analysis made of these stories by researchers. There are two interrelated binaries that dominate discussions of 'race', and which are challenged by the array of empirical work already accomplished. The first binary is that between bodies and cultures. A strong theme in this book is of the ideological work accomplished in racism aimed at linking physical appearance to a static and predetermined culture: at dissolving the social into the natural. In this way, a person's cultural scope can be read off the body. This is what we do when we look at someone and think, there goes a 'white', 'Latino/a' 'black' person, etc. The visual supply of racialised conclusions structures the way we categorise. The second set of binaries is between different racialised bodies. Each racialised group has a line drawn around it, inside which are its physical, cultural and social characteristics. There may be some overlap culturally, but in this model there is always a distinct set of characteristics. This way of imagining 'race' is endorsed and bolstered by the rule of hypodescent. However, the research around mixedness explodes those simplistic associations and dichotomies.

First, let's look at some observations on 'race' and culture. Winddance Twine's 'brown-skinned white girls' (1996) live in principally white suburban American space and have absorbed class privilege. Their brown skin is due to their mixed parentage (in each case, one of their parents is African American), yet their socialisation has been very similar to that of their white schoolmates and friends because of social class and geographical location. When they move to a different type of urban space and embark on lives as students in a multiethnic context, they reconstruct their identities to reflect their bi-raciality or blackness depending on the individual case. Parents are aware of the possibility of their African American children not being black 'enough'. In theory, culture can remove a black person from blackness or restore them to it. Dalmage's (2000) white parents who live in suburbia take measures to racialise their bi-racial or adopted African American children by taking them to black churches, play groups and other cultural settings in order for them to normalise blackness. Some of the black middle-class parents interviewed by Karyn Lacy (2007) also deploy similar strategies, going out of their way to socialise in neighbourhoods where they no longer live, but where friends and family do live, so they do not become too distant from their cultural blackness. So this is not only an issue for parents of bi-racial children, but for those of black children in socio-geographic positions that are overwhelmingly white and middle-class. Whiteness as a set of norms and values is not only available to people of European ancestry. Bodies that are racialised can be socialised into any culture. If this is true then, how can assumptions be made about people with parents from different racialised groups? What would be their *natural* culture? Some of that experience of identification is picked up in fieldwork and it constitutes a negotiation between: the image such individuals have of themselves; the image other social actors have of them; and the prevailing ways of making social sense of racialised identities in the places where, and at the times when, that person lives/works/is educated, etc. These identities are contingent and not set in stone. Even when they begin in one place, they can sometimes be readjusted in the light of experiences, knowledge, etc. – this is something which emerges clearly from the stories told to researchers (like those of the 'brown-skinned white girls' and 'Kathy' above).

Before we move on to the next section, it should be noted that there is a very uneven coverage given to the various combinations of ancestry in the existing work on 'mixed race'. The main thrust so far has been the experiences of people with one black and one white parent. This combination of heritages is the most frequent one in the UK, and one of the rarest in the USA. In the latter, it is made more interesting by the position of blackness being so looked down upon in comparison to other identities. There is much less work done with Asian-White and Asian-Black people, although there is some more of this now being published, especially in the USA (Root, 1996; Mahtani, 2002a, 2002b). In the UK Census' 'Mixed' section, there is no specific named box to tick if one of your parents is not black or from the Indian sub-continent ('Asian' in British terms). You have to opt for 'Other Mixed'. Indeed, the least researched group consists of people with neither a black nor a white parent, which is a point made by Mahtani and Moreno (2001), but which has not yet been picked up on in any meaningful way by researchers.

DEMOGRAPHICS AND POLITICAL INVESTMENT IN RACIAL IDENTIFICATION

The Census is not a neutral instrument reflecting social facts, but an indicator of what are considered as political problems to be quantified and made the subject of a discourse. The categorisation of populations into ethnic and racial groups using the Census is particularly fraught with problems over who decides what the categories are, and who decides who is placed in which category. As 'race' is a social not a biological fact, there is no consensus or scientific basis for these categories, which means they are open to change. Indeed, the census categories have evolved considerably in North America and the UK over the years. In the former, there were, as of the 2000 Census, over 100 ways to identify oneself racially and ethnically, as respondents are allowed to fill in more than one box (Box 6.2). The starting point of this logic is that 'races' are real entities to which people can choose to belong.

Box 6.2   Categories in the US Census 2000[3]

This Census showed the population of the USA to be 281.4 m, with 274.6 m identifying themselves as belonging to one race, and 6.8 m as belonging to more than one race.

White
'The term "White" refers to people having origins in any of the original peoples of Europe, the Middle East, or North Africa. It includes people who reported "White" or wrote in entries such as Irish, German, Italian, Lebanese, Near Easterner, Arab, or Polish.' (Census Bureau, *The White Population*: 2000, p. 1, www.census.gov/prod/2001pubs/c2kbr01-4.pdf)

216.9 m (211.5 m white only, + 5.4 m ticked 'white' plus another 'race') = 77.1 per cent of the US population.

Black/African American
'The term "Black or African American" refers to people having origins in any of the Black race groups of Africa. It includes people who reported "Black, African Am., or Negro" or wrote in entries such as African American, Afro American, Nigerian, or Haitian.' (Census Bureau, *The Black Population*: 2000, p. 1, www.census.gov/prod/2001pubs/c2kbr01-5.pdf)

36.4m (12.9 per cent) (34.7 m + 1.7 m Black and another 'race')

Hispanic (for breakdown, see www.census.gov/prod/2001pubs/c2kbr01-3.pdf)

35.3 m (12.5 per cent). But members of this group can tick any combination of boxes for 'race'. 'Hispanic' is therefore purely an ethnicity, in the terms of the Census.

Asian
'The term "Asian" refers to people having origins in any of the original peoples of the Far East, Southeast Asia, or the Indian subcontinent (for example, Cambodia, China, India, Japan, Korea, Malaysia, Pakistan, the Philippine Islands, Thailand, and Vietnam). Asian groups are not limited to nationalities, but include ethnic terms, as well.' (www.census.gov/prod/2002pubs/c2kbr01-16.pdf)

11.9 m (4.2 per cent) (10.2 m Asian only + 1.7 m more than one race)

Other groups
6.8 m chose to identify with more than one racial group
4.1 m identified as American Indian/Alaskan (of whom 1.6 m chose more than one race) and **0.87 m** chose the 'Other Pacific Islander' category.

Almost 7 million people (2.4 per cent) thus identified themselves as bi- or multiracial. The inclusion of such a category came as the result of lobbying by groups such as the Association of Multiethnic Americans (AMEA) and Project R.A.C.E (Reclassify All Children Equally).[4] We will look at the arguments for and against such a category below.

In the UK, the options have also grown since the first question on ethnic group was introduced in 1981. Ostensibly, the purpose of the British Census categories is to provide information for planning purposes and to enable the equal opportunity

Table 6.1   **Percentages of each 'racial' group in the US Census 2000**

Race	Percentage
White only	75.1%
Black only	12.3%
Asian only	3.6%
American Indian/Alaskan	1.5%
Pacific Islander	0.1%
'Some Other Race'	5.5%
More than one	2.4%
Total	100

Source: Grieco and Cassidy (2001: 3)

NB 'Hispanic' can cover any 'race'.

legislation to have a baseline against which to assess the recruitment, promotion, etc. of minorities. Lobbying has also procured representation for various groups, such as the Irish (O'Keeffe, 2007) and Mixed/Dual heritage people whose backing for separate categories came from the (now defunct) Commission for Racial Equality (CRE) and the support organisation People in Harmony (PiH). The approach adopted here is a separate category rather than the tolerance of ticking more than one box (which is the American solution).

Box 6.3   Ethnic categories in the England and Wales 2001 Census

White
British
Irish
Any Other White background

Mixed
White and Black Caribbean
White and Black African
White and Asian
Any Other Mixed background (*please write in*)

Asian or Asian British
Indian
Pakistani
Bangladeshi
Any Other Asian background

Black or Black British
Caribbean
African
Any Other Black background

Chinese or other ethnic group
Chinese
Any Other background

Source: 2001 Census of Population (1999) Cmnd 4253, cited in Owen, (200l: 147).

The arguments put forward by the advocates of a separate category for the 'Multiracial Movement' in America and the CRE/PiH in the UK are similar. First, the person can identify according to their personal choice, rather than be obliged to tick a box that does not correspond to a set of experiences that differs from one of the 'un-mixed' categories. It is argued that the binary construction of 'race' in America – the rule of hypodescent – solidifies all the stock racial group boundaries. Self-identification with a range of appropriate labels is conceptualised by the Multiracial Movement as a right being withheld from all who might fall into that category:

> Opting for a 'check one or more' race format over the traditional single-race, 'check one only' box format on the Race and Ethnic Question, represents a long overdue victory for those who have stood for, lobbied, or otherwise endorsed the acknowledgement, celebration and respect for human diversity. What has been dismantled by this shift in public policy is the mythical notion that race is fixed rather than fluid, or that any governmental agency's perception of racial identity takes priority over an individual's right to self-identify. (Douglass, 2000)

Explicit multiraciality, it is maintained, challenges monolithic and dichotomous understandings of what 'race' is, and better reflects the fluidity of 'race' in twenty-first century America. There are also people who point to the increasing numbers of multiracial individuals and couples as evidence that America is 'post-racial', a line of colour-blind argument (see Chapter 9) that will only become more strident as the USA is now led by its first African American President.

The arguments against such a re-categorisation are based on critiques of the political framework within which such claims are made, and disputes over what

Table 6.2   **Percentages of each ethnic group in the UK Census 2001**

Ethnic group	Percentage of total	Percentage of minority population
White	92.1	n/a
Mixed	1.2	14.6
Asian	4	50.2
Black	2	24.8
Chinese	0.4	5.3
Other	0.4	5
Minority	7.9	100

Source: Office of National Statistics (www.statistics.gov.uk/CCI/nugget.asp?ID=273)

the objectives are. The American debate is particularly split, with the Multiracial Movement being accused of wanting to abandon African American political goals and get closer to whiteness, as the 'New Coloured People' (Spencer, 2000) or the 'neo-mulattoes' (Horton, 2006). Gordon (1997: 67) critiques multiracials for not wanting to be black, which he argues is one of the two fundamental principles of racism (the other is wanting to be white, which he acknowledges does not have to be the case for multiracials). Moreover, Rainier Spencer (2006) points out that as such a high proportion of the African American population are 'mixed' in any case, what is the difference in racial logic, between bi-racials and 'mono-racials'? Concern is thus expressed about the consequent fragmentation of the African American population, which might impact upon the implementation of equality legislation and policies, by providing the political right with justifications for deprioritising them. Moreover, as the number of racial interest groups multiplies, yet the proportion of people claiming whiteness holds up, it becomes more difficult to mount coherent projects for racial equality. In summary, the Multiracial Movement is accused of sapping the demographic strength of black America, in a context where this merely means that the dominant position of whiteness goes unchallenged.

Is 'multiracial' a unitary category?

According to the fieldwork, there are areas of similarity in the experiences of multiracial and 'mono-racial' minorities. These can be summarised as degrees of rejection by the major racialised groups, not only the dominant one, with the added weight of constituting a racialised minority. The striking thing about reading the accounts of identity among 'mixed race' people is the scope for altering the cultural orientation that is not available to people who are not mixed (although even in describing this I cannot shake off the terms and ideas that make these experiences intelligible).

'The common characteristic that multiracial people share is that they have had to learn to thrive in a society that does not acknowledge their multiple heritages or acknowledge that they are an emerging community', argues AMEA President Leonora Gaddy (AMEA, 2001). Yet in the same article, another AMEA activist, Matt Kelley, is quoted as saying that multiracials are 'people of color', and warning the other racial communities to 'Stop pushing us out. Widen your definition of your community to include us'. Kelley's comment is more revealing of the ambiguity of 'mixed race' as a community which appears simultaneously to be part of other communities, and comes together around a political objective. This seems to be a 'status group' in the Weberian sense, which in its campaigning for Census recognition, becomes a 'party' (Weber, 1946).

The complexities of the US situation are evident from the many contributions to the growing literature (Zack, 1993; Root, 1996; Ifekwunigwe, 2004; Davis, 2006). Yet there is a concentration on black–white bi-raciality that does not correspond to its numerical frequency vis-à-vis other combinations, and the lack of international perspectives. The black–white dynamic is more fraught with power discrepancies, the legacies of slavery and 'masculine insemination' than the other possibilities. There is a lack of attention to mixtures that have *no* white component. This in itself indicates that the racialised line that is most absorbing for researchers and activists appears to be the one dividing whiteness from its Others. Is this a way to accord more salience to the phenotypical element of 'race', and therefore create a paradox? By saying 'mixed race' is challenging the idea of 'race', do we not call into play the very thing that is supposed to be effaced: the relevance of the natural world (which presents bodies in particular ways), and again subject these bodies to the same visual regime of racialisation? Might this actually bolster the hierarchies integral to racism rather than stripping it of its power to wound?

Historian George Sanchez concludes that mixing alone does not threaten power: 'Racial mixing has never in itself destroyed racial privilege, as the places of Africans and natives throughout nearly all Latin American countries has proved' (Sanchez, 2004: 278).

NEW NATIONS, NEW PEOPLE? CHALLENGES TO THEORIES OF NATION AND RACIAL IDENTITY

Do mixed-race people represent the post-racial future: the end of 'race' as a salient social division? If one argument is that mixed-ness per se challenges the social viability of 'race', then increasing numbers of mixed-race people logically must constitute a more potent threat to existing racial divisions.

In the experience of societies in which mixing has been ongoing for centuries, such as some of those in Latin America, a complicated set of patterns has emerged. Brazil is the example usually cited. However, if mixed-ness is a majority experience, it does not seem to have altered the overarching social hierarchy: whiteness equals power and blackness does not (Miller, 2004). There is a very large range of terms for identifying one's 'race' in Brazil, and on further inspection, they turn out to be a long list of ways to say that one is not white. As in many other Latin American republics, the official ideology is one of embracing *mestizaje* (Spanish) or *mestiçagem* (Portuguese) (mixed-ness), but the reality as translated into policies and actions is about constructing a nation around European norms, both ideological and physical. This has included encouraging European immigration in the nineteenth century (Garner, 2007a), implementing eugenics policies (Stepan, 1991; Dávila, 2003), and the development of cultural norms that favour European culture, especially the features of its beauty contestants (Edmonds, 2007).

In the nation-building story, blackness and whiteness mark degrees of modernity. For example, Weinstein (2003) argues that the state of Sao Paolo illuminates the process of making claims about which discourses are modern (free trade, democracy) and which are to do with tradition (slave populations, degeneracy). Claims were usually made by Sao Paolo elites by using models of development in which Sao Paolo is put forward as the only modern area of Brazil, particularly in relation to the backward, mainly black Bahia province to its north-east (ibid.: 249).

The short experiment of the *Estado novo* ('New State', 1937–45) which emphasised mixed-ness of course did so at the expense of black organisation, and focused away from divisions of 'race' and class. This made the space for political blackness relatively limited (Hanchard, 1998, 1999). Black cultural and political movements are quite a recent phenomenon. Yet, in the last few years, some states in Brazil have celebrated a 'Mixed Race day' holiday (*Dia do Mestiço*)[5] since 2005–6 after lobbying by the *Movimento Pardo-Mestiço Brasileiro* (Brazilian Brown–Mixed Race Movement) which is campaigning for separate representation to black Brazilians (against the government's practice of counting them as black, even when they have no black ancestry). It is easy to see why black Brazilian political organisations might feel threatened by this, having worked long and hard to create a non-white space for countering white European dominance. They might see this as similar to the *Estado novo*'s project of not seeing the outcomes of racial discrimination. Indeed, if mixed-ness is virtually the norm, is it so challenging to the racialised status quo?

We have to re-focus on the different levels of discourse and experience that this kind of question evokes. Individual people, as we have seen, do not have predetermined trajectories in which their racialised identity remains stable. It is contextual and developmental, based as much on ascription as self-construction. So, if people identify as mixed, *pardo*, *mestizo*, etc. in their nation states, in order to have their experience validated, this is one level of discourse. Some of those people may, depending on the context in which their status is worked out (see Box 6.1), also be absorbed into a white dominant majority or elite.

Indeed, this is one strand of Eduardo Bonilla-Silva's predictions for the future of the USA, his 'Latin-americanization' of 'race' (2002). In this structure, a continuum of racialised positions is complicated by increased mixing and variable identification by Hispanics and Asians. However, at the bottom, socio-economically, remain those with darker skin. The middle of the spectrum is thus extended but the principle lines remain intact. Some lighter-skinned people may become 'honorary Whites', but changing where the boundaries are established does not mean that the boundaries disappear. Racism reworks itself to structure relations in different periods.

Indeed, we may already have passed the point at which mixed-ness stops being a threat to the racial order, given the ideological work that such bodies perform in advertising. Danzy Senna's acid remark (2004: 207): 'If you spot a Cablinasian[6], please contact the Benetton Promotions Bureau', neatly encapsulates the commodification of 'beautiful' mixed people who are the future of the country (Ropp, 2004: 266), and who come to stand in as visual metaphors for globalization (Sanchez, 2004). Indeed, Sanchez goes on to state that not only will it still be dark-skinned and indigenous peoples who are at the bottom of the pile in terms of access to power and other resources (near the poorer whites, mixed and others), but there is also a question of timing (ibid.: 279). Is 'mixed race' in the US linked to America's imperialism, as a result of the military occupation of the Philippines, Vietnam, Japan, Korea, etc., just as the '... territorial and sexual' conquest of Mexico and of Native Americans led to *absorption* within a white-dominated United States (see Chapter 3)?

CONCLUSIONS

Mixed-ness per se really challenges only the existing sets of categories, not the category of 'race' itself. It is clearly open to regressive as well as politically progressive 'racial projects'. In the Latin-americanization thesis that seems to be shared in different ways by critics of the Multiracial Movement, you still have Whites at the top and Blacks at the bottom. The guys in the middle might be playing musical chairs, but it is not in any substantial way that the category 'White' seems to be diminishing through the mixed category, and what Christian (2004) foregrounds as 'white supremacy' is still the crucial framing element. Indeed, paying attention to 'mixed race' is a fine line to walk without actually reinscribing 'race', rather than deconstructing it: 'Indeed for racial boundary crossing to matter at all, difference has to be constantly maintained so that the act of crossing bears significance to the society' (Sanchez, 2004: 279–80).

However, there are personal and political collective identifications involved in this puzzle. People identifying as bi-racial on a personal level and acknowledging their mixed family may also identify with one or other of their parents' groups, depending on the context, as does President Obama. The two options need not be in tension but are often spoken about as if they are.

Once more, in the discourse about mixed-ness, other key dimensions of identity such as class and gender, seem to have become submerged as we are drawn into 'race' talk. It may seem an odd thing for a scholar of racism to be criticising an over-emphasis on racialisation, but in the logic of my argument, made throughout this book, I think it reads predictably. Racism intersects with gendered and classed oppression, and losing sight of the intersections of those forms of discrimination leads us away from the concrete experiences of the people we study as sociologists. Rockquemore and Laszloffy (2005), Small (2001), Tizard and Phoenix (2002) and Ali (2003), for example, all argue that gender and class, respectively, also structure the lifeworlds of 'mixed-race' people.

NOTES

1. This is the frequent refrain of Helen Lovejoy, wife of Reverend Lovejoy in *The Simpsons*, one of my children's favourite television shows.
2. This is something akin to the storyline of James Weldon Johnson's novel, *Autobiography of an Ex-Colored Man* (1912).
3. Breakdowns of various categories can be accessed through the Census Bureau website at: www.census.gov/population/www/cen2000/briefs/index.html
4. See AMEA: www.ameasite.org/ and Project RACE: www.projectrace.com/
5. See www.nacaomestica.org/mixed_race_day.htm
6. 'Cablinasian' is the racial identification that champion golfer 'Tiger' Woods attributes to himself. It covers Caucasian-Black-Native American-Indian-Asian.

7 Institutional Racism

In earlier chapters, I outlined the development of the idea of 'race', provided working definitions of racism and explained the process of racialisation. We now turn to the concept of 'institutional racism', a term that has come to occupy an increasingly significant space in public discourse in the English-speaking world since it was coined by American authors Stokely Carmichael (Kwame Touré) and Charles Hamilton in their 1967 work, *Black Power* (see Chapter 1). We shall look at definitions, and note the two broad strands of the core idea (which is a separation of *individual* from *collective* forms of racial discrimination) that have developed in two different directions.

DEFINITIONS

The definition put forward by Carmichael and Hamilton (1967: 6) deals with the parallel processes of individual and collective forms of action, the latter being exemplified as follows:

> ... when in ... Birmingham, Alabama – 500 black babies die each year because of the lack of proper food, clothing, shelter and proper medical facilities, and thousands more are destroyed or maimed physically, emotionally and intellectually because of conditions of poverty and discrimination in the black community, that is a function of institutional racism.

Compare this with the MacPherson definition (1999: para 6.34), which is now used by the British government as the basis of the 2000 Amendment to the Race Relations Act:

> The collective failure of an organisation to provide an appropriate and professional service to people because of their colour, culture or ethnic origin. It can be seen and detected in processes, attitudes, and behaviour which amount to discrimination through unwitting prejudice, ignorance, thoughtlessness, and racist stereotyping which disadvantage minority ethnic people.

The key elements are a failure to act properly and unintentional actions. We will come back to these below when we look critically at how this definition is put into practice.

WHAT DOES 'INSTITUTIONAL RACISM' MEAN?

Carmichael and Hamilton repeatedly associate social structures with systemic forms of discrimination and disadvantage. For example, they make very close links between the economic structure of the USA and the patterns of racialised discrimination they describe. Their concept is an analytical tool that contributes to understanding the collective practices of a society, and the thrust of their argument constitutes part of what I refer to here as 'structural' racism (see below pp. 108–15).

What we now call 'institutional racism' in Europe is not *necessarily* this at all, but rather a *legal concept* that has developed since the mid-1970s. To make sense of this confusion, we need to understand one crucial distinction.

The original distinction (Carmichael and Hamilton, 1967) was made between 'individual' and 'institutional' forms of racism in the American context. This meaning of institutional racism was dominant until the mid-1970s, when some European countries started to introduce legislation to combat racially discriminatory practices in the provision of services and access to resources such as employment and housing. One example is the UK's Race Relations Act (1976), which built upon previous legislation from the 1960s that made it illegal for individuals or organisations to discriminate on the grounds of 'race'. The Netherlands ratified the International Covenant on the Elimination of All Forms of Racial Discrimination (United Nations, 1965) in 1971, and it was officially transposed into Dutch law in 1976. Moreover, the 1983 Dutch constitution made discrimination illegal and formulated a general objective of equality. Since this period, the use of 'institutional racism' in the European context has tended toward a legal instrument rather than a social scientific analytical tool, and we have to understand where it went after this fork in the road.

LEGAL TERMS AND PRACTICE

The UK and Dutch governments were among the earliest to deploy specific legal forms as a response to the changing social realities of their populations in the late 1960s and early 1970s. A generation of people born to post-war migrants from the former colonies of the Western European countries were beginning to contest the informal segregation and discrimination that their parents' generation had faced (Sivanandan, 1990). Liberal politicians and civil society organisations supported the legal moves to ban discrimination, on principle, by the use of legislation. Since that point, the story of institutional racism has been the slow adoption of a principle and, with it, a set of organisations and agencies to monitor and implement equality plans at national and European Union level. The idea of racial equality has become a mainstream one within the European Union now, and member states have had to implement the ICERD by transposing it into national law. There are three things to note about this:

1. The definition that derives from institutional racism in this context is necessarily simple – it has to be operational in a court of law.
2. In doing this, the concept of 'race' has to be uncritically accepted. If not, how could you prosecute an organisation for institutional racism without proof that someone was being discriminated against on the basis of 'race'?
3. There is an intersection between racial equality and some other grounds for discrimination, which are organisationally brought together due to legislation.

Box 7.1   Case study: The Equality Authority, Republic of Ireland

To illustrate these points, we will look at the example of the Irish **Equality Authority**,[1] the semi-state agency set up in 2000 to monitor the effectiveness of new legislation on discrimination in the provision of services and the access to employment. The Republic of Ireland was one of the last EU member states to ratify the CERD. The model the Irish adopted was to organisationally combine the nine grounds for discrimination enshrined in legislation within one body – the Equality Authority.[2]

1. Definitions, reports, publications
The definitions of discrimination and 'indirect discrimination' used by the Equality Authority (2006) demonstrate its focus on the specific areas for which it was established: employment and the provision of services. The following definitions must be capable of being proven or disproved in a tribunal setting:

'Discrimination is defined as the treatment of a person in a less favourable way than another person is, has been or would be treated in a comparable situation on any of the nine grounds which exists, existed, may exist in the future, or is imputed to the person concerned. The instruction to discriminate is also prohibited.'

'Indirect discrimination happens where there is less favourable treatment in effect or by impact. It happens where people are, for example, refused employment or training not explicitly on account of a discriminatory reason but because of a provision, practice or requirement which they find hard to satisfy. If the provision, practice or requirement puts people who belong to one of the grounds covered by the Acts at a particular disadvantage then the employer will have indirectly discriminated, unless the provision is objectively justified by a legitimate aim and the means of achieving that aim are appropriate and necessary.'

2. The 'Race' grounds
'Race' is the most frequently used grounds for Employment-related casework, for example the 2006 casework includes 103/404 cases on these grounds (26 per cent, of which 40 per cent are to do with working conditions), while in Equal Status (provision of and access to services), the proportion is lower (41/366, that is, 11 per cent in 2006). In Ireland, the 'race' grounds are not used for Travellers (an indigenous nomadic minority group). They have successfully campaigned to be recognised as an ethnic group, whose culture diverges from the mainstream dominant one. This legislation has instead been used primarily by migrant workers (including white Eastern Europeans). Travellers account for only 2/404 (0.55 per cent) of

Employment cases, but 88/366 (24 per cent) for Equal Status. Also, more than half the cases dealt with under the Intoxicating Liquor Act 2003 (which addresses treatment in hotels, restaurants, pubs and nightclubs) are to do with Travellers' claims of discrimination.

Officially, then, there is a discrepancy here. An indigenous cultural minority, the Travellers do not apply for justice through 'race' grounds, yet white European groups such as Poles and Lithuanians do.

CRITICAL RESPONSES TO THE LEGAL FORM OF INSTITUTIONAL RACISM

Confusions

Another point to note is the *combined effect* of differing forms of discrimination, which has been identified by the Equality Authority (Zappone, 2003). A small proportion of claims are based on multiple forms of discrimination, even if they are not always deemed to have been proven. In 2006, in the case of *Czerski* vs *Ice Group*, a Polish woman claimed that she had been overlooked for a factory job (Equality Authority, 2006: 34). She had been employed in a similar position with a different company since 2000. When she asked why she had not been interviewed, she was told there was heavy lifting involved and the firm were looking for male employees. Moreover, she had only been able to find one employment-related referee (as opposed to the two requested) due to the relatively short period she had been working in Ireland. The Equality Authority found that there was not enough evidence to back up the claim on the basis of gender, but there was sufficient to support indirect discrimination by 'race' because it was easier for an Irish national than a non-Irish national to find the required number of employment-related referees, and that no argument had been put forward by the employer that the demand for two referees was more justifiable than one.

Looking at the work of the Irish Equality Authority, even as briefly as we have done, throws up some of the issues that arise when the concept of 'institutional racism' is applied within a legal framework. There first have to be definitions that can be proven or disproved in a tribunal (the Equality Authority is not a court of law but a tribunal whose rulings can ultimately be rejected). In this process, 'race' is necessarily used in an instrumental and essentialist way. In other words, it gets 'reified'. The term 'reify', taken from the work of Marx, means turning something that is produced by ideology (rather than a real thing) into an object itself. Reification therefore occurs when an abstract concept (e.g. one created to describe a relationship) is treated as a concrete thing. George Lukács (1971: 83) contends that:

> Its basis is that *a relation between people* takes on the character of a thing and thus acquires a 'phantom objectivity', an autonomy that seems so strictly rational and all-embracing as to conceal every trace of its fundamental nature: the relation between people. (my emphasis)

In the case of 'race', this means that the social relationship (the idea that 'race' is a biological rather than a social fact that has been produced by centuries of unequal power relationships) becomes treated as a real thing with an autonomous existence, empirically provable and used as a given in a court of law.

The example of *Czerski* (see above) illustrates some of the limits and advantages of the use of institutional racism. On one hand, the practice of asking for a certain number of employment-related referees from within the nation state discriminates indirectly against workers who are just as capable as others, but whose employment history lies outside the State. Whether this is to do with 'race', however, could be seen as questionable, as anyone who had not been working in the Republic of Ireland for very long would presumably have encountered the same issue. On the other, the discriminatory practice seems more glaring in terms of gender, with the supposition that women cannot lift heavy weights being a long-standing justification put forward for the recruitment of male staff in industry. The complexity of the story requires attention to both practices (gender and nationality) rather than simply looking at the fact that Czerski was a foreign national. The same problem could theoretically have arisen for a returning Irish emigrant. Moreover, the fact that there is no 'nationality' grounds among the nine specified by Irish law means that a certain proportion of claims that might be dealt with under such a heading end up coming under the 'race' grounds instead. Of course, there are arguments about which groups of nationalities are more likely to be migrants in Ireland and to be affected disproportionately by such practices.

Returning to the legal definition, MacPherson's definition of a 'failure to act properly' is a partial one. Surely, the range of actions that can have a discriminatory outcome is broader than a set of inactions. Alongside the inaction are a set of actions as well. For example, in the case of *Buenaventura and 15 Others* vs *The Southern Health Board* (Equality Authority, 2006: 46), the sixteen Filipinos working as care assistants had been ranked 14–29 in the list of prospective candidates for full-time positions behind 13 Irish candidates. The Health Board told the Equality Authority tribunal that the Filipinos had been ranked below the Irish nationals *as a matter of course* because they had work permits. This was ruled an incorrect interpretation of a government guideline that had urged employers to look within the EU before employing non-EU nationals. All the Filipinos were, as of the 2006 report, in full-time employment with the Health Board.

Aside from this, there is a certain amount of confusion engendered by the idea of 'unwitting action'. It is always difficult to prove or demonstrate 'intent', either philosophically or in a legal context. When, in the wake of the MacPherson Report, the British police redefined a 'racial incident' as one in which the victim interpreted it as such, the emphasis shifts to an area where it is hard to go any further. How can this be proven or disproved in the majority of cases? One of the reasons that Robert Miles (1987) objects to the term 'institutional racism' is that it supposes that a racist outcome can be disentangled from other sources of discrimination such as class and gender, whereas for him (and others – see the 'intersectionality' interpretation in Chapter 3), these forms of discrimination are bundled together.

Moreover, as Floya Anthias (1999) argues, there is a difference between organisational processes whose result is the exclusion of particular groups, and policies that are implemented on the basis of individual police officers' assessments of situations. She writes of the MacPherson Report that:

it fails to distinguish between mechanisms that indeed unwittingly exclude and disadvantage groups through criteria which are non-ethnic but where ethnic categories may be over-represented (for example, in terms of skills, language, period of residence, lifestyles, etc.) and mechanisms that actually specifically and 'wittingly' are applied to different groups on the basis of ethnic membership or its perception (this includes 'stop and search' of more black people than white, more arrests, etc.).

Opponents of the concept of institutional racism, and there are many, often argue that it injects 'race' where it has no place, thus perpetuating racism rather than addressing it. They say that tarring all the employees of an entire organisation with the same brush, as 'institutionally racist', is unfair and counter-productive. The line of argument used by the then British leader of the Opposition, William Hague, in a speech about institutional racism delivered in December 2000 (which caused a minor controversy) was that the institutional sensitivity of having to tread carefully around minorities, and of the requirement for employees to undergo training, in racism awareness and such like, gives minorities 'victim status', and actually ends up preventing the police from doing their job. A set of essays arguing along these lines can be found in Green (2000). The basic argument is that focusing on 'race' detracts from the ideal outcome, which is justice for all. Ignatieff's essay, for example, critiques the Report's recommendation that the victim should define the incident's nature:

> The MacPherson definition will 'racialise' every encounter between the police and the non-white public to the benefit of neither, while the white public, often badly treated by the police too, will feel that they have no recourse for the indignities they suffer – and will resent the perceived 'positive discrimination' towards non-whites. (Ignatieff, 2000: 22)

Indeed, the logics of the critiques of institutional racism as a concept are diverse, but the colour-blind one outlined by Ignatieff is a common thread. It supposes that we have passed through the phase of correcting the most discriminatory aspects and emerged the other side on a roughly level playing field. Green, in the same volume (2000: 38–40), twists this logic further to construct it as a system of racial preference geared to giving an advantage to ethnic minorities. He approvingly cites economist Thomas Sowell (1990) who theorises that the claims of indigenous and minority groups in the political realm are not in fact for equality, but for racial preference. In this interpretation then, institutional racism is a concept whose use actually enables a reversal of the (begrudgingly acknowledged) discrimination prior to its introduction into the public domain. It is hard to see how two parents' quest for a properly conducted investigation of the murder of their son is a claim for *differential* treatment. Indeed, the basis of the original claim was for justice like anyone else, which is exactly what Ignatieff seems to be arguing for. However, the misreadings upon which these sorts of criticisms are based are revealing about the very heart of what we are looking at: the idea of a level of social action which it is beyond an individual's power to alter significantly. The first thing to note is that neither the MacPherson Report nor its predecessor, the 1986 Scarman Report (which had first raised the possibility of institutional racism if not naming it as such), state that individual employees of institutionally racist organisations are racist. The whole point of the way these reports establish the concept of institutional racism involves distinguishing collective practices and a culture that discriminates from the actions of all individual officers. The latter can act in discriminatory ways without this affecting the practices and culture.

The second point is that the object of the concept is to make 'race' visible as a factor in how an organisation and its staff operate. In public cultures like those of the UK and the USA in the later twentieth and early twenty-first centuries, the norm is for 'race' to be avoided. From the perspective where not talking about 'race' solves the problem of racism, the opposite, that is, re-introducing 'race' as an explicit topic in public policy and discourse, actually encourages racism. This 'race-neutral' or 'colour-blind' approach argues that, for example, police practices should be geared toward serving everyone regardless of 'race'. However, this supposes that using the term 'institutional racism' necessarily impedes this outcome, and that the type of inequalities that separate people's experiences do not play a role in how they are policed. Simply put, the power relations (of class, gender and 'race') in the wider society already have a major role in how different groups are policed. The objective of using the concept of 'institutional racism' to understand power relationships is to reduce that inequality.

Yet, a major problem here with 'institutional racism' as a concept in legal terms is ambiguity about the relationship of racism to power. The focus on unintentionally discriminatory actions carried out by an organisation (covered by the 'indirect discrimination' clause in Ireland) is a necessary corollary of the way the concept has been framed. Organisations that are not set up to be specifically racist can, in practice, discriminate in their service provision, employment procedures, etc. However, the term 'unintentional' poses a problem. On one hand, it gives the impression that racist outcomes are clearly identifiable effects of clearly identifiable causes that can either be intentional or unintentional. This is true up to a point because the legal framing has to make such outcomes empirically provable and/or deniable. If not, the legal concept would be unworkable in its own context. However, while broadly recognising power relations as important, this implementation ignores the power relations *outside* the particular company, government agency, pub, etc. that is being called to rights. Indeed, they are beyond the scope of the precise legal battle involved in the discussion at a tribunal. It is at this point that the distinction between 'institutional racism' as a legal concept, and 'structural racism' as a sociological one become apparent. The latter includes and emphasises what goes on outside the case in question.

INSTITUTIONAL RACISM AS 'STRUCTURAL' RACISM

Within sociology, there have been long-standing distinctions between various understandings of how society functions and what counts as knowledge. The different schools of thought have suggested variously that sociology is a natural science of society, with problems/truths that can be unearthed and analysed (positivism); that there is no single social truth but rather a competing set depending on the interpretation of individual social actors (interpretivism); or that no individual social actor is aware of all there is to be aware of, so that the most important role of a sociologist is to construct models of how society functions at a theoretical level (critical theory) through structures (Box 7.2). The account I am going to present you with in this chapter owes more to the latter than the former two ideas, but discounts neither the importance of the empirical (enshrined in positivism), nor the way groups make sense of their social positions. Indeed, in Chapter 8, there is far more on that. However, the idea that social processes function at a level above the individual is at the heart of this side of 'institutional racism', as coined by Carmichael and Hamilton (1967).

There are relatively few examples of individual states or sections of states with legal authority using division by 'race' as an explicit tool for organising the life of its people. Indeed, examples such as South Africa under apartheid (1948–94), the southern states of the USA (formally until the mid-1960s) and Nazi Germany (1933–45) are understood not as end points on a continuum, but as completely separate *sui generis* forms of governance. Indeed, they are in a way constitutive of racism: in these models, there is a superior and an inferior 'race', and life is organised around that principle. However, these examples are not by any means the whole story (as we noted in earlier chapters). The idea of institutional racism may well have been shaped by the experiences of activists in segregated southern US states but its general applicability lies in the form of structures.

Box 7.2 Structure and agency

Social structure may be seen to underlie important social systems including the economic system, the legal system, the cultural system and others. Examples of what are considered structures in sociology are: family, religion, law, economy and class. These are long-term observable patterns that are beyond the reach of an individual to alter. The structure allows us to understand the parameters within which we, as social actors, operate. In contrast, the idea of *agency* is the degree of freedom to act that each of the social actors enjoys.

Throughout the history of sociology as an academic discipline, there has been disagreement about the relative explanatory power of each. Some schools and methods lay the emphasis more on agency, some more on structure. Interpretivism would tend toward the former position and Marxism toward the latter, but this is merely a guide. There have also been attempts to formulate a theory in which these two understandings interact more explicitly, such as Anthony Giddens' 'structuration' (Giddens, 1984). For him, it is the fact of the individual social actors repeating the practices that actually makes the structures.

In terms of the sociology of racism, the utility of the idea of structures is that it enables us to move away from the older psychology-dominated paradigm of racism, which conceptualised it as the aberrant behaviour of individuals, that is, where agency was dominant over structure. Using the structural lens, we can identify patterns of action at social and national (as well as international) levels, which do not appear if we focus exclusively on some people's behaviour patterns. In short, the structural approach sees racism as a problem of society, manifest in the way things function normally: the agentic approach sees it as innate to particular types of abnormal individuals. Clearly, the type of solution proposed in each case differs.

We are now going to look at three interlocking areas of discrimination and suggest how they can be interpreted as examples of structural racism.

Loans for housing

In the USA, as in the UK, most people own their homes (around 69 per cent in both countries). The vast majority of home-owners need to borrow money to buy them, usually in the form of a loan from a financial institution. In two important pieces of work, George Lipsitz (1995, 1998) analyses the racialisation of the granting of loans for housing purchase. He found that even when the sample was controlled for social class (white working-class compared to black working-class applicants), more money was made available, for longer and under more advantageous conditions to white applicants than to black ones. Other research focusing on this has demonstrated similar findings. A study of housing on Long Island, New York carried out by the Institute on Race and Poverty (IRP, 2002) concluded two things. Firstly, that in the 1999–2000 period, the rates at which conventional home loan applications were denied rose by more than 20 per cent for both African Americans and Latinos. Secondly, that higher income had less impact on the likelihood of obtaining a loan for minority applicants. In 2000, for example, Latinos in Nassau-Suffolk County in Long Island who earned in excess of $91,800 were more likely to be turned down for conventional home loans than were whites earning less than $38,250. This kind of lending practice is a partial explanation of the patterns of racialised residential segregation observable in cities across the USA. Indeed, there is a clearly identifiable pattern of differential group access to home-ownership, which appears in Table 7.1, compiled from US Census Bureau data.

While the discrepancy between the different 'racial' groups is lessening over the 11-year period captured in the table, the differences are still statistically significant and point to structural discrimination.

Such practices have a major impact in determining who gets to live where. In the USA, the most expensive housing is generally found in suburban areas, and the failure to obtain loans means that black and Hispanic Americans remain primarily in cheaper neighbourhoods where they can afford to buy. Moreover, the difficulty in obtaining loans is only one of a set of obstacles to minority integration into more affluent neighbourhoods. 'Restrictive covenants, explicit or implicit threats of violence, and generally adverse social conditions kept blacks out of white areas', argue Cutler et al. (1999: 496). When placed alongside other segregationist practices such as redlining, this results in the development of areas that black and other minority people cannot easily access (Gotham, 2000). They are therefore over-concentrated in other areas. The practice of 'redlining', for example, lies at the root of later versions. Lipsitz (1995) identifies the functioning of the Federal Housing Authority (FHA), set up in 1934, which lent virtually exclusively to white families in the post-war period. He points to the organisation's area reports and appraiser's manuals (drafted by the Home Owners Loan Corporation (HOLC)) in the 1930s, as maps of discriminatory practice. The maps colour-coded 239 American cities into areas of greater or lesser risk for lending, not according to criteria related to people's capacity for repayment, but

Table 7.1 Home-ownership by 'race' in the USA, 1994–2005

Race	1994	1995	1996	1997	1998	1999	2000	2001	2002	2003	2004	2005	% change since 1994
White (non-Hispanic)	70.0	70.9	71.7	72.0	72.6	73.2	73.8	74.3	74.5	75.4	76.0	75.8	+8.28%
Asian American	51.3	50.8	50.8	52.8	52.6	53.1	52.8	53.9	54.7	56.3	59.8	60.1	+17.15%
Native American	51.7	55.8	51.6	51.7	54.3	56.1	56.2	55.4	54.6	54.3	55.6	58.2	+12.57%
African American	42.3	42.7	44.1	44.8	45.6	46.3	47.2	47.7	47.3	48.1	49.1	48.2	+13.59%
Hispanic or Latino	41.2	42.1	42.8	43.3	44.7	45.5	46.3	47.3	48.2	46.7	48.1	49.5	+20.14%

Source : US Census Bureau, 2005

merely the demographics of the areas concerned.[3] Areas in which minorities were concentrated thus frequently appeared in red on the maps, indicating the highest level of risk, and therefore, the smallest chance of obtaining loans, even for home improvements.

The combination of these structural patterns with the deterrent factor facing the first black families to move into an area (captured, for example, in Lorraine Hansberry's play, *A Raisin in the Sun*, 1959) means that there are tangible material and ideological factors at work, granting privilege to white Americans and impeding the mobility of African Americans and other minorities (Massey and Denton, 1994).

Oliver and Shapiro (1995: 95–7) provide an array of statistical evidence to back up their claim that if you look at wealth, rather than income, the economic positions of white and African Americans are even more starkly polarised. This is true even for middle-class subjects. Although the *income* discrepancy tapers to its lowest point: 0.76 (that is, where African Americans on average earn 76 per cent of what their white counterparts do), the other measurements of wealth used by the authors tell a different story. Net financial assets (NFA) (including property in the form of land, housing, stocks and shares, savings, etc.) and net worth are far lower for African Americans than Whites. Also, because of borrowing for house purchases, 63 per cent of black households own zero or negative NFA, while only 28 per cent of white ones fall into that category. More black households therefore require two people to be working, so if income were cut off, far fewer could remain solvent – either at current level or poverty level – than white households. The *closest* point between black and white middle-class couples in terms of wealth is in the group earning over $50,000, where the wealth ratio is 0.52. Further down the socio-economic scale, the discrepancies are larger than this, with white wealth averaging at eight times that of African American wealth.

Residential segregation

To illustrate the distinction between structure and agency in relation to housing segregation, we can first reduce them to their extremes and then suggest how they function in a more complex way. The patterns of segregation in urban America could be interpreted as outcomes of the long-term historical processes referred to above: a structural understanding in which the individual has no power to brook the rule. On the other hand, if housing location was merely a question of individual choice of an area to live in, a different pattern would emerge. One of the common-sense understandings of 'race' is that people stick together 'with their own', neatly explaining why there is residential segregation: it's all the minorities' choice. However, if social class rather than 'race' were thought of in these terms, it would appear more problematic: after all, everyone knows that different types of housing and locations command higher prices on the housing market. It is therefore a lot more difficult for those on more modest incomes to buy in an expensive area. However, while this is acknowledged, the key idea that seems more compelling for many people is the rule of individual responsibility. This means that you get what you deserve, both for hard work and for idleness. Forms of this logic appear in a lot of discussions about class and 'race' (Lamont, 2000; Bonilla-Silva, 2006). Yet, to go back to the examples captured in the research referred to above, if you are a Hispanic in Nassau-Suffolk County, earning US$90,000 and not getting loans that are offered to white people earning US$38,000, there is obviously a breakdown in that logic. This is not to say that the latter do not work hard for their incomes, but simply, that there is not a level playing field. This outcome has not emerged from nowhere. During the periods either side of the Second World War, there were higher levels of union membership among American workers than today, and far lower proportions of women in the workforce. The majority of these labour unions operated colour bars, excluding black and Hispanic workers from protection and access to much of the better-paid work. The benefits of industry were thus transferred *disproportionately* to white male workers. Additionally, the Federal Housing Authority channelled more money and loans into predominantly white counties, which then developed white suburbs, obtained government funding for services and often sought independent status (Lipsitz, 1998). Massey and Denton (1994) note that although black people also moved to the suburbs, this process was uneven. In the 1960–77 period, 0.5 million African Americans and 4 million white Americans moved to the suburbs from inner-city areas. Of the latter, 86 per cent were living in highly segregated areas (that is, those with a maximum of 1 per cent African Americans) by 1993.

So there is no simple automatic relationship between income, ambition and social mobility. That is an aspirational element of the dominant ideological model of contemporary classless and raceless society in which anyone can achieve anything if they try hard enough. This idea of personal development and responsibility becoming the basis for identification is largely covered by the 'individualisation' thesis most famously put forward by academics such as Ulrich Beck (1992, 2000). However, if you have less chance of accessing the type of employment that leads to loans being granted, and even then, less access to the loans on top of that due to the financial organisations' lending practices, then how, practically, do you move out of the ghetto? Your failure to move is refracted through the atomised prism of late capitalism in which people are seen as exclusive agents of their own destiny. If you are not successful, it is because there is something wrong with you, personally. This is true even for people who tick all the boxes for the American dream. Lacy's middle-class African American home-owners (2007) tell stories of being directed away from particular areas in their home search, of having estate agents question their capacity to buy property in some areas, etc. Indeed, they are quite aware that convincing white Americans of their middle-class status (and acceptability as potential homebuyers) requires specific patterns of dress and behaviour.

This leads us back to the sociological problem: is residential segregation in the USA caused by class inequalities or racism? If it were a question of class alone, we might predict three things:

First, as racialised minorities climb the socio-economic ladder, and can afford more expensive housing, segregation diminishes.

Second, attitudes to which 'race' lives where do not play an important role in choice of residential area. Massey and Denton's work (1994) indicates that for African Americans, class is irrelevant to their degree of residential segregation, although it is a factor for Hispanic and Asian Americans. The segregation indices for African Americans in three income bands are very similar, and very high, particularly in the Northern cities. Yet this is not true of all minority groups. For

Hispanic and Asian Americans, the degree of segregation reduces as upward social mobility increases. Racism seems therefore to be relatively more compelling in explaining patterns of African American settlement than it does in explaining those of Asian and Hispanic Americans.

Third, although it is often suggested that people choose to live with 'their own' (thus bolstering segregated patterns of settlement), the information collected from surveys on this topic shows that if people had a choice, the opposite pattern would be the outcome. African Americans express the most favourable responses to scenarios where a district is 50 per cent black. 'All black' or 'all white' neighbourhoods are the least enticing options (Massey and Denton, 1994). So while African Americans see a mixed neighbourhood as more appealing, white Americans see homogeneous white areas as the best option. In the same survey quoted by Massey and Denton (the Detroit Area Survey, 1976), half the white respondents said they would be unwilling to enter an area where 21 per cent of the residents were black, a number rising to 73 per cent for an area with a black population of 36 per cent. Maybe some do choose to live with what they consider to be 'their own' people, but it is not necessarily the minorities who self-segregate.

So, in summary, there are observable socially constructed mechanisms for restricting the housing mobility of non-white people, which develop from the practices of white decision-makers, and fellow white residents as well as their own individual choices. In these mechanisms, all white people, regardless of class and gender, are ostensibly granted an a priori advantage over everyone else, even if it consists primarily in *not* encountering as many obstacles.

The other side of this process is how the inner-city areas became more impoverished in the post-oil crisis era. Lipsitz identified four trends that result indirectly from the decline of industrial zones in inner-city areas (1995, 1998):

1. The process of urban renewal involved clearing former industrial belts of cities and replacing them with commercial and more expensive residential units. Many of the people previously living in such relatively cheap areas (disproportionately minorities) were displaced.

2. The business development in these areas means that greater taxes are levied (to pay for redevelopment) on a smaller number of households, as redevelopment reduced the number of residential units.

3. There is more commercial dumping of waste in the poorer areas, which are again disproportionately home to minorities. Even when such illegal dumping is penalised, the penalties meted out are weaker than those for dumping in mainly white, especially suburban areas.

4. The type of criteria used for the organisation of space in newly developed city centre areas are business-friendly. The priority is the defence of capital and high-return housing units built for the wealthier middle-classes, often in gated communities. For an in-depth argument about Los Angeles, for example, see Mike Davis (1992). He maintains that downtown space has been reorganised to suit business interests, so that the urban poor are policed away from the business core and the residential blocks. As a result, they enjoy increasingly smaller areas in which they are free from police intervention.

If we stand back from this chain of interrelated consequences, we can see that decision making on one issue (here the system of access to financial loans) has a series of ramifications. These work to prevent people from being as geographically and socially mobile as they would like. The areas that most minorities live in will be more likely to be deprived, where local taxes are higher, and there are associated social phenomena such as the increased probability of crime and under-funded and low-achieving schools. These in turn limit the choices open to people who are educated in them. In brief, there is a structural chain of consequences that ends up impoverishing the life chances of those with less likelihood of accessing funds for loans. In this ongoing scenario, those in the dominant racialised group (which for Europe and North America means white people) emerge as beneficiaries. This is true even if they neither support the idea of such a system nor benefit much from it in other areas. There is no such thing as a neutral white person in this process because it is a *social* process, which means an individual cannot remove him or herself from it, solely by wishing it away or changing behaviour *as an individual*.

CONCLUSIONS

We have identified institutional racism as an important development in both conceptualising racism and in public policy responses to inequalities. Both can be successfully covered under the title. However, while drawing from the same pool of resources for argument, these two spheres are quite different. The institutional racism concept used for public policy is basically a legal tool used to combat inequalities directly arising from employment and service provision by both state and private sector organisations, on a case-by-case basis. It is frequently discussed and critiqued in the media and the world of formal politics. The ideological battle consists here of a clash of two main sides. On one side are those who seek to valorise the concept's capacity to bring about more equal outcomes, and oblige organisations to address discriminatory practice as a matter of course. On the other, the arguments focus on the concept's alleged clumsiness and its inappropriate use: this term brands a whole organisation, it is claimed, where only a minority of individuals are actually behaving in racist ways. There are a number of ways to understand this struggle, but I suggest that a starting point for a sociologist is to focus on the main problem that 'institutional racism' has helped to resolve.

There are two distinct dimensions of racism – the individual and the collective. One makes no sense without the other. People must use the cultural stuff available to them, and that includes the ideas on 'race' that we recognise as dividing groups of people into categories based on appearance and/or culture. One of the most difficult things that undergraduate students and lay people experience in trying to come to terms with this topic is the idea that there is a level at which racism (like all other forms of discrimination) operates *counter* to individuals' intentions and regardless of their personal convictions. In the argument against institutional racism, there are individual actors who do bad things and those who do not. The objection is that within an organisation, the two are grouped together. Yet this type of response really misses the point of what the concept of institutional racism can do for us. 'Institutional racism' underscores the idea that the individual and collective dimensions of social action co-exist, yet are distinct at the theoretical level. It can therefore be said to be a real sociological concept that illuminates otherwise more muddied waters.

When 'institutional' is used as a synonym for 'structural', as it has been in the lineage of ideas derived from Carmichael and Hamilton (1967), the utility can be more widely applied outside the legal realm and in the social world, where, like class and gender, 'race' is one of the main vectors along which discrimination is channelled at a collective level.

NOTES

1. The nine grounds are: gender, marital status, family status, sexual orientation, religion, age, disability, race and membership of the Traveller community. The relevant pieces of legislation are the Employment Equality Acts 1998–2004 and the Equal Status Acts 2000–2004.
2. See www.equality.ie (Equality Authority definitions can be found on this website).
3. See cml.upenn.edu/redlining/HOLC_1936.html

8 Whiteness

Social scientists began interrogating what white racialised identities meant at the end of the nineteenth century. The first to do so were African Americans: W.E.B. Du Bois (1998 [1935]) and Ida Wells (1893) are the pioneers of the corpus. It could be argued that many critical studies that fall into the category of 'race' and ethnic studies between the early 1900s and the 1990s are about white identities. However, the renewed and explicit academic interest in 'whiteness' as a topic dates back to the work of American labour historian David Roediger, whose study of the white American working class called *The Wages of Whiteness* (1991) opened the door to a multidisciplinary migration towards the kind of issues he raised. The previous invisibility of whiteness in framing questions as being neutral, and forgetting pieces of history that reflected poorly on even the more radical white Americans, was an important step in shifting the analysis toward how the dominant groups in US society developed identities in relation to minorities.

This shift takes the focus away from minorities as somehow problematic per se, and pays closer attention to the ways that white people are racialised actors rather than neutral observers, and the complexities of the positions they hold. However, there have also been criticisms. Most important is the accusation that studies focusing on the way white people are divided by class and gender so that they do not all benefit equally from whiteness leads us to lose sight of the bigger picture: racisms work in the West by valuing whiteness over other forms of identity, and by generating a series of benefits and dis-benefits (Mills, 2004). However, the discourse that questions whether racism is still relevant in the contemporary USA is very widespread, and this forms the background to what we shall look at in the following chapter under the heading of 'colour-blind racism'. Moreover, there are other criticisms, namely that the whole problematic is tied closely to the USA and does not have much to say to activists and scholars in other places.

Additionally, there are serious political implications to stressing that 'white' might be a real identity. Groups from the anti-racist left to the white nationalist right often share the starting point that 'race' is a real thing, and that they are white. Their ideas of what to do about that might be very different, but the idea of white as an unchallengeable identity (reflecting Blackness, Asianness or Latino-ness, for example) might well be endorsed by studies of white identities unless they are very carefully qualified. So, as in the cases of all the topics looked at in this book, there are political stakes in studying, reflecting upon and being active around questions of racism beyond (as well as inside) the confines of the classroom.

In this chapter, the key elements of the American literature will be identified and summarised, before looking at the way in which whiteness can be used critically as an approach for examining contemporary Europe. This necessarily overlaps with what has been labelled the 'new racism' since the early 1980s (Chapter 9). Here, whiteness can be used, with clear caveats, to help understand current discourses about nation, 'race' and belonging.

AMERICAN WORK ON WHITENESS

There are a number of principal themes from the American literature on whiteness,[1] which I will explain here. In answer to the question 'what is whiteness?', I would argue that it is a number of things at once, and the most important of these are a power relationship; a frame for understanding social relationships; and a making explicit of how white identities are racialised. There is no one all-encompassing definition because the dynamics of power are very local and tied into the historical circumstances of a particular place.

Terror

The starting point for understanding whiteness in the American context is that of terror. For centuries, the use of violence against the population of Native Americans and enslaved Africans, then freed slaves generated understandings of interaction with white Americans among those communities based on fear and resentment. The narratives of the slavery period are full of this arbitrary use of different forms of violence: removal from land, psychological violence, rape, lynching. The systematic use of violence to keep order and control of the non-European population of the American colonies and then the nascent USA, is reflected in a vein of literature including essays, novels, poetry, theatre, political campaigning and social science going back more than a century. Writers such as James Baldwin, bell hooks and Toni Morrison have engaged directly with whiteness as it looms over the African American experience.[2] Baldwin, for example, identifying the psychological violence of racism, refers to the cumulative effect of 'the millions of details twenty-four hours of every day which spell out to you that you are a worthless human being' (1985: 404). Given this type of presence in the imaginary of people of colour, it may seem odd that the idea of invisibility has been used to characterise whiteness, but this is the next theme to emerge.

Invisibility/visibility

There are three ways in which invisibility crops up in terms of white identities. The first is the context of whiteness as the norm, and the second is to do with the power of whiteness to make itself the norm. The third is the power to make individuals who are not white invisible in a collective. These are connected. First, in a number of studies, white people say they do not think of themselves as being 'white', that is, as not having a racial identity, or that 'race' didn't matter where they grew up because there were no minorities there. This supposes that 'race' is only for people who are not white, so that a 'normal' identity is white. It therefore does not have to be addressed in racial terms. Many of Ruth Frankenberg's

(1994) Californian women speak about feeling white only when they arrived in larger multiracial towns where they were exposed to a greater variety of people. This experience is repeated many times in stories that white British people from provincial towns tell about when they visit urban areas with more obvious demographic diversity (Tyler, 2003; Byrne, 2006; Clarke and Garner, 2009). Ann Phoenix (1996, 2005) and Steven Farough (2004) find that her young people and his white males construct their identities as being individual vis-à-vis those of minorities as being collective and informed by 'race' in a way theirs is not. This becomes a different point when we talk about how norms are invisible. The dominant groups in society, whether by class, 'race' or gender, generate and sustain ideas that justify their dominance and make it natural and normal. Only people whose identities fall outside the dominant group therefore need to be defined differently. Richard Dyer's central point in his study of whiteness in film and photography (1997), is that white is the framing position: a dominant and normative space against which difference is measured. In other words, white is the point from which judgements are made, about normality and abnormality, beauty and ugliness, civilisation and barbarity. Simply put, whiteness is the default setting for 'human': everything else is deviant and requires explanation. Whiteness goes without saying.

However, one task of critical scholars is to articulate what 'goes with out saying', and therefore unpick what it means. Toni Morrison's essay on race in the history of American literature (1993) identifies African Americans as the invisible segment of the population. As we have noted from the work that links whiteness to terror, whiteness is far from invisible to people who are not racialised as white. The question of invisibility depends on who you are and what you are looking at. It also applies to the effects that whiteness can have on others. In Morrison's terms, it renders black people invisible.

The third function of whiteness is to make individual black people invisible vis-à-vis an idea of blackness, as in Ralph Ellison's *Invisible Man* (1952). This occurs in D. Marvin Jones' (1997) interpretation of the 1989 Charles Stuart case in Boston. Jones argues that 'race' as a social practice evacuates individuality from those objectified and reduces them to a list of imputed bio-cultural characteristics. Stuart and his brother murdered his pregnant wife, then wounded Stuart in order to trick the police. They then blamed the murder on a black man in jogging pants with a raspy voice. This led to a highly intensive police operation in the area where the killing had taken place, in which many black men were questioned. Stuart's brother later confessed that the scheme was a scam to claim life insurance. The surrounding media and political discourse had included calls for the restoration of the death penalty in the state. Stuart's story had been readily believed, despite a lack of evidence. He eventually committed suicide and Boston's black community reacted angrily to the scrutiny to which it had been unfairly subject. Jones asserts that assumptions of black criminality thus form the basis of white responses to black subjects at particular moments, when 'race' constitutes a line dividing innocence from guilt. White Americans are willing to accept the story because this is how they expect black men to act. The police and media response was founded on the idea that any black man could have killed the woman because it is in the nature of black men to do things like this. However, when discussing crimes perpetrated by white criminals, a different logic applies:

it is not *in the nature* of white people to do these things, although some may do. This is a significant distinction as it recognises Whites as individuals and free agents, but Blacks as a collective bound by nature.

CULTURAL CAPITAL

'Cultural capital' is one of the terms developed by Pierre Bourdieu (1986) to describe non-economic forms of 'wealth' distributed unevenly throughout society. It grants advantage that provides unequal access to employment, education, etc. Simply put, cultural capital can be thought of as consisting of ways to behave, think and express oneself that are valued, as well as the holding of types of knowledge that are valued hierarchically, especially that pertaining to high culture (Bourdieu, 1977). While the concept was first developed to enable an exploration of class distinctions and reproduction, it can also be used in relation to whiteness.

Du Bois first focuses on the non-economic advantages in being white in America, in his history of the Reconstruction (1998 [1935]), when he discusses what he terms the 'public and psychological wage' of whiteness. He was searching for reasons as to why the white poor in the southern states supported their elites against the newly freed slave population rather than allying with them to press for better living and working conditions. His conclusion was that whiteness insulated them from the idea of ever being slaves, the lowest possible status in American society. The distance between them and the former slaves was more important to them than that between poor and wealthy white southerners.

This 'psychological and public wage' has been looked at in a number of ways, and can be seen clearly in two pieces of work. One is the essay by Peggy McIntosh (1988), in which the author conceptualises privilege as a 'knapsack' full of things that give her advantages over people of colour. The list of 46 items includes things she does not have to do (act as a representative of her 'race'; take notice of minority groups' agendas or minority people without any penalty befalling her); things she can take for granted (move into an area that she can afford to live in) (see Chapter 7); being treated at least neutrally by her neighbours; curricula which reflect the contribution of people her colour; cosmetics and prosthetics which match her skin tone; and things she can do without worrying (move around different public spaces without being the focus of attention). McIntosh's list is a starting point for thinking about what she calls 'unearned advantage'. Frequently, models of racism we are presented with suggest that there are clear ways in which some groups are discriminated against, but do not make explicit how the dominant groups (usually white, but not always in every place) gain advantage from it. Reflection on this point brings us forward to a position where we can distinguish the intentions and ideas that individual people hold, from the systemic disadvantages and advantages that we are provided with. Charles Mills' neat summary of this, in his *Racial Contract* (1997: 11), is that the tacit contract to maintain a racially hierarchical society can be the object of criticism without it ceasing either to function, or to advantage white people as a group: 'All whites are beneficiaries of the Contract, though some whites are not signatories to it'. This does not mean that everyone in that category benefits equally, but that there is a benefit vis-à-vis groups racialised as not being white.

Amanda Lewis' study of three California primary schools (2003), for example, shows how teachers' expectations of behaviour, language use, achievement and family support follow a racialised pattern. The white pupils are not subject to the same kind of attention as their black and Latino classmates and this lack of scrutiny works to their advantage.

While the message emerging from work on schooling in both the USA and Britain (Johnson and Shapiro, 2003; Byrne, 2006) is that as a general rule, white parents seek schools with minimal proportions of minorities, there is also another side to cultural capital. Bourdieu (1984) uses it to talk only about the advantageous aspects enabling the middle classes to reproduce their patterns of education and thus employment. There is another scenario: the desirability of 'multicultural' capital. Diane Reay and her team's (2007) study of middle-class parents in England showed that there is a segment of that population who send their children to particular types of state secondary school, with a mixed class and ethnic composition. This strategy is aimed at extending the amount of cultural capital their children develop in terms of having experience of different types of people from themselves. This, it is argued, will be an asset to them in terms of employment and social networking in multicultural Britain. In the other form of cultural capital, there is a benefit to be accrued from non-elite culture. In their study of young people in a small provincial English town, Watt and Stenson (1998) show that the capital gained through having attended the town's multi-ethnic secondary schools enables the former students to negotiate urban spaces with more confidence than their middle-class suburban peers. The latter, due to the restricted social circles in their schools, have less knowledge of the town centre, of the different districts and of the people who live in them, making them wary of much of the town.

Contingent hierarchies[3]

In addition to a set of borders between people categorised as 'white' and 'non-white', there is another set of internal borders produced by racialisation. In other words, there are socially observable degrees of whiteness between the groups that seem to be unproblematically white. Examples here include Southern, Central and Eastern European immigrant groups in Western Europe and North America, Jews, Gypsy-Travellers/Roma, as well as the numerous and important divisions based on class, gender, sexuality, region, etc. identified in the literature on both America and Britain (Daniels, 1997; Nayak, 2003; Hartigan, 2005).

In European and North American societies, there is a history of imputing defective natural and cultural characteristics to members of the lower classes that goes back to feudal times in Europe. The thread of this is that there is a hierarchical socio-economic order in society, an order that reflects the natural traits of those groups. The hierarchy is thus because the dominant group deserve to be dominant, and the subordinate deserve to be subordinate. This is territory in which the social world is explained by the natural world, and culture is an expression of these distinctive 'natures' in which those groups are bounded by orders. The social mobility opened up by the end of feudalism and the beginning of the industrial world ended the notion that the feudal orders were completely distinct from each other. Instead, the new urban and to a lesser extent rural working classes were conceptualised by the dominant groups as both biologically and culturally inferior.

By the mid-nineteenth century, when ideas about class, 'race' and gender as social hierarchies were fully developed and linked to science (see Chapter 5), bodies of work dealing with the flaws inherent in working-class lives and culture were being published. Reports of the 'dangerous classes' linked their difficult economic positions and involvement in crime as deriving from genetic and cultural shortcomings not shared by the upper orders of society. Such flaws could be transmitted environmentally or through the bloodline, and some of the writing around the topic of racial purity in the late nineteenth and early twentieth-century, the period of social Darwinism and eugenics, focused on this reproductive mechanism. Eugenics-influenced discourse emphasised the perils of mixing good with bad genes. It was argued that antisocial behaviour derived from poor family etiquette and practices. In the scenarios popularised in the press, the idea of 'racial poisons' became significant, all the more so as 'weaker' blood was believed to multiply faster than the 'stronger'. Gertrude Davenport, the wife of America's leading eugenicist Charles Davenport, stated in a popular magazine in April 1914 that 'the greatest menace of imbecility is not that the imbecile may break into our house and steal our silver, or that he might set fire to our barn, but that he may be born of our flesh' (Hartigan, 2005: 95).

Similarly, in the Freudian fight for civilisation taking place within the Self, Winthrop Stoddard asserts that class status coincides with racial value:

> Let us understand once and for all [he warns] that we have among us a rebel army – the vast host of the unadaptable, the incapable, the envious, the discontented, filled with instinctive hatred of civilization and progress, and ready on the instant to rise in revolt. Here are foes that need watching. Let us watch them. (Stoddard, 1922: 87)

Of course, if the argument could be used to note a distinction between classes, then it could equally apply to different ethnic groups, even the nominally white ethnic groups. By the late nineteenth century, not only was there a notion of the racial superiority of whites over everyone else, but putative league tables of superiority within each of these broad 'races' had been put forward (see Chapter 5). The Anglo-Saxon was claimed to be at the summit of the white 'race', above the Celts, Latins, Persians and Jews (who sometimes appeared as a separate 'race' in the many attempts to classify human diversity that emerged from this period). In both Britain and North America, the racial status of ostensibly white groups such as the Catholic Irish, Eastern European Jews and Gypsy-Travellers has been the subject of discussion, social comment, social action and state policy. Indeed, Britain's first piece of immigration legislation, the 1905 Aliens Act, was formulated as a result of campaigning against the arrival of Jews fleeing persecution in Eastern Europe. In the contemporary UK, there has been a recent presence of Central and Eastern European migrants, often in areas where there had been little previous history of migration, such as the more rural east, and parts of the northwest. Many of the statements of hostility made about them resemble accusations of dirtiness, undercutting labour markets and lawlessness made about waves of immigrants going back to the Irish in the early nineteenth century.

This point leads us back to where we came in, with American labour historians' excavation of the relations between different immigrant groups and the host populations in American urban space (Roediger, 1991). The principal finding of Barrett and Roediger (1997) is that the cultural line separating white from black in the USA was not as clear as had been supposed. New European migrants who were neither protestant nor Northern European were not constructed as fully white (that is, fitting in with the dominant culture and capable of democracy). They often worked in jobs that free black Americans had done, lived in or near places that they had lived, and in the case of the Catholic Irish, were compared unflatteringly with black Americans (Garner, 2004). Indeed, so dangerous were Southern and Eastern European Catholics and Jews in the eugenicists' view, that the harshest quotas in the 1924 Immigration Act were applied to countries such as Italy, Poland and Russia.

The theoretical engagement with whiteness in the USA has produced a large number of books and articles that discuss and refine ideas (Nayak, 2007). However, for the purposes of this introduction, we are going to concentrate on some empirical fieldwork to get a feel for what can be analysed on the ground.

THEMES FROM FIELDWORK ON WHITENESS

There are a number of overlaps in the findings of the fieldwork carried out in the USA and Britain (Garner, 2009a). The theme of invisibility/visibility; the roles of cultural capital and shared values in making 'white' meaningful vis-à-vis others; the contingent class and ethnic hierarchies within the white group – all these appear with their distinctive accents. An emerging finding is that white is frequently now proposed as a disadvantaged identity in the face of government and cultural schema that favour minorities. This coalesces around affirmative action (or at least what people imagine affirmative action to consist of – for clarity, see McKinney, 2004; Dhami et al., 2006) in the USA and so-called 'political correctness' in the UK. Underlying this victimhood is a profound sense of not having benefited from social change, and loss of ground. However, the precise history of the USA and the experiences of colonial violence there have made terror and systemic psychological and physical violence more immediately relevant to accounts of whiteness as power. This is not to say that there are none of these things in Europe. Indeed, the more striking element of the European experience is of whiteness mediated through a colonial history into a postcolonial present. The following fieldwork will demonstrate some of these overlaps and distinctions.

CASE STUDIES

Hartigan's 'Racial Situations'

John Hartigan's ethnography of inner-city Detroit (1997, 1999) is focused largely on a district called Briggs, which is home to low-income white and black families. While there are other sections dealing with gentrification of a nearby inner-city area, and a struggle over schooling in a mainly white suburb, Hartigan develops his analysis primarily from his observations of life in Briggs. He finds that the way people there make sense of whiteness and blackness is a very complicated mixture of codes. Incidents can end up racialised, but do not necessarily begin that way. On the other hand, the cordial relations between black and white in the area are explained, he believes, by the long period of common socialisation: many of the inhabitants were at school with each other and have remained in the area. The personal knowledge they have of each other's family histories appears to keep people focused on individuals rather than on the collective narratives of black and white. In an earlier piece, Hartigan had reported that when he told some interviewees that he was studying 'race relations', they suggested he should go to a housing project across the highway, indicating that it was a zone too dangerous for whites (1997: 191):

> In this [their own] neighbourhood, they were one family among many, white and black, who held elaborate and lengthy knowledge of each other reaching back over the tumultuous past three decades. But across the intersection [that is, in that particular project] they were simply 'whites', partly for their skin color and partly in terms of location and being out of place.

The invisibility feared by Hartigan's white respondents thus thematically mirrors that of the black people who Jones (1997) maintains are objectified by whiteness.

In the codes of discourse and action that Hartigan identifies, the role of 'race' differs widely. It is sometimes irrelevant, sometimes part of the mix and sometimes the basis of action. There are different registers of language and behaviour that are acceptable in some contexts and not in others. Additionally, 'race' is frequently understood through the frames of class. An example of this is a multiracial baseball game played by the family of Hartigan's main white informant, Jessie (1999: 140–4). They arrange to play a serious game against a team of local black people whom they had met the week before. One of Jessie's brothers, David, refuses to play because he doesn't want to play against Blacks. His decision is viewed by the Briggs-based family as more evidence of David's weirdness and efforts to distance himself socially from them: David already lives elsewhere in a wealthier neighbourhood. More people join the game as the afternoon goes on, and by the end, the two teams are racially mixed. David's girlfriend, Becky, from a white suburb of Detroit, expresses her discomfort about the proximity of black people. This manifests itself in her leaving early and not wanting to lend her glove to black players, which is what she tells Jessie. The resulting family feud is interpreted through the lens of class. Jessie's Briggs-based family see Becky as a spoilt middle-class girl who is out to 'spoil' David too. Her inability to function in a racially mixed setting is seen by the family as proof of her snobbery (not her racism, which is not explicitly referred to as such). For Becky and David, argues Hartigan, their 'striving for social mobility and higher class standing was articulated through an assertion of the need for careful racial boundary maintenance by avoiding interracial situations' (1999: 142).

Lewis' 'Racialised School Situations'

Amanda Lewis (2003) argues that the school is not a racially neutral haven of equality but a site in which children learn about 'race', and the adults they encounter impose understandings of 'race' upon them and each other. Her study is of three primary schools in California: a mixed inner-city one, a mainly white suburban one and a special bilingual (Spanish–English) suburban one.

All the schools address the issue of 'race' differently, from denial that it is an issue at all through to explicitly placing racism on the agenda to be addressed. However, Lewis finds that despite the different starting points, there are common areas.

At the mainly white 'Foresthills' school, the consensus is that 'race' is not an issue because of the demographic composition of the school. Staff and parents are adamant that 'race' plays no part in their lives, and the school's addressing of multiculturalism and inequalities is rudimentary. However, Lewis asserts that this school encapsulates the dominant way of thinking about 'race' in America: colour-blind racism (see Chapter 9). The process of racialisation, and the discriminatory effects of housing policy over the past century, for example, have created white suburbs like Foresthills that provide the intake of this school. Moreover, this residential segregation is bolstered by social and workplace segregation, which means that the school's student body lives in virtual isolation from non-white people. The understandings of discrimination are that it is mainly just the response of minorities with a chip on their shoulder, and that in fact there are cultural deficiencies that give rise to the problems of poverty and segregation.

At 'West City', a school in a mainly white neighbourhood into which Latino and African American kids are bussed daily, 'race' is not denied as such, but given a cultural spin. Lewis finds that teaching staff have racialised expectations and understandings of the pupils' lives. Problems in school among African American children are understood by the mainly white staff as stemming from the dysfunctional families of the latter, and the lower value attached to education. The few minority staff in the school feel the pressure of having to be the ones who explicitly raise the issue of racism and racist assumptions, and the minority children generally do worse academically than the white ones. Lewis asserts that the combination of expectations, different assumptions and engagement of staff with the different types of pupil contributes to unequal outcomes. It is easier to attribute this to the children's culture than accept that there is something in their practices and assumptions that needs remedying.

'Metro2' is a special bilingual school sought after by white middle-class parents, and which contains a large proportion of Latino students. Although it serves a mixture of socio-economic groups, the white pupils are generally from the better-off end of the spectrum and their parents dominate the school's agenda. It is in part a study of how cultural capital functions in a school, even from the point of applying for a place, which requires handling a number of forms (Ball, 1993). Although the school is bilingual, Spanish is the official language and there is no English as a Second Language teaching available. English is the first language in only two classrooms. This means that the learners of Spanish get a better educational deal than the learners of English, who provide models to the other students but do not get the same service in return. Despite a lot more attention being paid to minority identities and the issue of social equality, the outcomes still tended toward those of the other school. 'The white children in this school', writes Lewis, 'were the only white children I interviewed who were aware of and able to talk about racism and discrimination as factors in mobility and opportunity' (2003: 108). However, the social segregation she witnesses, outside of formal lessons, takes place in the schoolyard, and outside the walls of the school. Even in the school itself, the racial lines are sometimes clear: the three spelling groups follow racial lines. Most of the top group are white, most of the few African Americans are in the bottom group and most of the Latinos are in the two bottom groups (ibid.: 115).

The interpretations of difference held by the white staff and parents of these three schools are based firmly in ideas about culture and responsibility. The concept of structural discrimination is acknowledged most often at Metro2, but this does not eliminate the cultural approach. This goes hand-in-hand with the colour-blind ideology, which asserts that it is solely people's merit that counts. Rather than being an aspiration, this is understood as a fact, and therefore collective failure is interpreted as the failure of individuals within the group. However, the phenotypical dimension of 'race' is still present. In the case of bi-racial children at Metro2, for example, this comes to the fore in a series of misrecognitions, when the culture and appearance of children does not tally with preconceptions (ibid.). Hector is a light-skinned Hispanophone Latino who is consistently seen as a white Anglophone, and not given credit for his English-language skills. Enrique's parentage is black-Mexican, and he is proud of his Chicano culture, however he is seen as African American and not acknowledged as a Latino. Finally, brown-skinned Omar, whose parentage is German-American and Bolivian, is questioned when he claims European heritage.

Tyler's semi-rural English middle classes

Katharine Tyler's ethnographies of the English village of Greenville in Leicestershire (2003, 2006) show that semi-rural space is defended using the development of middle-class values of belonging through adherence to ways of being and behaving. Tyler finds clear class distinctions within the village between the white inhabitants, but her fieldwork focuses on the ways in which racism is articulated there. There are a small number of wealthy South-Asian families in Greenville, and these are seen as 'abnormal' because they do not fit notions of respectability and normality. In other words, they do not engage in the usual activities there such as charity work (women) and going to the pub (men) (2003: 394). Particular episodes illustrate the way 'race' emerges in people's understandings of the Asians. One family extended its house against local opposition generated by anxieties of the villagers about what the space would be used for. The white villagers predicted that the house would be used as a combined residence, business premises and temple. One villager states that: 'They are very nice people but eyebrows are raised when the hordes of friends and relatives come from Leicester. It isn't done in Greenville' (ibid.: 405). Tyler concludes that 'wealthy Asians are thought to live in extended families, are perceived to be excessively wealthy, extravagantly religious, run disruptive businesses from their homes and cook smelly foods' (ibid.: 409). For the middle classes in semi-rural Leicester (a medium-sized city in the East

Midlands with a relatively large South-Asian descended population), tranquillity is a prized value. While solidarity (for the poor elsewhere) is demonstrated through the routines of charity work, the real test of belonging in Greenville is to attain invisibility. Talking of one particular Asian family in the village, one resident tells Tyler (ibid.: 400) 'They are as good as gold … we never see them'. Hiding oneself and keeping the noise down is viewed as the correct way to behave, a value that contradicts the justification given for not forging more intimate relations, which is that 'Asians don't mix'.

Byrne's mothers looking for the 'right mix'

Bridget Byrne (2006) studies white mothers choosing primary schools for their children in South London. She explains that she is seeking to counteract: 'the assumption … that we (everyday white people in Britain who are not particularly racist) cannot be interesting as "race" has nothing to do with us' (Byrne, 2006: 1). The analysis of how the 'we' she refers to is constructed is a project requiring her to hear and see 'race' in 'contexts where it is not explicitly felt as present' (ibid.: 2). Byrne argues that 'race' needs to be understood as performative, and 'more specifically as a product of perceptual practices' (ibid.: 74). She observes that questions about 'race' in her interviews were frequently met with a lowering of the speaker's voice. There were evasions (talking about other identities when asked directly about 'race'), and silences: talking about 'race' is awkward. Indeed, a common strategy deployed was not to see difference, that is, to talk as if whiteness is not a social location. Yet, in not seeing their whiteness, the women definitely see blackness. Black men, for example, emerge as simultaneously threatening and desirable. In narrating themselves, Byrne's white women subjects often evoke whiteness as an absence of 'race' during provincial, often rural, childhoods, followed by an awareness-raising confrontation in the cosmopolitan metropolis. For them, as for Ruth Frankenberg's interviewees (1994), 'race' is something seen and done only when face-to-face with the 'Other'.

At the 'core of motherhood', writes Byrne, 'lie the intersections of race, class and gender' (ibid.: 106). She proceeds to demonstrate this in her examination of the ways in which the social networks of both mothers and children, and the choice of schools, are highly classed and raced acts. While there are obvious cultural and material conflicts over resources, what is fascinating is the view of multiculturalism as a form of cultural capital. Many of the mothers are pro-multicultural: exposure to difference is deemed good for the children. Yet there is what former French president François Mitterand once termed a 'threshold of tolerance'. For these mothers, there has to be the 'right mix', which involves just enough minority (and/or working class) children to make it interesting, but not so many as to make them think that the school's standards will be brought down (even this is not true). Byrne's conclusion is that in the eyes of their mothers, children must learn to be white and middle class *in the right way*. Her emphasis on performativity leads her to state that: 'the security and stability of the white middle-class norm requires constant repetition and recitation in order for it to be ensured for their children' (ibid.: 137). The mothers thus nurture their children's whiteness by careful management of the contexts in which they learn about difference.

In all the snippets of fieldwork glimpsed here, the binding themes are the precarious invisibility and visibility of whiteness and the cultural capital this brings into play and the location in states where there is anti-discrimination legislation and a diminution of overtly racialised language. The understandings of what constitutes racism and what the 'problem' actually consists of are increasingly individual rather than collective, and locate problems in the past rather than the present. What I mean by this is that there is something paradoxical going on in white people's statements of identity. On one hand, they see themselves as individuals, and minorities (unless they know them personally) are conceptualised as groups. On the other hand, discrimination is seen as a thing of the past, which is now minimal and used as an excuse for not achieving by minority individuals. Whiteness studies has now been under way in its new form, as a reflexive body of work per se for nearly two decades, and according to Gallagher and Twine (2007: 5) is now beginning its 'third wave'. The corpus on whiteness as conceptualised and operationalised outside of the USA is growing, and the fieldwork reveals the complexities of local racial regimes and underscores the intersectional approach's claim (Chapter 3) that people live out intersections of identities. On some axes, they are dominated and on others, part of the dominant group. The ongoing power of whiteness, which is reflected in each of the chapters of this book, is not as invisible or as potent for all those racialised as 'white'. Indeed, in some cases it is more difficult to see how it benefits people on the lowest socio-economic rungs of the ladder. However, as has been argued since the beginning of social science's engagement with whiteness, its benefits are not confined to the economic sphere. Analyses that focus exclusively on that aspect will necessarily miss the point, which is that the ideological and social interpretations of white identities can (maybe provisionally) compensate for low status in the economic arena. There are pertinent critiques of the substance of whiteness studies. Two of the most glaring gaps in the work so far are the absence (with a few notable exceptions) of sustained studies of the intersection of gender and whiteness since the black feminist critique of the early 1980s, and the overriding concentration on working-class subjects as opposed to middle-class ones (again with a few exceptions) (Clarke and Garner, 2009).

NOTES

1. Interested readers can find a much more detailed investigation in Garner (2007a).
2. See Baldwin (1965, 1985), bell hooks (1992, 2000) and Toni Morrison (1993).
3. See also my amended chapter on 'Contingent Hierarchies' in Routledge's electronic resource: *The Social Issues Collection: A Routledge/University Readers Custom Library for Teaching* (www.socialissuescollection.com/).

9 New Racisms?

As some norms and values change from one period to the next in different social contexts, so the way 'race' is articulated through the ideological dimension of racism is transformed. In terms of ideas and practices of racism, there is no consensus about the precise changes, or how they are to be interpreted. However, there is a consensus that there is something to mark the late twentieth-century as distinctive in terms of identifiable differences from the previous period. In this chapter, we shall look at some of the suggestions advanced about what these changes are, and how to understand them in Europe and the USA.

We shall begin by looking at three European contributions to the theorisation of racism that have specifically identified elements that are 'new' in the period since the 1974 oil crisis: those of Martin Barker (1981), Etienne Balibar (Balibar and Wallerstein, 1991) and Pierre-André Taguieff (2001). After this, we will identify how elements of what they describe can be used in political discourse, first by representatives of the Far right, and then by other actors, before going on to see how the changes in formulating 'race' have taken place in the USA in the post-civil rights era.

EUROPEAN 'NEW' AND 'NEO-RACISM'

Martin Barker (1981, 1990) coined the term 'new racism' to describe the configuration of ideological force in which the neo-liberal market-driven Conservatives were at the beginning of their domination of British politics that would last until 1997. He links the discourse of sociobiology to the realm of politics. Sociobiology is a set of scientific approaches to human behaviour that emphasises genetics and group behaviours observable in both animal and human worlds, a kind of updated social Darwinism shorn of its explicitly racialised element (Morris, 1968; Dawkins, 1976; Wilson, 1976). There is a narrative about natural, primal drives to stay with one's own kind and defend the 'us' from the 'them'. The following quote from the work of Richard Ardrey encapsulates the sociobiological account of group dynamics:

> The biological nation ... is a social group containing at least two mature males, which holds as an exclusive possession a continuous area of space, which isolates itself from others of its kind through outward antagonism, and which through its defence of its social territory, achieves leadership, cooperation and a capacity for concerted action. (Ardrey, 1967: 191)

Barker's interest in sociobiological accounts of inter-group conflict lies in the idea that such conflicts are genetically programmed into us. Racism and nationalism are thus naturalised, that is, described as primal feelings that cannot be changed by social action. Worse still, from the social scientist's perspective, the act of aggression that locates danger in the out-group is actually explained as an act of 'kin altruism'. Racism is thus transformed from a form of hatred into merely a form of love for one's own people: a refrain used by far-right politicians since the 1980s. Les Back (2002) talks of this in his study of far-right internet dating sites, where he states that 'hate speaks the language of love' (see Box 9.1).

French political scientist Pierre-André Taguieff first located the development of two parallel forms of racism in the 1980s (1990, 2001). He began talking about what he termed 'differentialist racism', which can be distinguished from 'discriminatory racism'. The latter is framed within an imperial/colonial relationship that understands human diversity as being explicitly on a scale running from civilised to barbarous, and is as much about biology as culture. Indeed, Taguieff stresses the overlap and flow between the two spheres. 'Racism', he argues, 'does not just biologize the cultural, it acculturates the biological' (1990: 117).

'Differentialist racism' then is what he observed in the French and wider European context from the 1980s onwards, that is, a political instrumentalisation of the key terms of the previously anti-racist language of respect for difference and cultural diversity. In the French republican context, talking explicitly about 'race' in the political discourse is not acceptable. The far-right Front National (FN) (among others) developed a form of argument around difference ('le droit à la différence') in a cultural setting that implicitly places Christian, Catholic, white Europe on one side and everything else, especially Islam, on the other. This line of reasoning is linked by Taguieff with the far right's other areas of interest, such as anti-statism and nationalism.

So from being the clarion call of left progressive forces, the 'right to be different' becomes a slogan that encapsulates the nostalgic and reactionary imagining of communities as pure and monolithic blocs that should not be spoiled by mixing. Cultures are understood to be exclusive and static groups of people, unchanging across time and place, so that FN leader, Jean-Marie Le Pen can state that 'I love Maghrebins [people of North African, usually Muslim origin], but their place is in the Maghreb' (Taguieff, 1990: 116). So from this perspective, each culture has its own characteristics and specific location. The movement of peoples entailed in the post-Second World War migratory landscape can only disrupt this. Differentialist racism is not ostensibly about biological 'race' at all, but about defending the right to have a distinct culture. This is the dimension of the ideas that political groups want to project. That discourse is both populist and extremely disorientating for anti-racist movements that have been using similar logics (the right for minorities to express their cultural differences), and cannot adapt to the new context. However, argues Taguieff, this is really about mixing, which is the obsession of differentialist racism. It claims that cultures cannot mix without damage being done. At the root of the defence of culture is a vision in which the proximity of cultures alone necessarily leads to conflict, and this conflict is accelerated by mixing between people. This mixing and the process of métissage that it brings about is anathema to the differentialist racist point of view because it destroys the supposed purity of the original culture and leads to its degradation. It is ultimately driven by a phobia about race mixing, and therefore about the biological aspects of 'race' rather than only being about culture. Indeed, Taguieff's argument neatly underlines the new and not so new elements of the 'new racism'. While the appropriation of the anti-racist left's vocabulary and its reorganisation into a white nationalist ideology is specific to the period, the theme of civilisations failing due to mixing and losing their purity can be traced back at least as far as de Gobineau's work in the 1850s.

We shall now turn to another French thinker, whose work focuses on political theory at a further level of abstraction. Etienne Balibar's broad argument is that like class and nationalism, racism is on one level 'functional' to capitalism: the salience and content of the ideologies change as the forms of capitalism alter (Balibar and Wallerstein, 1991). In the late 1980s, what he calls 'crisis' racism (1991: 219) deflects anxieties about the decline of the economy and life chances onto migrant groups, so that they are blamed for bringing disorder and economic problems and lowering the West's cultural level. In his discussion of new forms of racism, Balibar begins by locating the phenomenon historically:

> This new racism is a racism of the era of 'decolonization', of the reversal of population movements between the old colonies and the old metropolises, and the division of humanity within a single political space. (1991: 21)

The main argument of the new racism is 'differentialist' (see above), that is, that cultural difference in the world's populations is not only evident, but desirable and necessary. When the distance between the geographical spaces in which the world's cultures are lived out shrinks, then it is a natural step for this to lead to conflict between cultures defending themselves. In this logic, those who advocate the bringing together of cultures and indeed their mixing (the anti-racists) are actually generating racism. The perspective that seeks to keep cultures separate is thus the true anti-racism.

The dominance of the cultural element of racist ideas (at the expense of the pseudo-biological element that had been the focus of discourses of 'race' until the Second World War) is not new per se. As Balibar notes, European anti-Semitism is essentially cultural in character and goes back to medieval times. The obsession with the cultural field means that the idea of 'racism without races' (1991: 21) derives from this long-standing stream of racism. However, for Balibar, what distinguishes the twentieth-century forms of 'new racism' is the naturalisation of conflict around cultures, alongside the implicit, rather than explicit, hierarchisation of cultures. All forms of racism include the idea that the world's cultures are hierarchically related, in other words, there are some superior ones and some inferior. Although the new racism proclaims itself egalitarian but separatist, Balibar notes that the idea of superiority pervades it, emerging 'in the very type of criteria applied in thinking the difference between cultures' (ibid.: 24). All integration or assimilation of people whose origins lie outside Europe is seen as progress for the latter.

The legacy of the 'new racism' is that the cultural frame still dominates the language and politics of the mainstream and far right in Europe. Political parties such as the Italian *Lega Nord* (LN), the *Alleanza nazionale* (AN) and the MSI (with its links to Mussolini's Fascist Party) have shaped the country's debates on immigration and national identity. Since the 1990s, civilised Italy (the North) is put forward as having to defend its cultural integrity against both the backward cultures of the South (especially for the LN/AN) and foreign ones brought in by people from outside the EU, or *extracommunitari*. This discourse is particularly focused on African and Eastern European immigrants, sparking frequent discussions of citizenship, immigration legislation and initiatives for integrating immigrants. The 'honest national' discourse, however, can readily link space to 'culture' (a surrogate for 'race'). Sometimes there is a Freudian slip, as Umberto Bossi, Secretary General of the Italian Lega Nord demonstrates in an interview with *Epoca* magazine in (20 May 1990):

> The cultural differences are too much. The difference in skin colour is detrimental to social peace. Imagine if your street, your public square, was inhabited by people different from you: you would not feel part of your own world.

This is a statement formulated as a reasonable argument, and one hears echoes of this in fieldwork with white Europeans since the Second World War. The weight lies in the term 'different'. Some differences are ignored and others are seen as unbridgeable, and the link between space, 'race' and culture seems very clear.

In summer 2008, a spate of attacks on Roma and Sinti Gypsies in Italy was also justified by this logic: the Roma/Gypsies are constructed as being unbearably different. They are represented as bearers of pre-modern culture, dirt, disease, immorality and crime. In opinion polling, very hostile attitudes toward even non-Gypsy Romanian nationals and Italian Roma were expressed at the time. The Italian administration of 2008 is a coalition between a populist conservative party run by media tycoon Silvio Berlusconi and the right-wing Lega Nord. The Interior Minister, Roberto Maroni, belongs to the latter. His response to the arson and attacks in Naples and Rome was to condone them, and to institute fingerprinting for all Gypsies (Milne, 2008). The response of the people who engaged in the attacks was to boast that they were ethnic cleansing, and supporters of the anti-Gypsy campaign have been described as patriots. Again, the theme is of the protection of values out of love for one's country rather than hatred for others.

Box 9.1   Not hate but love: the British National Party

The British National Party (BNP) is currently the most well-organised and popular far-right party in the UK. It has undergone a series of changes since 1999, when its leadership was assumed by Nick Griffin, a moderniser who has brought the presentation of the party toward the mainstream in order to compete more effectively for votes. Their motivation, it is argued, is not hatred, nor is it racism, but love for one's own country and one's own people. Their website FAQs section included the following question and answer:

> Q: 'The politicians and the media call the BNP "racist"? Is this true?'
>
> A: 'No. "Racism" is when you "hate" another ethnic group. We don't "hate" black people, we don't "hate" Asians, we don't oppose any ethnic group for what God made them, they have a right to their own identity as much as we do, all we want to do is to preserve the ethnic and cultural identity of the British people.' (BNP website, in Atton, 2006: 577)
>
> Like the French Front National in Taguieff's work, the BNP has appropriated the Left's language. It uses 'equality', 'community', 'identity' and 'rights' to establish the departure point of their claims that white British people are the collective victims of racism and oppression in 'their own' country.
>
> The BNP's site thus constructs white identity as repressed and in need of defence. White British identities are perceived in this view as being under threat from minorities. Indeed, 'racism', argues Chris Atton, 'is presented as a reasonable reaction to the imputed racism of the Other' (2006: 580). Minorities come out of this argument as not suffering from racism at all, but in fact being those who exert it against the indigenous population, with the assistance of politically correct authorities and other institutions. Thus, the adoption of previous left-wing and progressive concepts has enabled the far right to recast its potential voters as the abandoned, oppressed majority. This is an image that a considerable number of people seem to recognise, and which emerges strongly in qualitative interviewing of white UK people (Clarke and Garner, 2009; Hoggett et al., 2008).

CULTURE, BLOOD AND NON-BELONGING

The establishment of an imagined natural bond exclusively tying a people to a place, and defining the bloodline of the people within the framework of the nation state is the legacy of the eighteenth century (see Chapter 4), building on the ideological work done by the French and American revolutionaries. Remember how Herder's natural set of analogies renders this perfectly:

> The most natural state ... is one nation, with one national character ... a nation is as much a natural plant as a family. Only with more branches. Nothing therefore appears so directly opposite to the end of government as the unnatural enlargement of states. The wild mixture of races and nations under one sceptre. (Herder, 1784–91: 249–50)

In contemporary Europe, this bond justifies 'defensive' strategies of securing territory against the encroachment of those perceived as non-members of the nation. By its act of opening the possibility of dialogue (or miscegenation), the transgression of members of the *ethnos* (those outside the democratic, rights-exercising community) into the *demos* (the democratic, rights-exercising community) legitimises verbal and physical violence as a response. The neatest summary of the relationship of 'race' and culture as tools of domination in Western thought is provided by Robert Young (1995: 54) in this thought-provoking account of the genesis of culture in colonialism:

> Culture has always marked difference by producing the other; it has always been comparative, and racism has always been an integral part of it: the two are inextricably clustered together, feeding off and generating each other. Race has always been culturally constructed. Culture has always been racially constructed.

What is important for us to grasp is the way that the discourse of 'new racism' wields the power to enact constrained and sublimated violence: a discourse that hinges on an assumed membership of a culture amongst its audience, the perception that this culture is threatened, and upon a broad belief that 'white' European/ North American Christian culture is superior – although people may deny thinking that one 'race' is superior, as political leaders making the transition into respectable politics may stress. They are not inferior or superior, just different. And it is the quality of this difference, its absolute 'unbridgeableness', and its bearers' incapacity to transcend it, that makes the deployment of cultural difference as an organising principle so treacherous.

The vagueness and popular understandings of culture as static enable them to be easily accessed by people seeking to demarcate themselves from their Others. The now defunct National Socialist website dedicated to Ireland (www. nsrus.com), whose banner heading was 'No to a Black Ireland', contained a forum ('Concerned Citizens') from which the following was posted on 1 March 2002:

> Now the Government is spending millions on anti-racism. How in the world can you lump totally backward cultures and modern cultures in together and expect them all to get along. That's impossible. It would take generations and by then you would not have a white society and you would not have an Irish culture.

The discourse here evinces the usual anxieties over mixture, and disappearance of cultural specificity that can be found in writings going back to the nineteenth century (the former), and anti-immigration discourse since the 1950s in Europe (the latter). Moreover, the putative pathological incapacity for intra-cultural dialogue, and the chasm separating cultures (developed vs undeveloped) is a synonym of 'race'. Take out the term 'culture' here, and replace it with 'race', and the message remains unaltered.

Indeed, the unvoiced supposition in the cultural struggle is that difference overrides similarity. While it is relatively easy to pinpoint the reliance of far-right political parties in Europe on new racism, it is also instructive to look at some of the ideas that form the basis of the way people discuss immigration in the mainstream political arena and the challenges this presents for society. One such example is David Goodhart's well-known provocative article in the political journal *Prospect* (2004: 30–7), which questions the capacity of Britain to sustain its welfare state in the face of increasing ethnic diversity (Box 9.2).

> ## Box 9.2   Goodhart's: 'Too Diverse?'
>
> 'The diversity, individualism and mobility that characterise developed economies – especially in the era of globalisation – mean that more of our lives is spent among strangers. Ever since the invention of agriculture 10,000 years ago, humans have been used to dealing with people from beyond their own extended kin groups. The difference now in a developed country like Britain is that we not only live among stranger citizens but we must *share* with them. We share public services and parts of our income in the welfare state, we share public spaces in towns and cities where we are squashed together on buses, trains and tubes, and we share in a democratic conversation – filtered by the media – about the collective choices we wish to make. All such acts of sharing are more smoothly and generously negotiated if we can take for granted a limited set of common values and assumptions. But as Britain becomes more diverse, that common culture is being eroded.' (David Goodhart, 'Too Divese?' *Prospect* magazine, February 2004.)

The ethnic/cultural form of diversity above all others, Goodhart maintains, is inimical to social solidarity. The rest of the article is constructed around this assumption, and it is what I want to draw attention to. In support of his main thesis (diversity diminishes solidarity), Goodhart cites increasingly hostile opinions toward immigration, and toward perceived free-riding in general as ways in which British taxpayers are losing sympathy with the national trend toward diversity of values. However, the empirical basis for suggesting that people's values differ very much *by ethnicity alone* are scant. In the fullest comparative exploration of ethnic minorities (Modood et al., 1997), it is clear that there is both a spectrum of cultural overlap with mainstream British values as well as distinct areas of difference. Yet the former is much larger than the latter. This is not to suggest that, hypothetically, what culturally separates a British Muslim from a British Sikh, and both from a secular White Briton, for example, is not important to each of them, but that the assertion that there is so little in common as to raise problems about social solidarity cannot so lightly be assumed. What, for example, if these three were all men, or all women, all from the same town, all sat next to each other in a school classroom? Moreover, Modood's argument (2004) that Muslim solidarity might be increasing as a function of post-2001 attacks and suspicion, and that segregation in the northern English towns that witnessed rioting is a result of poverty and white flight rather than a case of Muslims simply 'choosing' to live separate lives, is borne out by the fieldwork carried out by Phillips (2006) and Hussain and Bagguley (2005) respectively. Typically, Goodhart refers to Robert Putnam's (2000) highly influential work as an example of diversity reducing solidarity. However, even Putnam now argues that while diversity leads to social isolation and lower levels of trust, both between and within ethnic groups, and he makes two important qualifications (Putnam, 2007). The first is that this phenomenon is only a short-term one. Over generations that situation dissipates. Secondly, there are institutional success stories that show that such attitudes can be overcome by contact on an equal footing, like the US armed forces. Goodhart's assertion that 'most of us prefer our own kind' (2004: 31), in an article devoted to the salience of ethnic difference in public policy, seems to signify that it encapsulates a special kind of difference that is more problematic than class, age, gender or religion, for example. He then makes a jump to advocating the exploration of a two-tier system of welfare in which migrants access a lower level of resources (which is already the case). For the first part of the article, we have been reading 'ethnicity' as a code for 'race', yet here it equates with migrant status (labour migrant or asylum seeker). However, the proportion of Black, Asian and Minority Ethnic (BAME) people in Britain lies at around 7 per cent (2001 Census). What place, therefore, do those who are British but 'ethnic' in these terms, occupy in the progressive dilemma that Goodhart illustrates? What is assumed about their values being different? Different from whose? Are class values so close in a nation experiencing a reversal in the direction of social equality in terms of wealth and income, that we can assume that the white populations are homogeneous, and necessarily different in important ways from those of BAME British of the equivalent social class? The object of this commentary is to highlight the lack of evidence to back up a serious assertion that both has and has nothing to do with 'race'. Goodhart's piece demonstrates elements of the new racism: culture is the great divide; the lines between the domains of the physical (colour) and the psychological (humans are prone inevitably to in-group and out-group divisions and social action (Goodhart, 2004: 31)), are blurred. This is refracted through entirely mainstream and acceptable political discourse. Indeed, in recent fieldwork with White UK people (Clarke and Garner, 2009), the cultural heritage of Britain is very clearly seen as a resource to be defended against encroachment (particularly from Muslims).

We shall now turn to the forms of racial discourse observed in the USA as being constitutive of a new formulation. There are similarities to the European forms, but also some clear differences.

THE NEW RACISMS IN THE USA: COLOUR-BLINDNESS, APATHY AND WHITENESS AS A BURDEN

A number of American scholars have identified a pattern of indifference, ignorance and disengagement with racial topics on the part of white people since the 1990s (Bobo et al., 1997; Carr, 1997; Crenshaw, 1997; Kenny, 2000; Gallagher, 2003), but here we will look at three illustrative pieces of work, each illuminating one strand of the central problematic: colour-blind racism. These are Eduardo Bonilla-Silva's *Racism without Racists* (2006); Tyrone Forman and Amanda Lewis' article on 'racial apathy' (2006); and Karyn McKinney's ethnography of white undergraduates' responses to a course on 'race' (2004).

What exactly is 'colour-blind racism'? Isn't colour-blindness something positive to be aimed for? Not in the terms of the scholars who use the concept, as the emphasis is placed more on the blindness side of the equation. Forman and Lewis summarise colour-blind racism's central beliefs as the following:

(1) most people do not even notice race any more; (2) racial parity has for the most part been achieved; (3) any persistent patterns of racial inequality are the result of individual and/or group-level shortcomings

rather than structural ones; (4) most people do not care about racial differences; and (5) therefore, there is no need for institutional remedies (such as affirmative action) to redress persistent racialised outcomes. (Forman and Lewis, 2006: 177–8)

The most in-depth and provocative exploration of colour-blind racism (henceforth CBR) is Eduardo Bonilla-Silva's *Racism without Racists* (2006). The original was published in 2003, and the second edition is the one I am using here. Like Joe Feagin (2006: 126–8), he argues that there are dominant frames (or pathways for creating meaning available to people), and in relation to CBR, there are four central ones: abstract liberalism, naturalisation, cultural racism and minimisation of racism.

In abstract liberalism, ideas associated with liberalism such as individual rights and freedoms and the free market are used to argue against policy remedies for collective inequalities. Affirmative action, for example, is seen as an infringement of the rights of individuals and the scapegoating of people in the present for past actions (Harris, 1993). This view of competing individuals ignores or neglects the structural aspects of racism that were identified in Chapter 5. 'Naturalisation' is the argument that residential and other forms of segregation are explained by people's 'natural' drive to live with their own kind. This transforms the white suburb and the minority inner-city 'ghetto' into identical products of choice. Cultural racism is the attribution of cultural deviance and backwardness to minorities, which explain patterns of social exclusion that have outlived the civil rights era. Examples of this can be seen in Lewis' (2003) study of Californian primary schools looked at in Chapter 8. Finally, the minimalisation frame diminishes the significance of racism and racist acts. This can be done by narrowing the definition of racism to include only explicitly racist acts, by arguing that this is all in the past, suggesting that only a few aberrant individuals are now actually racist, or, lastly, blaming minorities for being over-sensitive and seeing racism where it does not exist.

In his qualitative interviews, four principal storylines emerge. Bonilla-Silva maintains that the stories people tell about 'race' are the emotional glue (2006: 72) that binds their claims about what that means in their lives. The stories are both a means to demonstrate to the interviewer that the speaker is not racist, and to show how the speaker is positioned vis-à-vis the contemporary question of racial inequality. The three-part structure of the mechanism is first to confess that a friend or relative holds or held racist views. Then an example is given of these views or actions, and finally the speakers distance themselves from this view. The substantive content of the four principal storylines that surround this 'trinity' structure are reducible to the following. The first is 'the past is the past', whereby the speaker supposes an absolute rupture between the past and the present, in which racism ceases in 1964. An overlap with this is the next storyline: 'I did not own slaves'. As the past is the past, the speakers distinguish themselves from any responsibility for past discrimination (even genealogically), and thus inoculate themselves against further claims for compensation or personal responsibility. The third line is comparative: 'if other ethnics made it why not Blacks?' Here the parallel drawn is between Irish, Italian, Jewish and other white ethnic groups in American history and their successful rise through society after an initial phase of poverty and discrimination. This supposes that the obstacles in front of all groups are the same, which, like the first two, ignores the structural element of racism that was identified in Chapter 5. The final line, which we shall see in more depth in the work of McKinney (below), is 'My job/promotion went to a Black man'. Here, the sense of entitlement of white interviewees is revealed through their assertion that either their job or promotion was unfairly given to an unqualified minority. In these stories, notes Bonilla-Silva, the minority is always assumed to be less qualified than the speaker. So these recurring lines shape the mainstream white response to discrimination in the post-civil rights era. And that response says that 'race' no longer matters, but the authorities and minorities with a chip on their shoulder make it matter, in ways that are perceived to be disadvantageous to white people in general.

The question of how living in segregated ghettos affects black and Latino people's outlook on 'race' is frequently posed in America, and assumptions are made about its role in cultures of poverty and dependency. Yet, what happens to white people's racial solidarity, asks Bonilla-Silva, when they live in segregated white areas? The most obvious thing is that they think that segregation is perfectly normal and not to do with racism. The residential segregation is mirrored in the workplace, friendship and leisure activities, and this too is seen as unproblematic. Instead, the cultural generalisations: 'they are lazy', 'they are not like us', 'we are nice people' take the place of interactions and feed what Bonilla-Silva refers to as the 'white habitus': the norms and values of white segregated living. Indeed, the answers to the question on intermarriage in the survey reveal this absence of interaction. 'People cannot like or love people they don't see or interact with', he concludes (2006: 124).

Yet there is also a stream of white people in the survey who question the existing status quo, who see structural discrimination as a reality, and understand that they have a role in challenging it. Contrary to the received wisdom that suggests that more educated middle-class people are more tolerant and liberal, he finds that working-class women are more likely to show empathy and understand discrimination. This he attributes to their increased interaction (as equals) with minority women, especially in the workplace. The other thing Bonilla-Silva finds that might appear surprising is that minorities themselves are invested, albeit to a lesser degree, in the four pillars of CBR. While it is clear that they see racism as pervasive and structural, which is not the case for most white respondents, the 'cultural racism' and 'naturalisation frames' emerge as directly influencing minorities. Abstract liberalism also influences them indirectly. Given this proof of the penetration of CBR, Bonilla-Silva concludes: 'I regard the ideology of color-blindness as the current dominant racial ideology, because it binds whites together and blurs, shapes and provides many of the terms of debate for blacks' (ibid.: 171). A dominant ideology, he reminds us, 'is effective not by establishing ideological uniformity, but by providing the frames to organize difference' (ibid.) Why is this important? Because having shifted from the paradigm in which Whites were argued to be superior and others inferior, the new form of racism (as ideology) is equally unconducive to solving racial inequality because it allows people to live out their lives as if it had already been eliminated, and thus lets it continue by not supporting attempts to introduce reform. Bonilla-Silva sums this up:

By regarding race-related matters as non-racial, 'natural', or rooted in 'people's choices', whites deem almost all proposals to remedy racial inequality necessary as illogical, undemocratic, and racist 'in reverse'. (ibid.: 209)

Tyrone Forman coins the term 'racial apathy' (2004) to cover what he understands as a new form of racial prejudice in the USA: one that is growing and has negative consequences for equality. He followed this up with an article co-written with Amanda Lewis (2006), whose work on California schools has already been highlighted. The bare bones of the argument are the following. In the post-civil rights era, the form of racial attitude identified in surveys has been less to do with maintaining actively antipathetic attitudes toward minorities, but with indifference. First, the increasing proportion of non-committal answers to survey questions seems to hide more negative than positive attitudes, while second, the level of apathy about racialised inequalities outstrips that expressed in relation to other forms of inequality (2006: 179). There is a correlation between apathetic/indifferent answers on the question of discrimination against racialised minorities and hostility toward public policy measures aimed at reducing it. Therefore, this indifference is not neutral, but culminates in hiding negative feelings about helping to reduce inequalities. This structured and very selective apathy condones the racial status quo and acts against remedial policy. This can be linked to work on prejudice suggesting that the distancing between dominant and minority people takes the form of placing the latter in a position where they are understood as so different from the former that no empathy can be achieved. Second, it depends on 'strategic evasion' of the realities of social inequality (Bobo, 2004).

However, this is all derived solely from large-scale survey data ('Monitoring the Future' (an annual survey of high-school seniors, whose sample was around 2500) and the 2005 Chicago Area Survey, whose sample was 279 adults aged 21 and over). Forman and Lewis go a step further and interview white people in a Mid-Western town who used to go to a high school that was racially mixed prior to desegregation in the 1950s, and who graduated in 1968. This choice was made in order to understand how a group that can be expected to have more positive and engaged association with minorities, thinks about 'race relations' in the twenty-first century. While a few interviewees still maintain connections and interactions with minorities, and are interested in overcoming inequalities, most are now suburban-based and racially apathetic.

The general pattern is one of withdrawal into 'a culture of avoidance' (ibid.: 188) of contact with non-whites, a lifestyle of 'not seeing', 'not knowing' and 'not caring', which, the authors claim, is not arbitrary, but chosen and cultivated through choices of residential settlement and school attendance. One interviewee goes as far as to say, of his interest in events: 'If it doesn't happen on my driveway I'm not interested' (ibid.: 189). In the interviewees' social understandings, the long period of discrimination in American history has ceased and its relevance has been erased. History starts after civil rights (the mid-1960s), which means that all that happened before is discounted in explanations of poverty. In this way, the reasoning is that individuals have the choice to engage at school, to get qualifications and to work hard for a living. Not all those who refuse to take these choices (as the argument runs) are African Americans or Latinos, but the latter are more likely to because of cultural deficiencies. We noted in Chapter 7 that there are reasons why residential segregation is so high in American urban spaces. To recap, the white suburban space in which they live has been created by generations of state intervention (through the Federal Housing Association, by lenders' racialised policies on mortgage lending, both described by Lipsitz (1998)), and white middle-class adults' choices of living there. This makes it not only more difficult for minority families to access the funds (as their wealth is on average eight times less than white families (Oliver and Shapiro, 1995)), but also creates a space which is perceived as monolithically white and unwelcoming. One of Forman and Lewis' interviewees expresses shock that an African American work colleague refuses to drive out to her house. The suburbanites then justify this segregated pattern of residence as arising from blacks' unwillingness to live with them, which is again disproved in Massey and Denton's data (1994).

Forman and Lewis conclude that 'racial apathy' is not merely an absence of information, but a cultivated resource of whiteness. It is enabled by a package of socially produced ignorance or 'mis-cognition' that allows people to claim they are nice and have good values, while actively dis-engaging or de-racing their lives to make their physical and mental surroundings into white places that at best maintain the status quo of racial inequality, and at worst exacerbate it.

Karyn McKinney's (2004) work on white undergraduates' responses to her teaching on racial equality in the USA provides further evidence of the way that the meanings of 'race' have been profoundly altered in the post-civil rights era. She bases the book on the journals that her students wrote on their reactions to her teaching and their reflections on their racialisation as white. In one chapter, McKinney brings together the pieces that cluster around the theme of whiteness as an economic liability in the contemporary social world. The feelings of whiteness 'under siege' coalesce around the topic of affirmative action. The students express anxieties about losing out to people of colour in university entrance, scholarships and employment. They perceive that the balance has shifted from a time when there was discrimination against minorities (in the past), which is now over, to the present, when the odds are stacked against them on the basis of their whiteness. One student, Jerry, even goes as far as to say that for the first time, he wishes he was black:

> Had I been black I would be a National Merit Scholar and had I been black I would not be taking a small loan to be here … I am sure that when I do graduate college and attempt to trade bonds, on Wall Street, I will probably, for the second time wish I was black. (2004: 163)

The context, as Jerry notes, is of perceived competition. There are two main findings. The first is that the principal competitors are African Americans, and second is the baseless assumption that affirmative action always constitutes quotas and rigid targeting practices (Dhami et al., 2006). From this evolves the script that the speaker or a friend or family member lost out to an unqualified black applicant. Indeed, such is the recurrence of this script (also noted by Bonilla-Silva) that 'unqualified' becomes almost redundant. The scenario is always one in which the qualified white male is sacrificed to the quota-related success of the perennially unqualified Other. This sense of entitlement, in which the competition is always given unfair advantage, can only be understood as a result of the failure of the white students to grasp the reality of discrimination going on at a national level. They see affirmative action as 'quotas', and imagine that there is a level playing field that no longer requires compensatory action, despite the consistent patterns of racialised inequality identified in surveys on employment, income, wealth, access to loans, etc. However, the students in McKinney's survey are very poorly informed about the field that inspires such distress and resentment in them. The type of knowledge that the students do not have would significantly alter the frame they use to think about competition. There are substantial amounts of legacy quotas (for children of alumni), gender-based advantages and a relatively tiny proportion of minority-only scholarships (4 per cent of all scholarships in higher education). Moreover, the points systems for assessing students' applications are based neither solely on grade point average of SATs nor on ethnicity.

From the conviction that there is no longer discrimination against minorities requiring remedial action derive the attitudes expressed by students, according to whom existing practices comprise 'reverse discrimination'. This is not only labelled unfair but immoral and seen as running counter to the American ethics of hard work and responsibility. Indeed, the contemporary period for these young people is characterised by meritocracy: open, free education, and the opportunity to achieve regardless of origins. The colour-blind norm, then, banishes 'race' from the public domain. Those that refer to it in order to further themselves are 'hypocrites' or the real racists, because 'what racism is now' (McKinney, 2004: 162–3) is discrimination against white males.

The racialised frame thus switches, according to McKinney, to one in which white racial superiority is ostensibly denied, and instead, judgements are made on the basis of a bogus collective appeal by minorities for the redress of grievances that are no longer pertinent. She writes:

> The argument is not necessarily that people of color are 'lazy', or 'unmotivated', or whatever other traditional stereotypes are employed, but that *if they are not*, why do they, in today's meritocratic society, request or need 'extra help' in the form of affirmative action, 'quotas' or scholarships … This linguistic maneuver is characteristic of the new discourse of whiteness. It affords these white respondents and others in their generation a supposed neutral stance in the problem of race: they are the defenders of people of color against claims of innate inferiority, but are also, in effect, judge and jury of the legitimacy of their stories, able to silence or at least discount parts of them that violate today's racial discursive etiquette. (2004: 181)

That etiquette is the colour-blind one that best represents American values. Indeed, on the basis of McKinney's work, colour-blindess seems to have assumed a significance far outweighing actual discrimination: ' … for many white people, it is not continuing inequality in current race relations, but the inappropriate invocation of race that threatens American democratic values' (ibid.).

These three pieces of research using different methods: quantitative survey data, qualitative interviews and learning journals/ethnography, have provided us with different perspectives on how 'race' is experienced and understood by white Americans in the early twentieth century. The argument is put forward that 'colour-blind racism' is a new departure specific to the post-civil rights era. It depends on a refusal to acknowledge the continuing significance of racism in distributing differentiated life chances, and stems in part from the very segregated lives that most white Americans live. Most live in areas where minorities account for fewer than 1 per cent of their local neighbours, and go to schools where an average of 80 per cent of their peers are also white (cf. the experiences of African Americans, of whom between 16 and 25 per cent attend schools that are virtually 100 per cent minority). The dominant discourse of colour-blindness also treats 'race' per se as a taboo topic, so that talking about the existing inequalities is constructed both as exaggeration and the unjustified deployment of 'race' to further the agendas of people who are not prepared to work hard for their goals. Instead, 'race' is addressed indirectly, through talk of 'bad schools', 'certain people', 'crime', etc. The aspiration toward colour-blindess, where people are always, to quote Martin Luther King, judged by the 'content of their character' has been ideologically conflated with the undoubted but slow and uneven actual movement in that direction. Ultimately, this mechanism works counter-productively: the idea that a level playing field already exists hampers discussion of what it would take to practically reach that situation.

CONCLUSIONS

Is there anything 'new' about 'new racism'? It is clear that there is an emphasis being placed on the role of culture in defining difference, as opposed to phenotypical difference. However, with regard to the historical record, I would argue that the period when bodies were so important to racial ideologies at the expense of culture, might well be the 'blip', while the reliance on culture comprises the continuity. The period prior to the eighteenth century witnessed both the development of anti-Semitism and the British colonisation of Ireland, for example. Both these seem to me to be performing the same discursive and material functions as racism does from the late eighteenth century. Using the term 'new racism' can best be seen not as ushering in a completely new way of talking about 'race', but as recognising a new historical configuration. There is the post-Nazi taboo on using 'race' explicitly in the public arena. We have also witnessed half a century of post-colonial developing-world immigration into Europe; the decline of the welfare states; and the economic restructuring that followed the 1970s' oil crisis, with European and North American economies moving painfully away from manufacturing toward the service sector. The 'new racism' describes how long-standing currents of ideas and practices have been reformulated to be effective in a different age, with cultural difference as its core concept.

10 The Racialisation of Asylum

In the chapters on racism, 'race' and racialisation, I suggested some ways to understand these processes and power relationships so that it became clearer how much the social and biological elements could either be separated or linked through the notion of culture. In other words, attributing insurmountable cultural difference to two sets of bodies can be just as much about 'race' as looking merely at the physical externality. In current discourse about difference, threat in the West is now voiced around innate characteristics and cultural deficiencies more than around physical difference (Chapter 9). Or, the other way round, two groups who are nominally racialised as 'white', for example, can construct the differences between them as being properties of culture and civilisation, and no less profound than physical differences which in this case are absent (for example, European anti-Semitism and the triangular relationship of British, Catholic Irish and Protestant Irish in Northern Ireland). In this chapter, I want to demonstrate that a category of people whose origins and phenotypes are extremely diverse can *also* be racialised, that is, socially constructed as a homogeneous group, with characteristics that set them apart from social norms. This category is that of the 'asylum seeker': a bureaucratic invention deriving from the post-Second World War process of managing population displacement across European national borders that had occurred during the conflict there. I will use the United Kingdom as a case study to illustrate particular elements and trends of this process, but some of these will also resonate in other states.

WHAT IS ASYLUM?

Originally, the word asylum was the equivalent of *sanctuary*. In Medieval Europe, a person being sought by the law could take refuge in a church. The ensuing state of asylum/sanctuary was determined by the space of the church building, where secular and religious authority is separate but equal. The person in sanctuary was balanced between the two, and therefore temporarily out of reach of the secular authorities.

The contemporary use of the word differs from this in its precise derivation from international treaties, and is predicated on the modern world's organisation into nation states. The term 'refugee' has been used for centuries to describe people fleeing their homeland because of persecution, but also now has a precise meaning of someone who has been granted an internationally recognised status to remain protected in a nation different from their own. So the Jews fleeing Spain at the end of the fifteenth century, the Huguenots fleeing France and the Low Countries in the sixteenth century, and those people displaced by the fighting in the First and Second World Wars could well be described as 'refugees', but not 'asylum seekers' because the term only has meaning in the 1951 Geneva Convention and the 1967 New York Protocol, to which most countries are signatories (see Box 10.1).

After the United Nations' ad hoc attempts to deal with displaced populations in the 1919–50 period, an international treaty, the Geneva Convention, was signed in 1951. This set out rules and regulations for the international functioning of a refugee and asylum system. In this system, a process was set out whereby internationally displaced people would apply for the formal status of 'refugee' in another state. This person, having once applied, was granted the status of an 'asylum seeker'. The rights and responsibilities of people with this status were determined by the nation state in question, whereas those for people who had successfully been granted UN 'refugee status' were set out by the Convention and updated by the United Nations. So, as well as requiring a world of nation states, the asylum system also pre-supposes a world of international law (with international rights pertaining to *categories* of people as well as individuals), adhered to by nation states recognising the United Nations as an adjudicating authority. I am stipulating this so carefully because the (usually very confused and poorly informed) debates on asylum that take place on a national level seem to understand the global asylum system as falling entirely into the realm of national governance, whereas this is not the case: important aspects of it, logically, fall under international not national law. Asylum is an international issue. So, to clarify, for the rest of this chapter, I will be using the terms 'refugee' and 'asylum seeker' in the sense in which they are used in precise relation to the Geneva Convention and New York Protocol, where an 'asylum seeker' is an officially recognised person with a case to prove. If this case convincingly demonstrates that the person has, in the words of the Convention: 'a well founded fear of persecution because of race, religion, nationality, membership of a particular social group or political opinion', then he or she may be granted the status of 'refugee'. However, this does not apply to the far larger number of people who are displaced from their homes, but remain within the borders of their countries of origin, described by the UNHCR as 'internally displaced persons' or IDPs.

Box 10.1   Information about asylum seekers and refugees

The international asylum and refugee system is based on two international agreements: the 1951 Geneva Convention and the 1967 New York Protocol (www.unhcr.org/protect/PROTECTION/ 3b66c2aa10.pdf).

A special unit within the United Nations, the United Nations High Commission for Refugees (UNHCR) is charged with monitoring asylum and refugees across the world. Statistical bulletins and summaries going back to 1994 can be obtained from the UNHCR website: (www.unhcr.org/statistics.html). The UNHCR uses a number of different definitions that go beyond simply 'asylum seeker' and 'refugee' to cover the various categories of people who are generally labelled 'refugees':

- 'Internally Displaced Persons' (see www.unhcr.org/basics/BASICS/405ef8c64.pdf)
- 'Refugees' (see www.unhcr.org/basics/BASICS/3c0f495f4.pdf)
- 'Stateless' (see www.unhcr.org/basics/BASICS/452611862.pdf)

In terms of national statistics, the information is generally held by whichever government department is responsible for managing asylum.

- In the UK, this information is available from the Home Office's Research and Statistics Division (www.homeoffice.gov.uk/rds/immigration-asylum-stats.html).
- In the USA, see the Department of Justice, Executive Office for Immigration Review (www. usdoj.gov/eoir/statspub.htm).
- In Canada, see Citizenship and Immigration Canada (www.cic.gc.ca/english/resources/ statistics/menu-fact.asp).

So, we have established that an asylum seeker is officially recognised by the State in which they have lodged an application for refugee status. The British rules on this dictate that an application can be made on arrival or 'in-country', which means at an appropriate place like a police station, as well as at a port or airport. The application has to be made within a certain period of time after entering the country. The person is then processed, registered and issued with identity documents, and given official leave to remain pending a decision. It is therefore impossible to be simultaneously 'illegal' and an 'asylum seeker', as the fact of being recognised as an asylum seeker necessarily means that a claim for refugee status has been lodged and registered. Indeed, to get away from the idea that a person, rather than a status, can be 'illegal', I will use 'undocumented' for the remainder of this chapter.

To set the parameters of the international problem of asylum, refugees and displaced persons in context, I have included some headline figures and trends in Box 10.2 below.

Box 10.2   Overall trends in asylum seeking

In the industrialised countries, there was a dramatic rise from the early 1990s to a peak in the 2001–2 period. After this, the levels dropped consistently before flattening off. In the first half of 2008, for example, of the industrialised countries, the USA received by far the most applications (around 15 per cent), with Canada (around 10 per cent), France (9 per cent), the UK (8.5 per cent) and Sweden (7.7 per cent) next. While the exact positioning of these nations within the 'top five' might alter over time, they are usually the top five. However, there are two things to remember: first, these percentages are of the number of applications to the 44 *industrialised countries* (not all the countries in the world) that return figures to the UN. This accounts for between 20 and 25 per cent of all people 'of concern' to the UNHCR. This is because the vast majority of displaced persons do not seek asylum: either they merely take refuge in a neighbouring (usually developing world) country, or remain within their own state. The UN estimates that as of 2007, only around 14 per cent of refugees live outside their region of origin, and that refugee-generating regions retain between 83 and 90 per cent of the people displaced (UNHCR, 2008: 7).

Those seeking asylum in the West comprise only a small fraction of the world's displaced persons. Claims that they are flooding the West are therefore statistically unfounded. Asylum seeking is driven by political and economic instability. This is reflected in the trends over time that show greater numbers of displaced persons at moments with particularly acute instability (war, internal political conflicts, economic crises, etc.), and geographically, with war zones the most likely to be places from which people flee. The other important factor is natural disasters. Indeed, globally, the top countries of origin of asylum seekers in early 2008, for example, were Iraq, Russia, China, Somalia, Pakistan and Afghanistan. All of these areas were theatres of armed conflict in the previous months with the exception of China, whose asylum dynamics were driven by political persecution of dissidents and natural disasters. Local variations can be noted (e.g. Zimbabweans claiming asylum in the UK since 2004, for example), but the overall trend in the industrialised world is governed by the prevalence of crisis and political instability. However, when we look at the overall figures that include displaced persons (forced to leave their country for another, but not seeking asylum) and internally displaced persons (those remaining within their own country's borders), another pattern is striking.

The 2007 provisional figure for people under the UN's responsibility was around 51 million, 26 million of whom have been driven out by war and 25 million by natural disasters.[1] The countries with the largest number of people seeking refuge and IDP are found in those *adjoining* war zones: Eastern and Central Africa (around the Democratic Republic of Congo and Sudan); the Middle East (next to Iraq and Iran); Pakistan (neighbouring Afghanistan); and the South American neighbours of Colombia, where there is something akin to a civil war. The top refugee-hosting nations in the world, as of the end of 2007, were, in descending order: Pakistan, Syria, Iran, Germany, Jordan, Tanzania, China, the UK, Chad, then the USA. It should also be noted that every year, thousands of refugees are voluntarily resettled in their countries of origin through UN programmes, and that figure is now the highest it has been since the early 1990s.

THE EUROPEAN CONTEXT

Before looking at the British case in more detail, I want to set out a European context. Although there is officially no explicit pan-European immigration and asylum policy decided by the EU, there are a series of practices and processes that engage EU member states in cooperation with each other, and also with so-called Third Countries (states outside the EU) over these issues (Garner, 2007b).

In a 2003 White Paper, the British government proposed the concept of 'safe havens' for asylum seekers, a strategy comprised of two elements: 'Regional Protection Areas' (RPA), near or inside countries producing refugees; and 'Transit Processing Centers' (TPC), outside EU borders, in which refugees in transit, as well as those deported back from EU countries, would be interned pending an examination of their asylum claims. Although this proposal was officially withdrawn later that year, and rejected by the European Parliament in 2004, it still resulted in the development of pilot projects between individual governments and countries outside the EU. The relationship entails funding and training given to the immigration officials in the 'Third Country'. Moreover, as demonstrated by Migreurop's map,[2] the number of detention centres has rapidly expanded in the past few years, and the outsourcing of border control functions offshore (the 'Mediterranean solution') is beginning. The message to emerge from such strategic distancing of asylum seekers from Europe is that they are dangerous and 'unwanted', in Christian Joppke's (1999) terms.

There is also a range of organisational input into constructing an EU policy and a means of implementing it; these include the Schengen Information Systems (SIS) (marks I and II), FRONTEX (the EU border agency) and the two five-year 'Tampere programmes' (1999–2004 and 2004 onwards), agreed by the Justice Ministers of EU member states. These agreements prioritised EU-level cooperation on securing external borders against infiltration from the south and the east.

This strategy is therefore based on EU-level cooperation – with regard to expertise and information-sharing, collaboration with non-EU states to police the external borders more effectively, and even the performance of some detention and application-processing functions that were previously the sovereign domain of EU member states. Examples of this type of work are evident in the increasingly fraught relations between Morocco and Spain over the enclaves of Ceuta and Melilla in North Africa, funded pilot schemes to establish processing centres in Libya and the Great Lakes region of Africa (and engage in joint naval exercises with the former). The Italian government's reliance on Libya involves disregarding the UN Convention on Human Rights. This constitutes an important shift from the policy where all applications were dealt with within the country in which the application was made.

THE UNITED KINGDOM AND ASYLUM IN THE 21ST CENTURY

The UK figures bear out most of the trends highlighted above. The numbers of applications fell after 2002 and levelled off. The top six sending countries (2007) were war zones, had seen natural disasters or witnessed other political instability: Afghanistan, Iran, China, Iraq, Eritrea and Zimbabwe. The profile of asylum seekers is mainly male (70 per cent), and under 35 years of age (80 per cent).

One of the key distinctions in the British case is that an agency was established by the government to coordinate the provision of housing and benefits for asylum seekers (who are prohibited from taking paid work or undertaking vocational training) in April 2000. This National Asylum Support Service (NASS) was originally set up to manage the 'dispersal' programme (Robinson, 2003). The concentration of asylum seekers around the ports and airports of south-east England was considered potentially harmful in that it might provoke resentment against the government in these areas, already the most expensive part of the country to live in, when local taxes had to rise to pay for accommodation, etc. Accordingly, the dispersal programme spread asylum seekers around the country by allocating them to accommodation within various local authorities. Asylum seekers cannot be housed in social housing, but NASS works with local councils to find appropriate private-sector accommodation. This is usually either through landlords known to the local authority, or through outsourcing to large companies such as Adelphi and Clearwater, which locate blocks of housing, sometimes in hotels and motels, sometimes in disused premises.

NASS covers benefit payments to the majority of asylum seekers. Benefits are capped at a maximum of 70 per cent of the basic state benefit (Income Support) and dispensed on a case-by-case basis, sometimes with payments 'in kind' such as direct payment for housing, utility bills or the purchase of pieces of furniture. As of the end of 2007, the agency had just under 44,500 people on its books (including unaccompanied minors). It was responsible for housing just over 29,000 in England, 3900 in Scotland and 2200 in Wales. The rest were living on subsistence-only payments, and not in NASS accommodation. The largest concentrations were in the provincial cities of Birmingham (1950), Manchester (1310) and Leeds (1760).

Moreover, within the 2095 in detention under Immigration Rules were 1455 people who had sought asylum. These were mainly male (86 per cent) and from China, Nigeria, Pakistan, Jamaica and Iraq.

People granted 'refugee status' before 2005 have it permanently. Refugee status gives its bearer international travel documents, the right to family reunion in the UK, and allows the refugee access to most of what UK nationals are entitled to. They can also accrue residence for naturalisation once this status is gained. However, those granted refugee status since August 2005 have it for a five-year period, to be reviewed in the case where their country of origin is deemed safe for return.

Having set out the context for the British asylum situation, we shall examine the argument that 'asylum seekers' as a group have been racialised. This requires establishing the range of responses to this category of people. As we have seen, even in the top six countries, we have groups that are quite differently phenotypically from one another. My case in no way revolves around asylum seekers looking similar to each other: quite the opposite. The racialisation of asylum depends on this spectacularly diverse category being filled with homogeneous characteristics through a complicated process involving a number of actors: the State, the media, political parties, independently organised campaigning groups and only marginally asylum seekers themselves. This is a function of their powerlessness: they are structurally prevented from undertaking paid employment or studying, and they are allocated housing through NASS. The small amount of agency they have available does not enable them to set up national or even local campaigning groups themselves.

The State plays a critical role, introducing legislation that sets out the rules for manoeuvre, the rights available to asylum seekers and the responsibilities of local authorities. Since 1999, there have been four principal pieces of legislation (in 1999, 2000, 2002 and 2004). Among other things, these laws have removed entitlements, imposed stricter regulations and made it more difficult to successfully apply for refugee status. No single government can alter the rules for claiming asylum beyond a certain point because they are overseen by the UNHCR, but modifications can be made in the following areas:

- the level of proof required
- the time limit for holding refugee status
- the a priori rejection of cases from particular countries (deemed safe)
- the 'fast-track' hearing of cases from particular countries (deemed safe)
- the withdrawal of state support for those who have exhausted the appeals process (almost a quarter of initial decisions are appealed, signalling some flaws in the process)
- the detention of asylum seekers thought at risk of absconding.

The last of these important acts of government is the establishment of detention for some asylum seekers. The government is empowered under immigration rules to hold people who are undocumented, or whom it feels might try to evade deportation once papers have been served. Yet, as we have seen, there is another batch of around 1500 people who have only applied for asylum, yet are detained either in special centres or in prisons, without having broken immigration rules. Other than people suspected of terrorist offences, this is now the only group that can be imprisoned without having been charged with a crime under British law. Usually these are single men and they are frequently dealt with by private-sector employees of security firms with contracts to transport and guard detainees. The differential application of the law to them is part of a pattern (see Agamben's theory of 'states of exception' below).

Media images of asylum seekers

Studies of media coverage of asylum in Britain (Buchanan and Grillo, 2004; Finney, 2004; Crawley, 2005; Finney and Peach, 2005; Jempson, 2007) have found consistent patterns in the representation of asylum seekers:

- The first thing to note is the reflection of power relations in that asylum seekers themselves are very rarely interviewed. They are instead spoken about or for, by officials from governments, NGOs or campaigning groups (both for and against). Asylum seekers thus have a minimal input into the way they are represented in British media, and therefore little capacity to counter the weight of negative images.

- They are conceptualised as an undifferentiated mass of single males whose presence is synonymous with an invasion (Jempson, 2007): terms such as 'mass', 'invasion', 'deluge', 'influx', 'tide' and 'overwhelmed' frequently appear in headlines to do with asylum.

- The terminology is often inaccurate and loaded. The differences between asylum seekers, refugees and economic migrants are often blurred by using them as synonyms of each other, while pejorative epithets are added. The Cardiff School of Journalism study (Buchanan and Grillo, 2004), for example, found 51 terms used to describe asylum seekers over the period of its research. Many of these were derogatory and meaningless, like 'asylum cheat'. The terms 'illegal refugee' and 'bogus asylum seeker', for example, are two of the most frequently recurring. The term 'illegal refugee' is an oxymoron: refugees cannot be 'illegal' because they have been granted an internationally recognised status by the British government and are awaiting decisions on their application. Moreover, the term 'illegal', when applied to people, actually refers only to documentation.

- There is a fixation with the costs of asylum to the UK economy and often misleading references to people receiving benefits.

- There is a lack of contextual information to help people understand government statistics, which again are presented in ways to make reporting as sensational as possible.

- There is a critique of asylum-seekers' right to be in Britain, which is conveyed in the 'illegal' and 'bogus' terms.

- Asylum seekers themselves have criminality imputed to them. When an asylum seeker commits a crime, or even is suspected of doing so (in unsubstantiated allegations, such as 'eating swans' in 2003), this is used to reflect on everyone that holds this status, as if criminality were an innate characteristic of all.

The actual effects of the media on individuals are of course contested, and there are considerable differences in the way local and national, print and broadcast media, for example, deal with the topic (Finney and Peach, 2005). However, it comes through clearly in the discourse that many of these messages structure lay people's responses when they oppose asylum seekers being located near them. This is also true in the case of Portishead, below when they are opposed to offices dealing with asylum seekers being located near residential areas. Similar themes and ways of understanding to those used in print media are very apparent.

Confrontation

While the dispersal programme was notionally designed to reduce local hostility toward asylum seekers in the south-east of England, it actually generated more, by raising the possibility of asylum-seeker settlement near to communities that had thought themselves distant from inner cities, minorities and the social problems associated in people's minds with asylum. The government was pursuing two lines of operation in its attempts to hold asylum seekers to specified locations. One was the NASS/local authority route, often farmed out to private property agents. This might involve the block booking of hotels, or the use of disused amenities. The second was to consider the change of use of existing government properties or even the construction of purpose-built facilities. Since 2002, confrontation between the State, anti-asylum groups, and to a lesser extent, pro-asylum groups has taken the form of local campaigns of opposition to planning applications. In most cases, this led to plans being scrapped. In the 2003–5 period, such campaigns were run by local action groups in small towns and villages in provincial England, e.g. Bingham (Nottinghamshire), Bicester (Oxfordshire), Saltdean (Sussex), Throckmorton (Worcestershire), Lee-on-Solent (Hampshire) and Portishead (Somerset).

The key explicit themes mobilised in the campaigns of opposition to planning permission were the 'inappropriate' use of space, the lack of available infrastructure and the threats posed to the peaceful existence of the community by the accommodation of asylum seekers. Underlying this, I will argue, was an ongoing racialisation of asylum seekers, whose outcome was that campaigns against the facilities were just as much about locals' projected fears of asylum seekers as they were about the facilities themselves.

Until the late 1990s, hostility expressed toward migrants in opinion polls was subsiding (Finney and Peach, 2005). Groups singled out previously for greater public displeasure were the 'unemployed' and 'single mothers'. 'Asylum' as a policy area did not really register until this period, at which moment the blurring between immigration and asylum, and the focus on it in the media, combined to make it a hot topic. Opinion polls and surveys carried out by large polling organisations such as YouGov, ICM and MORI since 2002 recorded increasing levels of anxiety about immigration, asylum and associated topics (see Box 10.3).

Box 10.3   Understanding opinion polls on social attitudes

Opinion polls dealing with attitudes toward asylum seekers and immigrants and other groups are often published. In Britain, since the late 1990s, attitudes as measured in these polls have become more hostile overall to most minority groups. However, while this might well be an empirical trend, as sociologists, we need to go into the study of these polls with some considerations about how they function. We should always be very careful about taking opinion poll findings as meaning exactly what they say.

The way questions are introduced, framed and indeed their very wording can influence people's responses. For example, if a respondent is provided with a list of 'important issues' to choose from, you might well get a different answer than if you just asked for the person to tell you what they thought were the most important issues. If the list does not include some of the most frequently referred to (e.g. the economy, crime, education), but does include immigration, then people are more likely to opt for that answer. Moreover, the wording of questions can reflect the agenda of the sponsor (*The Sun* newspaper, the anti-immigration campaigning group Migration Watch UK, the Commission for Racial Equality, for example).

Finally, questions that ask people to 'agree' or 'disagree' with a statement frequently assume knowledge that the respondent does not have. If you ask people, 'are there too many immigrants in your local area?', then to answer properly, you logically have to know how many there actually are (and people notoriously over-estimate this), quite apart from the fact that there is no consensus about how many is 'too many', or what that question even means in political terms.

Additionally, sample sizes have margins for error. This means that due to sample size, the differences in percentages of people giving a particular answer are only statistically meaningful *beyond* that discrepancy. In a sample size of 1000 (margin of error = +/– 3 per cent) which is the industry minimum for polling organisations in the UK, a difference of less than 6 per cent can be accounted for just through sampling, and thus might well have nothing to do with the substantive issue at hand. When that 1000 sample is broken down (perhaps by gender, age or socio-economic group), the margin for error rises because the sample is decreasing. So in a sample size of 100 (usually a sub-group of a larger one, for instance, 'people in socio-economic group C1'), where the margin of error is +/– 7 per cent, any difference of less than 14 per cent can be explained by sampling. However, what we *can* say about the polling results is that the percentage of people admitting anxiety about immigration and hostility toward immigrants is, in general, rising. This might in part be due to its treatment by the print and, to a lesser degree, the broadcast media.

The second trend is that the group of traditionally more liberal respondents, Labour voting graduates, have also become more hostile. This is identified in the 2003 British Social Attitudes Survey (MacLaren and Johnson, 2007). This means that the assumption that there is much greater hostility expressed by the poorer socio-economic groups than the wealthier is now much more qualified: the difference is merely of degree.

Indeed, in the existing qualitative interviewing, similar ideas are expressed but often differently, and around different resources. The main fears are centred around entitlement to resources such as housing, benefits and employment. However, middle-class respondents who have little or no experience of social housing or welfare benefits talk of these issues more abstractly (Clarke and Garner, 2009). They tend to focus equally on culture and space as resources. Miranda Lewis (2005) concludes that 'attitudes are very largely based on perceived economic consequences rather than actual knowledge or experience' (ibid.: 12), and that 'relative deprivation can produce discontent and anti-immigrant sentiment where there is no evidence of an actual negative economic impact' (ibid.: 13). She notes a class-specific set of concerns: 'people living in social housing, BME groups[3] and young people are particularly concerned about the impact of asylum seekers upon employment, housing and welfare. People from higher income groups are concerned about the impacts they perceived asylum seekers to have on services such as education and health' (ibid.: 27).

So we are beginning to note that the perceptions do not have to be accurate. The negative feelings toward asylum seekers exist despite confusion about what an asylum seeker actually is (rules governing their actions, where they come from, why they are in the UK in the first place) and what exactly their economic impact is locally. The *figure* of the 'asylum seeker' exists independently of real people whose status is that of 'asylum seeker'.

Racialisation

I defined racialisation (Chapter 2) as a process by which 'race' becomes a salient element of social relationships, and 'race' as a set of attributed characteristics (in the context of a power relationship) that become attached to each member of the group regardless of class, age or gender.

The vectors of racialisation are numerous: media, the State, local authorities, contemporary ideologies, people's experiences and available language. We have also noted that 'asylum seeker' is a bureaucratic category, not a stable identity: there is no restriction on colour, age, class, gender, religion, etc., and although there are more frequent profiles (men under 30), we would find a selection of people drawn from the world's population among the asylum-seeking group at any given moment. We shall look at a representative selection of comments made in the context of objections to planning permission for facilities for dealing with asylum seekers in the 2003–4 period, and then I will summarise the key themes I have identified as being significant in the racialisation process.

Attitudes

The first few comments were made in letters to Rushcliffe Borough Council (Nottinghamshire) in respect of an application by government to build a detention centre near the village of Bingham on Ministry of Defence land (Hubbard, 2005).

- 'The rural area is quite unsuitable for such a masive venture, housing mainly men who have little or no concept of our rural way of life … We as a nation are very tolerant but this is going too far.'

- 'How do these refugees get into Britain? Illegally in most cases. If they are pre- pared to enter the country illegally, they may commit other crimes.'

- 'My 13 year-old daughter is now allowed to walk anywhere in Bingham. I fear this will not be the case should the centre go ahead. A good majority of these people will be single men. Without their wives and girlfriends, our children will be in danger of falling foul of their sexual advances.'

The next batch is drawn from letters written to North Somerset Council objecting to a change of use of a building on a small industrial estate within a newly built residential estate in the small town of Portishead. Around 200 letters of objection were received by the council, which ultimately voted by the Chair's casting vote to reject the Office of the Deputy Prime Minister's planning application. This decision was overridden, and the office opened in November 2005.

- 'Should incidents occur and be reported in the media there is a concern that the potential stigma and perception by those outside of Portishead in relation to the Asylum screening centre will result in a reduction of house prices, people's investments and long term future.'

- 'Having moved to Portishead 18 months ago to invest in my families' right to a better quality of life I find all the past years of hard work, saving and moving to what I thought was an up and coming area, all to be taken away. The decision to be made by councillors, most of whom, probably do not live in the affected area. How would you truly feel if it was next to your home? Something you've worked for all your life to be wiped out from underneath you.'

- 'Why is the proposed centre in the middle of a residential area? It is full of children, which at present can safely be allowed out to play. If the proposal goes ahead can you guarantee the safety of our children, I don't think you can with the sort of people you are planning to dump on our doorstep.'

The comments are made in the context of a series of criticisms levelled at the location of such an office in a residential district (the original office had functioned in the town centre with little comment for years prior to 2004). The arguments against the office are expressed around the following topics:

- The transport links to Bristol (nearest city) are too poor.
- There is insufficient parking on the estate.
- This constitutes inappropriate use of a building for a suburb/village/residential area (depending on the author's perception).
- Pollution (noise, light, sound) would be generated by the new office.
- Danger (theft, traffic, violence) would be generated by the asylum seekers.
- There would be a betrayal, by developers, the local council and central government, of the people who had bought homes on the estate.

It is important to note that racialisation occurs as a thread in other processes and is rarely a clearly defined linear narrative. Many of the objections here could be conceived of as having nothing to do with 'race'. Indeed, only a very small number of letter writers explicitly mentioned 'race'. However, this would be to de-contextualise the comments from the discourse on asylum that has been going on for the previous five years at least. The anxieties about the dangers of asylum seekers passing through the residential area are based on a set of assumptions that mark them as pathological. As in the case of Bingham, they are presumed to be men with no sexual restraint who will endanger young women and children. Moreover, they are a priori considered criminals, and sometimes potential terrorists, whose behaviour can be predicted, or in alternative logic, people about whom nothing is known and therefore must be assumed criminal. This means that they are undeserving, and certainly should not be prioritised over locals in terms of resources. The thought of spending money on 'strangers instead of Portishead' strikes one objector as 'such an abomination'. Another argues: 'there is potential for increased crime which often arises when you have a stark contrast between those seeking asylum and those who have paid their taxes and have worked hard to build up a life and home for themselves'. Indeed, the recurrent theme of betrayal at the hands of authorities and developers functions through claiming the unfair imposition of something unarguably wrong. Had we known beforehand, runs part of this argument, we would not have bought homes here. The betrayal is only resonant because the imposition is so great: while nobody actually knows anything about the asylum seekers who will be visiting the centre (and the majority of whom are resident in Bristol), the assumptions are for the worst possible scenarios, paid for by increased local taxation and accompanied by a fall in house prices, two themes particularly important for Britain's middle classes.

Moving from these two case studies (Bingham and Portishead) to the national arena, the key themes then in the media, State and negative public responses to asylum in Britain in the twenty-first century are:

- Non-productivity: asylum seekers are seen as a drain on society. They do not (are not allowed to) work, and must be kept at the taxpayers' expense. This is taken as the rationale for becoming an asylum seeker in the first place.

- Culpability: asylum seekers ('asylum cheats', 'bogus refugees' and 'illegal asylum seekers') are presumed criminal and possibly terrorist just by dint of the fact that they have applied for asylum in the UK. Media coverage and the policy of detention can only have exacerbated this presumption.

- Gendered threats: asylum seekers are viewed as bringing a series of threats to the areas where they are located. These threats are to do with violence, crime, sex and disease. Thus, the most likely victims of such threats are women, children and homeowners. The capacity to constitute threats is partly a function of the spare time they have because of not working. As Buchanan and Grillo (2004) observe, the standard representation of the asylum seeker is that of the wild, anarchic, male menace, and this image has clearly permeated into the public's understanding, hence the fear of attacks on children and women that are associated with the location of asylum seekers in new vicinities. In brief, as a result of racialisation, asylum seekers are collapsed into an amorphous group who 'won't fit in' to white English space, whether it be rural or suburban. The correct place for such people, it is argued in the objections, is in urban areas where there are already other minorities. This ignores the fact that a sizeable minority of the asylum seekers are Europeans, and that many come from rural backgrounds. However, it is assumed that their otherness makes them incompatible with certain types of space.

Compare this with the *actual conditions* in which asylum seekers live. Their powerlessness within the bureaucratic process and structural isolation lead to high levels of stress, and an above-average incidence of psychological problems. They cannot integrate through the workplace; they have difficulty integrating through social networks except those to do with benefits or childcare, and remain isolated from consumption patterns. They exercise little choice in where they live, as they are dispersed by NASS early in their application process. Their capacity for agency is therefore severely reduced. Moreover, a substantial proportion of asylum seekers have come from war zones, have experienced brutality or have left close family behind. While people assume that they are living easy lives supported by the taxpayer, this is not the case. 'Social isolation and poverty have a compounding negative impact on mental health, as can hostility and racism' (Burnett and Peel, 2001: 545). The bureaucratic category of 'asylum seeker' is turned into a racialised category that provokes hostility among many, even though the group itself is very diverse. How can we theorise this?

Interpreting hostility

A number of avenues suggest themselves here. Žižek (1989) argues that groups assume the function of being a focus for hostility, and that this is not really to do with the group's characteristics, but more to do with the majority's need to find an object to define themselves against. Žižek's example is European Jews in the 1930s. By developing anti-Semitism into nationalist ideologies, the far right in the inter-war years was able to successfully define its national projects as being aimed at removing particular behaviours (attached to Jews) from the pure nation. In other words, it is not anything that asylum seekers do that provokes hostility, but instead the majority's need to reaffirm that they are fixed to place, work hard and are entitled to a safe life. Asylum seekers, however, remind us of the political chaos outside and the enforced mobility that propels people around the globe to escape it.

Mary Douglas (1966) argues that dirt is impurity (disorder) in Western cultures, and that the idea of 'matter-out-of-place' can be applied to people. A shoe in a shoe cupboard is 'in place' and part of civilised order, yet a shoe in a bed, for example, is 'matter-out-of-place', bringing dirt and disorder into the clean, ordered space. This principle is clearly at play in the way people defend rural and suburban spaces against asylum seekers, suggesting that their correct location is in (dirty and disordered) urban centres where there are other people like them. We could even say that campaigns against asylum are attempts to return the disorder to the disordered world beyond the borders of Western democracies.

David Sibley's (1995) relational approach owes a debt to the work of psychologist Melanie Klein. He maintains that spaces are 'produced' by class, 'race' and gender relations. 'Family', 'suburb' and 'society', he argues, 'all have the particular connotation of stability and order for the relatively affluent' (Sibley, 1995: 43). On the evidence of other fieldwork (Clarke and Garner, 2009), we could also add 'village' to this list. The process of definition is relational, as with Žižek (1989). 'Collective expressions of fear of others, for example, call on images which constitute bad objects for the self and thus contribute to the definition of self' (Sibley, 1995: 45). He refers to planning regulations as a way for the middle classes to keep the poor out of rural England, using the language of 'pollution' (ibid.: 59), but this could also be true of asylum seekers. The pollution spoken of by petitioners in the twenty-first century explicitly invokes light, noise and traffic. However, implicitly, as much of the anxiety is expressed around 'matter-out-of-place', the residential estate is to be polluted by dangerous bodies that belong elsewhere. Indeed, in the work referred to here, the middle-class ideological labour of self-distancing (from impurity and dirt) is threatened by the British State's superior mobilisation of resources and authority. Only in Portishead, however, has the State emerged as too strong for the opposition. In all the other cases, plans to build an asylum centre or convert an existing building have been abandoned.

Much has been made of Zygmunt Bauman's use of the concept of the 'stranger' to refer to asylum seekers. This idea, developed from the work of Georg Simmel, is that modernity is increasingly characterised by encounters with strangers, who are categorised as 'friends' or 'enemies'. This relationship is relational, that is, mutually constitutive: there would be no friends (in-group) if there were no enemies (out-group). However, Bauman asserts that the social construction of difference means that particular people fall between the categories of friend and enemy, into the new category of 'stranger', who crosses the threshold to stand simultaneously next to both friends and enemies. This has significant consequences for the social order in Bauman's work. He develops the idea to study the construction of 'the Jew' (1989), 'the vagabond' (1998a) and the 'new poor' (1998b), for example, arguing that assimilation and genocide form the two poles of the spectrum of ways in which the stranger must be dealt with to restore order. The stranger is thus a 'by-product' of the order-making process: a figure constituting not merely a social but a moral relationship, involving emotional attachments to place and people.

In the case of asylum seekers then, one can note the bureaucratic process which creates the 'asylum seeker' as a category, not a set of diverse individuals. One can also see that the category is unsettling because is it is comprised of neither normal 'labour migrants' nor 'citizens'. They can be kept at arms' length by state policies, and emotionally distanced as potentially representing deleterious aspects of social behaviour: rape, theft, pollution, violence (especially attacks on children). However, if we are to think of asylum seekers as 'strangers' rather than 'enemies', which is closer to the way they seem to be conceptualised in contemporary Western societies, we need to see them also in the process of integration, so that they are creating relations with 'friends'. This might be the case in places where they are allowed to live near UK nationals on a similar economic level, but there is very little literature on this (Qureshi, 2007; Bowes et al., 2009).

Italian philosopher Giorgio Agamben (1998, 2005) argues two key points that are relevant to asylum. In *Homo Sacer* (1998), he argues that there is a status of person that, like the obscure Roman condition of *homo sacer* (who has lost citizenship rights through committing criminal acts), can be included in law only in the form of their exclusion. This is the opposite of the status of sovereign, who is both within and outside the law. Agamben asserts that ever since, as the result of power relations in the modern State, people have been categorised into two main groups: 'bare life' and 'citizens'. 'Bare life' are bodies that are not allowed to access the 'good life' that is available to citizens. On one level, asylum-seekers' legal status and powerlessness represents a form of bare life: they are excluded from citizenship in its broadest sense, and marked principally by what they cannot do. The option of their detention without committing a crime is evidence of such a marginal status, which links into Agamben's other main idea relating to State powers: the state of exception (2005). Sovereign powers can be used to suspend law and make a 'state of exception' (that is alerts over terrorism, war footings, martial law) into the norm. Agamben argues that Nazi Germany was a 12-year long state of exception, for example, and that the Bush administration's treatment of prisoners taken in Afghanistan and held in Guantánamo Bay provides an example of the state of exception. 'What is new about President Bush's order', Agamben maintains, 'is that it radically erases any legal status of the individual, thus producing a legally unnameable and unclassifiable being. Not only do the Taliban captured in Afghanistan not enjoy the status of POW's as defined by the Geneva Convention, they do not even have the status of people charged with a crime according to American laws' (2005: 3).

The parallel with asylum seekers' status is provocative. As Western states alter their asylum regimes to make the status of asylum seeker less attractive, those applying for asylum have increasingly tenuous links to human rights. On one level, they can be detained without being charged of a crime, and on another, they can be processed by officials belonging to states where they have not even applied for asylum in the first place, as is the thrust of one strand of European Union policy (see above). In those processing centres, the state of exception theory dictates that although they are applicants to a specific state within the EU, and subject to a specific human rights regime, they are physically detained within the national territory of a non-EU state, and possibly outside that human rights zone. What is the legal status of such individuals?

The anxieties expressed over asylum seekers are therefore not necessarily anything to do with asylum seekers as individuals, but centre on the category of 'asylum seeker', into which fears are projected. Is this racist? Yes. Whatever else it consists of, the attribution of assertions about the natural behaviour of particular groups, using racialised representation of 'Others', is a racist practice. I have argued from the first page that one dimension of racism is an ideological one that alters from one historical moment to another, and from one place to another. One version of it in the early twenty-first century world is to provide a valve for contemporary insecurities over such things as property investments, terrorism, children's safety, losing ground, vulnerability to economic and political forces and powerlessness in the face of social change, to be focused away from the sources of those problems onto other people who are victims of even more radical economic and political instability. In doing so, those who define themselves through the values of industriousness, quietness and family invoke their communities as exclusive. Elements from all the analytical perspectives outlined above can teach us something about how asylum seekers are racialised.

CONCLUSIONS

The formal 'asylum system' only functions in a world of nation states with international agreements and standards. It is therefore a creation of what sociologists call 'modernity', and indeed dates back in its present form to only the post-Second World War period. In this global system, most of the people displaced do not reach the West at all, but end up migrating within their country of origin, or settling in a neighbouring developing-world country.

The status of asylum seekers in the West places them in a position parallel, not equal to, the rest of the population: there are separate regimes for benefits and the control of movement and detention, all in all what Foucault would term a different 'disciplinary regime'. This legal process (regulated internationally at the overall level and nationally in terms of the specifics) creates a category: 'asylum seekers', which corresponds to a very diverse group of individuals covered by it. Racialisation turns the mass of cultural diversity that is 'asylum seekers' into a homogeneous group occupying a space of danger, deviant behaviour and cultural otherness.

Different groups 'enact' their identity on this construct in order to establish and/or sustain their own power and ideology of community. For example, the State exerts its control of borders and movement by separating asylum seekers out from citizens in rights regimes and applying differential regulations to them. Opposition to 'asylum seekers' is based on a hierarchical and exclusive bounded community which projects its own anxieties onto 'asylum seekers'. Supporters of asylum seekers may also to some extent enact their identities, through the values of solidarity, inclusiveness and a more fluid and less hierarchical concept of community.

However, once the category of 'asylum seeker' is broken down into individuals and their stories, a different dynamic takes over. Even politicians committed nationally to harsher asylum and immigration regimes can support the rights of individual asylum seekers to remain in a country, as demonstrated in the example of former Conservative shadow Home Office minister, Ann Widdicombe. She supported the campaign of Verah Kachepa, a Malawian asylum seeker from Weymouth, Dorset to stay in the UK. Ironically, an image taken of her and Ed Matts, the prospective parliamentary candidate for the South Dorset parliamentary constituency campaigning for Mrs Kachepa to remain in the UK, was doctored in the 2005 election campaign[4] to show them campaigning for tightened immigration controls. I think this episode illustrates all too graphically the way that more powerful social actors enact their identities on the category of 'asylum seeker'.

In the next and final chapter, we shall turn to another example of the racialisation of a diverse category: Muslims, with a look at Islamophobia.

NOTES

1. The figures from the UN are usually grouped with those for the special agency set up to deal with Palestinians (the United Nations Relief and Works Agency for Palestinian Refugees in the Near East (UNRWA)).
2. The French NGO, Migreurop, has published a map called 'Foreigners' Detention Camps'. It is accessible from: www.migreurop.org/IMG/pdf/carte-en.pdf
3. BME stands for 'Black and Minority Ethnic' groups, the current expression used in public discourse to cover people who do not tick the box 'White UK' in the Census (see Box 6.3).
4. The messages on the placards the two were holding were changed: from 'picture of family' and 'Let Them Stay', to 'Controlled Immigration' and 'Not Chaos and Inhumanity'. See www.guardian.co.uk/politics/2005/apr/12/election2005.uk1. At the 2005 election, Matts came second, with 37.9 per cent of the vote going to Jim Knight (Labour), a drop of around 3.7 per cent on a night when the Conservatives' vote rose nationally by 3 per cent.

11 Islamophobia?

The term 'Islamophobia' emerged relatively recently.[1] However, it covers a phenomenon which is far from new: the process of homogenising Muslims and attributing negative, backward and exotic otherness to them as a group. We will critically present some definitions of Islamophobia and its establishment as a genuine phenomenon in the twenty-first century. Clearly, there is racism addressed towards Muslims, and has been for some time, so the question is, do we need this new term? If so, what does it describe? What does it do? Could it be dealt with under 'racism'?

In this chapter, we are going to exmine the history of the relationship between the 'West' and the 'East', to summarise, and to observe some of the specifics of how Muslims in the West talk about their own identities. The first section refers to two controversial pieces of work (Said's and Huntington's) that bring out different aspects of the overarching relations at play in the construction of Islam. The second section tries to begin the work of separating the idea of 'fundamentalism' from Islam. The third looks more closely at definitions and their limits. We then discuss two arenas that might shed light on some of the cultural tensions: socio-economic indicators and dress codes. Finally, I offer some ways to think critically about Islamophobia as a set of ideas.

It has already been established in previous chapters that the distinction between phenotype and culture as the basis of discriminatory discourses and practices is actually a false dichotomy. In reality, they are two faces of the same phenomenon that have become increasingly entangled in the forms of 'new racism' emerging in the West over the last three decades (Chapter 9). There is even a case to say that culture preceded physical difference as the basis of discrimination: Balibar (Balibar and Wallerstein, 1991) suggests that anti-Semitism is paradigmatic of this, while Garner (2004, 2009b) points to the colonisation of Ireland and the racialisation of the Irish in the USA and Britain as later versions. Moreover, following on from the discussion at the end of the previous chapter, in which a highly diverse group of people are clustered together under a temporary administrative status, this chapter provides another case study of Othering: the construction of Islam, a diverse set of practices with different sects or streams, crossing all the world's continents and involving people from all of what were labelled in the nineteenth century: the 'races' of the world.

BIG THEORIES: 'ORIENTALISM' AND CLASHES BETWEEN CIVILIZATIONS

Said: the idea of 'Orientalism'

Edward Said (1979) argues that over a period going back to the late eighteenth century, expert knowledge, developed in the academies of the West, created an exotic object: the 'Orient'. This space was completely different from the West: backward rather than modern and full of people ('Orientals') who are congenitally corrupt rather than honest; indolent rather than industrious; fanatical rather than objective; and selfishly dangerous rather than altruistically interested in the truth. I have used pairs of adjectives deliberately. Said's contention is that Western scholars have created the imaginary place, 'the Orient' and the people who populate it, 'Orientals', as opposites of the cherished image they have of themselves as Westerners. This process and set of practices is what he terms 'Orientalism'.[2] Indeed, the question of power to create representations lies at the heart of Said's thesis:

> ... the phenomenon of Orientalism as I study it here deals principally, not with a correspondence between Orientalism and Orient, but with the internal consistency of Orientalism and its ideas about the Orient ... despite or beyond any correspondence, or lack thereof, with a 'real' Orientalism. (Said, 1979: 5)

The representation is highly sexualised, as demonstrated in the paintings to which Said refers[3] and the 'anthropological' travel writings generated by scholars' engagement with the Middle East. Oriental men are conceptualised as weak and effeminate, yet a danger to white women, whom they covet. Oriental women, on the other hand, are mysterious, submissive and exotic. He finally contends that the policy-making circles of Western powers have understood the East in this orientalist fashion because of the provision of this kind of information from experts.

Said's work has become a cornerstone of postcolonial studies, attracting a plethora of critical writings. Overall, there are some obvious gaps in the work, such as his overriding focus on the Middle East at the expense of other parts of Asia and North Africa (indeed omitting a large part of the Muslim world), the lack of follow-up to the gendered understandings he identifies in the writings of European and American scholars, and the implicit claim that everyone from the West who studies Eastern cultures is an Orientalist. Elsewhere, he is at pains to critique essentialist understandings of culture and people. Scholars who argue that the 'Orient' has a similarly reductive and politicised understanding of the 'Occident', that can be referred to as 'Occidentalism' (Carrier, 1992; Buruma and Margalit, 2004), may well have a point. Said's work is also open to the critique that the 'West' is as much of a misrepresentation as the 'East'. However, it is not clear that the power relations are the same: the Muslim world's relative economic and political weakness (with the exception of the oil-rich Gulf States) vis-à-vis the imperial and neo-colonial West means that, as Werbner (2005) points out, the anti-Americanism of Muslims can serve as a protest against geopolitical domination rather than the response of equals.

However, what remains is a thought-provoking argument that threads power relations to images circulating freely in Western culture, and which lie at the root of prejudice against Islam and Muslims.

Huntington: the 'Clash of Civilizations' thesis

Political scientist Samuel Huntington (1993) published an article in the journal *Foreign Affairs* using a phrase drawn from a paper by 'Orientalist' scholar Bernard Lewis (1990) a few years previously. It was in part a response to historian Francis Fukuyama's thesis of 'the end of history' (1992), which claimed that liberal capitalism had defeated communism and that global *ideological* conflict was now to all extents and purposes over. The journal article received so much acclaim that Huntington worked the paper up into a full-length monograph (1996). His argument is straightforward. After the Cold War and the fall of the Berlin Wall, the world will realign along cultural (or civilisational lines):[4]

> It is my hypothesis that the fundamental source of conflict in this new world will not be primarily ideological or primarily economic. The great divisions among humankind and the dominating source of conflict will be cultural. Nation states will remain the most powerful actors in world affairs, but the principal conflicts of global politics will occur between nations and groups of different civilizations. The clash of civilizations will dominate global politics. The fault lines between civilizations will be the battle lines of the future. (ibid.: 22)

The blocs Huntington labels 'civilizations' are 'the highest cultural groupings and the broadest level of identity short of that which distinguishes humans from other species' (ibid.: 24). 'Fault line conflicts' occur between neighbouring countries belonging to different civilisations (e.g. India and Pakistan) or within states that are home to populations from different civilisations (e.g. the former Yugoslavia). 'Core state conflicts' are on a global level between the major states of different civilisations (e.g. the Iraq war). Yet, the principal confrontation, he maintains, will be between the Judeo-Christian West and Islam (ibid.: 31–9). The conflicts between Islamic and other civilisations are particularly intense and violent. 'Islam', he asserts, 'has bloody borders' (ibid.: 35).

While Huntington found favour within neo-conservative policy circles especially, his thesis has been roundly criticised over two main areas. Firstly, his conceptualisation of civilisations assumes homogeneity and ignores internal divisions. These blocs appear vast, discrete and culturally static. There are two forms of conflict arising: the divisions within the region of the world he terms 'Islam' can be ethnic as well as religious. It is questionable to imagine that a swathe of the world running from Northern through Eastern Africa to the Middle East, the Indian sub-continent and Indonesia has no internal divisions. The references he uses are drawn entirely from elites and from overviews of conflicts. Indeed, there is no empirical basis put forward for stating that this is in fact the primary way in which billions of people identify themselves. Secondly, the attribution of all conflict to exclusively cultural differences ignores any political, ideological or even economic basis for differences that might arise. In Huntington's perspective, everything is pursuant to clearly defined cultural boundaries. The idea that countries can contain people from different cultures without conflict, or that political ideas can be implemented at different times in different places, is absent. Indeed, Huntington's broad thesis actually chimes with that of the Islamist organisations deploying political violence (that is, groups that claim Islam as their source, but whose objectives are wholly political), a point made by Said (2001) in his review of Huntington's book. This brings us neatly to the question of 'fundamentalism'.

'Fundamentalism'

One of the ideological outcomes of the latest phase of political conflict between Islamist groups and nation states both in the Islamic world and the West, is the collocation 'Islamic fundamentalism'. Yet the term 'fundamentalism' was coined in relation to protestant churches in the USA in the 1920s as a mark of differentiation from what were seen as liberal and deviant churches. In Steve Bruce's (2000) work, like that of Karen Armstrong (2002), examples of fundamentalism are drawn from the major world religions. Bruce concludes that fundamentalism is 'a rational response of traditionally religious peoples to social, political and economic changes that downgrade the role of religion in public life' (Bruce, 2000: 116). Indeed, he points out that seen from the viewpoint of the 'fundamentalist', it is the people who do not observe the scriptures that are deviant. The norm of detaching oneself selectively from such texts is relatively recent in the Judeo-Christian world: the nineteenth century is seen as the secularising century. However, he does argue that monotheistic religions (Christianity, Judaism and Islam) can give rise to more intense and dogmatic forms of fundamentalism. Eisenstadt (1995) uses the term 'fundamentalism' to refer to the attitude of religious groups that reject complex traditions, including scholarly and juridical interpretive ones, in favour of a 'return' to an idealised era or scriptures, often, he adds, with the added agenda of imposing their vision through political or violent means. In relation to contemporary acts of political violence committed by individuals or groups that see themselves fighting back for Islam against the West, Eisenstadt's definition at least captures the political dimension. Bruce's fundamentalism is exclusively religious. In Bruce's terms, an Islamic fundamentalist could well have an interpretation of the Qu'ran that leads him or her to despise aspects of Western civilisation, but they would not act on this in the kinds of ways that others deploy political violence.

Parekh's early exploration of the subject (1991) tends toward Eisenstadt's. In fact, he argues that far from being traditionalist and conservative, fundamentalism is an attempt to engage with modernity: it provides a reading of scripture designed to be the basis of political activism engaging with the secular world, rather than humble contemplation; it has to understand the secular rules of the game and utilise modern technology in order to assail these norms. He makes a very useful distinction between 'ultra-orthodoxy' and fundamentalist understandings of the scripture, and forward-looking 'politico-religious projects' (Parekh, 1991: 41) based on a narrow and selective reading of scripture. Indeed, Parkeh asserts that only religions 'of the book' (Islam, Christianity and Judaism) can experience 'fundamentalism' in the terms he sets out, because they are based around the direct inspiration of one set of writings that is understood as the word of God revealed. Other religions can have political movements based on writings, but not with a relationship established between scripture (as the word of God) and political action. The degree to which the various groups within the Islamic faith either do or do not reflect the 'true' messages of the Qu'ran, or what that means, lie well beyond the scope of this book. There are obviously a number of different paths within Islam; Sunni, Shi'ite, Sufi, Wahhabi, etc. that have different emphases, traditions and understandings about what exactly constitutes ethical behaviour. If you add to this that the religion includes white Europeans and North Americans as well as Black Africans and African-descended people, people of Middle Eastern, North African and Indian sub-continental origin as well as Indonesians, this world faith starts to become less easy to visualise as a monolithic bloc, and that is even before we start to think about linguistic, regional, class and gender distinctions in the way Islam is experienced. In a way, the *homogeneous* global community of all Muslims is, like Marx's international proletariat, a virtual reality, an aspiration of activists. What I am seeking to do here is suggest an accurate understanding of what the term 'Islamic fundamentalism' might actually mean: groups of people who see their position as at the vanguard of this *ummah*, taking the battle to the West and to those seen as its acolytes, with a long-term objective of overthrowing non-Islamic states and replacing them with states run according to what they think is a specific interpretation of the Qu'ran. It is to be noted that in this definition the political project dimension (as in Parekh (1991) and Eisenstadt (1995)) is the most significant. Indeed, the groups and individuals actually signified by the term 'Islamic fundamentalist' in this sense are those who actively support or condone political violence used not just against Westerners, but against other Muslims who are deemed not Muslim enough.

However, the most salient point about current discourse on Islam is that no definition is offered. The vaguer the term remains, the easier it is to stretch it to fit anyone, including the overwhelming majority of Muslims: people who have no interest whatsoever in the political project of overthrowing states and replacing them. Indeed, Quraishi's (2005) study suggests that Muslims feel their religious identity is 'soiled' as a result of depictions of adherents to Islam being considered fanatics, terrorists or fundamentalists. What the linking of the terms 'Islamic' and 'fundamentalist' actually accomplishes in contemporary discourse is to fuse in the minds of the Western public two different communities. On one hand, we have Muslims in general (in all places at all times), some of whom might well have a developed critique of some Western practices and values derived from their reading of Islam (as do many Christians and Jews). On the other, there are the small number of people committed to a politics of violence and the establishment of an Islamic state to replace both existing states in Islamic countries, and Western states. The latter group are nominally part of the first. However, a parallel would be to say that as most Nazis were European Christians, then all Christians are racist extremists, for example.

This focus is not meant to turn the gaze away from the political violence enacted by nation states, either against their own citizens or those of other countries. The 'war on terror' has involved a variety of state terrorist practices: the bombing of civilian populations; the suspension of the rule of law; imprisonment outside international law; shoot-to-kill policies; racial profiling. Indeed, the relationship of state and non-state forms of violence to one another needs to be thought of as more intimately linked. Al-Qaeda did not materialise out of nothing; it has a lineage going back to the Muslim Brotherhood in Egypt and the attempts to eradicate it by the Egyptian State. There are also links between superpowers' incursions into Muslim countries and the sponsorship of and recruitment to organisations wedded to political violence (Hiro, 2002).

We have noted Said's (2001) claim that both Islamophobes and Islamists believe the world is neatly split into two main civilisational blocs in confrontation. There is a kind of symmetry of understandings here. For the latter, the West indiscriminately oppresses Islamic people, both in the West and in the Islamic world, thereby creating the *ummah* of oppression and resistance. Those who justify attacking people and objects within Muslim states in retaliation for bombings aimed at Westerners are also buying into this idea that *all* Muslims everywhere are fair game because they are somehow the cause of the actions of tiny numbers of people. In Adams and Burke's research on post 9/11 attitudes in England (2006: 992), 'Andrea' expresses exactly this sentiment:

PB: How do you feel about the media coverage?

Andrea: They was showing [Muslim people] being quite scared to go down the street, because they were getting attacked, Muslims over here, and spat at. I must admit, if I was walking down the street and I would see one of these, you know those dresses that they wear from head to toe, and I'd get angry cause I'd think, you know, 'your bloody beliefs, and all the rest of it, that did all that'. Even though I'd know they weren't personally to blame I'd still feel 'if it weren't for you bloody people'.

PB: You felt an anger towards ...?

Andrea: But it is a contradiction because I did, yeah, but at the same time I do know there are normal nice people that don't agree with it as well.

The readiness with which one can switch between these discourses is a clue to the normative racialisation of Muslims. As with asylum seekers, a diverse group of ethnically distinct people can be categorised as innately dangerous. The cartoons of the Prophet Mohammed in the Danish newspaper in 2005 work on the same principle. The Prophet in that case represents all Muslims. He is carrying bombs to signify that in this world view, all Muslims are potential terrorists. The discursive process of making the terms 'Muslim', 'fundamentalism' and 'terrorist' adhere to one another is engaged in by the media and the State in its formulation of security policy that profiles all Muslims as potential terrorists, and it becomes the norm: to the point where it is accepted policy to make (male) bodies racialised as Islamic into a priori objects for punishment and suspicion (Bhattacharyya, 2008).

The outcome is to reduce the complexity of Islam to a one-dimensional figure that signifies terror. This is not to deny that some Muslims have used political violence to intimidate and kill opponents, just as have people from other religions and secular groups. The point is that the process of linking those three terms turns all Muslims everywhere into potential terrorists, or 'suspect communities' (Hillyard, 1993) regardless of their personal convictions, or at the very least into accomplices who should publicly denounce links even if there are none.

DEFINITIONS OF ISLAMOPHOBIA

In 1996, the Runnymede Trust established the Commission on British Muslims and Islamophobia and published its report, *Islamophobia: A Challenge for Us All*, a year later (Commission on British Muslims and Islamophobia, 1997). The report set out eight distinctive features of Islamophobia. Each of these features contained 'closed' and 'open' views toward Islam. The common reading was that the closed views should be interpreted as prejudiced, whereas the open views should not. However, if these are the only options, this presents a problem. Where can opinions between these two end points on a continuum be classified? Few binary systems represent all the shades of the social world (see Figure 11.1).

Islamophobia or Muslimphobia?

There is much debate over what racist dispositions Islamophobia constitutes. In his analysis of the literature, Millward (2008) suggests that 'narrow' and 'broad' positions can be adopted.

Fred Halliday (1999) exemplifies Millward's 'narrow' position. He contends that Islamophobia denotes a fear of the religion of Islam (ideas and practices) rather than fear of Muslims per se, which should be labelled 'anti-Muslimism' (Halliday, 1999: 898). This is also the stance of Miles and Brown (2003), for example. Their question is, should Islamophobia be included under the term 'racism' because it is about a religion rather than a 'race'? Earlier writing had put forward the idea that it could not be considered racism because of the cultural, rather than racial, target. Muslims as a group are multiracial, therefore, the logic ran, Islamophobia could not be about 'race' (if 'race' is understood only as phenotype and not to do with culture).

Taking on a 'broad' position, Modood (1997: 4) argues that it is about both religion and 'race'. Islamophobia, he asserts, is more a form of 'cultural' racism than a religious intolerance. He, like Barker and Balibar in their different ways (Chapter 9), argues that cultural racism is a form of 'new' exclusion which is as pernicious as 'traditional' forms that focused on the body (Modood, 1992, 2007). We have seen that in the 'new racisms', the ideological centre has shifted so that 'race' seems now to be as much about insurmountable cultural differences as biological difference. These unbridgeable differences are often expressed around membership of national communities, so that the excluded group have some flaw(s) that mark them as undeserving of membership, such as African Americans in the literature on 'colour-blind racism', and European Muslims in the 'new racism'.

Figure 11.1 **Closed and open views of Islam**

Distinctions	Closed views of Islam	Open views of Islam
1. Monolithic/diverse	Islam seen as a single monolithic bloc, static and unresponsive to new realities.	Islam seen as diverse and progressive, with internal differences, debates and development.
2. Separate/interacting	Islam seen as separate and other – (a) not having any aims or values in common with other cultures; (b) not affected by them; and (c) not influencing them.	Islam seen as interdependent with other faiths and cultures – (a) having certain shared values and aims; (b) affected by them; and (c) enriching them.
3. Inferior/different	Islam seen as inferior to the West – barbaric, irrational, primitive, sexist.	Islam seen as distinctively different, but not deficient, and as equally worthy of respect.
4. Enemy/partner	Islam seen as violent, aggressive, threatening, supportive of terrorism, engaged in 'a clash of civilisations'.	Islam seen as an actual or potential partner in joint cooperative enterprises and in the solution of shared problems.
5. Manipulative/sincere	Islam seen as a political ideology, used for political or military advantage.	Islam seen as a genuine religious faith, practised sincerely by its adherents.
6. Criticism of West rejected/considered	Criticisms made by Islam of 'the West' rejected out of hand.	Criticisms of 'the West' and other cultures are considered and debated.
7. Discrimination defended/criticised	Hostility towards Islam used to justify discriminatory practices towards Muslims and exclusion of Muslims from mainstream society.	Debates and disagreements with Islam do not diminish efforts to combat discrimination and exclusion.
8. Islamophobia seen as natural/problematic	Anti-Muslim hostility accepted as natural and 'normal'.	Critical views of Islam are themselves subjected to critique, lest they be inaccurate and unfair.

Source : Commission on British Muslims and Islamophobia (1997) *Islamophobia: A Challenge for Us All*, Runmymede Trust. Reprinted with permission.

The issue of what exactly Islamophobia does is addressed directly by social anthropologist Pnina Werbner (2005: 5–6). She suggests that there are two broad conceptualisations of racism. One states that there are a variety of unique forms of racism, each specific to a group of targets and the historical context in which it arises (this is exactly the line I pursue in this book). The other tends to see these specifics as simple layers of artifice cloaking the basic function of racism: to subjugate and/or destroy the Other. If the latter idea is correct, what is the point of using Islamophobia as a way to understand discourse and social action? To answer this,

Werbner proposes a way to see what is specific about Islamophobia to the contemporary period. Her rationale involves using three 'logics' of racism (ibid.: 7) drawn from the work of Wieviorka (1995) and Bauman (1993). These are:

- self-purification = physical expulsion/elimination
- subordination = physical exploitation of labour
- assimilation = cultural destruction.

Corresponding to each of these logics, she designs a fantasised figure representing the type of person to which this logic is principally addressed: the 'slave', the 'witch' and the 'Grand Inquisitor'. However, these, she adds, are not merely fantasies but real fears displaced onto real people, and 'what these people come to represent symbolically' (Wernber, 2005: 7). The symbolic threats are described in language drawn from psychoanalytic accounts of racism.

In the case of the subordination logic, the figure is the slave: out-of-control, order-threatening and perpetrating revenge through violence, theft and sexual aggression. Corresponding to the logic of assimilation is the witch, who:

> crystallizes fears of the hidden, disguised, malevolent stranger, of a general breakdown of trust, of a nation divided against itself. Your neighbour may be a witch who wants to destroy you. He or she is culturally indistinguishable in almost every respect because the witch masquerades as a non-alien. (ibid.)

Here one thinks of Jews in Europe and various trading 'middleman minorities' (Bonacich, 1975), such as the Chinese in Malaysia and the Caribbean, Asians in the USA, Indians in East and southern Africa, etc.

The logic most pertinent to Islamophobia, argues Werbner, is reliant on changes in the dominant ethos and values of Western society. Sexual threat and libido in the permissive West are now less threatening, while a society based on individual capital accumulation and consumption as an aspiration and measure of social worth renders the 'greedy' middleman minorities somewhat less terrifying than a century ago. So the figure that must be expelled in the act of self-purification is the 'Grand Inquisitor'.

This figure is chosen because Europe's intellectual history since the Middle Ages has been aimed at escaping the Inquisition, that essentialising, rights-denying, difference-swallowing space of punitive clerical control. 'What is scary about Islam', she contends, 'is the way it evokes the spectre of puritanical Christianity, a moral crusade, European sectarian wars, the Crusaders, the Inquisition, the attack on the permissive society' (ibid.: 8). The function that such a figure performs is to create a bloc out of groups that are usually in tension with each other: the political far right, middle-class elites and the unsatisfied working classes.

> The Islamic Grand Inquisitor is not a disguised and assimilated threat as the Jew was; 'he' is not subservient and bestial like the black slave. He is upfront, morally superior, openly aggressive, denying the validity of other cultures – in short, a different kind of folk devil altogether. (ibid.)

This thought-provoking train of ideas indicates that there is a purpose for the term 'Islamophobia', in that it suggests something specific to the historical moment. However, despite the sophistication of this model, the class and gender aspects of the puzzle are not developed. We shall return to that in the conclusion. However, while there is some technical dispute over whether Islamophobia is a form of, rather than a separate concept from, racism, there is something of a consensus that the 2001 attacks in the USA marked a point that has seen a change in the way Muslims are perceived in the West. While Meer (2006) and Modood (2005) both claim that there have been positive changes, with more exposure of a variety of Muslims in the public domain meaning that it becomes more difficult to collapse them all into the category 'fundamentalist', more scholars see 2001 solely as the starting point of a worsening of the hostility shown toward Muslims. A rise in the number of attacks on Muslims across the West was observed in the immediate period after the September 2001 attacks (Allen and Nielsen, 2002). The media and the far right are identified as playing an active role in the development of anti-Islamic opinions (McDonald, 2002; Richardson, 2004; Larsson, 2005; Sheridan, 2006). The effects of this are clear in fieldwork done with white UK respondents in contemporary Britain, where Muslims have assumed the position of most threatening Other (Clarke and Garner, 2009). Abbas (2007) is therefore summarising other scholars' thoughts when he contends that both the volume and level of anti-Islamic sentiment in Western societies have intensified.

However, while there might be consensus that there is more hostility toward Muslims than before, and that this is linked to various responses to the attacks on Western targets since 2001, there is also a line of critique that suggests there are limits to the utility of Islamophobia. Can the term also be used, for example, as a way to silence criticism of practices that some consider unacceptable, or as a useful 'straw man' on which to blame everything negative in Muslims' lives? In other words, does every criticism or negative action toward Muslims or Islam constitute Islamophobia? Are Muslim women campaigning to be able to worship in mosques they are excluded from using Islamophobic arguments? Are Muslims who target other Muslims in wars, and with political violence, etc., Islamophobic? There are voices that make qualified claims of this kind, such as Malik (2005), and others who point to the potential dangers of it (Richardson, 2004). Religious authority of any kind comes into its most serious tension with secular society over how a body of ideas can be criticised when there seem to be opposite ways of understanding social relations: over the separation of the public and private spheres, over the role of women, over the way the leading figure in a given religion can be spoken of or represented. I think as students of the sociology of racism, we ought to exercise caution here, because the problem is that in the actual discourses that occur, arguments move very quickly from the specific to the general. In other words, attention has to be paid to not generalising a specific practice to all Muslims (or Jews, or Christians, or Sikhs, or Hindus and so on) everywhere, at all times, as we will see below in Delphy's (2006) engagement with the French law of 2004 against wearing headscarves to school. This is especially true when the same practices are also engaged in by people who are not part of the faith group under scrutiny.

We shall now look at two areas that should help us establish some contours of the discourse on Muslims that are useful to any discussion of Islamophobia. The first is an exploration of the issues around one of the most contentious interfaces between Muslim and secular societies in recent years: dress codes. The second is a brief socio-economic outline of Muslims in the UK, and especially London, which presents a dimension that is usually left out of the culturally focused discourse of difference that constitutes the basis for Islamophobia.

Islamic women's dress

Women wearing traditional Muslim dress (including anything from a headscarf (the famous *foulard* in French), through to the *jilbab* to the full dress, *niqab* and *burqa*) raise questions about what types of difference are permitted and not permitted, about public and private space, and about gender relations. Westerners generally read such codes as over-dressing and narrowly as signs of oppression and excessive religiosity in secular settings. Here, we return to Said's observations about the West's power to construct Islam. The West's construction of the Orient is gendered as well as racialised: the univocal interpretation of Muslim women as submissive and oppressed is expressed in terms of clothing as reading it as the outward manifestation of their oppression by Muslim men. This is not to say that women have not been the subject of violence perpetrated by men as 'punishment' for not dressing in the way they are expected to by some men with a particular understanding of the Qu'ran's injunction to dress modestly. The point is that the most oppressive behaviour becomes generalised in the discourse as the most frequent, as the norm. The second element of this process is that women who claim they choose to dress with headscarves, *jilbabs*, etc. to demonstrate their piety, are dismissed as being submissive and backward, or as just doing it to please Muslim men. In fact, empirical research, where Muslim women actually talk about their dress codes reveals a highly complex set of factors. The wearing of particular clothing at particular times can be about the choice of which self to present at a given moment and why. Individuals do not all dress the same way all the time. In terms of clothing, public space seems demarcated much more strongly from the private space than is the norm in secular understanding, and political choices sometimes overlap with religious ones, as Rinaldo (2007) concludes in her study of women in Indonesia:

> Among women's groups in Indonesia, the veil serves both to inculcate piety *and* to express identity, both intentionally and unintentionally. If we were to study these women only in terms of identity politics, we would certainly overlook their religious devotion and their efforts to produce themselves as pious subjects. But to examine them only in terms of their religious piety would be to neglect crucial elements of their political commitments … Perhaps because of this complicated function and this very public role, clothing is an important part of how subjectivity is produced and reproduced. (Rinaldo, 2007: 18)

Clare Dwyer's (1999) interviews with young Muslim women in Britain reveal a continuum of practices that revolve around dressing to fit different contexts (school, leisure outside family, leisure with family, private space). The choices are sometimes to do with resistance, and sometimes bowing to expectations, but they are made within the context of a consensus that there is an obligation to wear at least a headscarf in certain contexts in order to retain the identity of a Muslim woman. This consensus is clearly not shared by every Muslim. As seen in the case of France and the 2004 law, there is a variety of interpretations among leading Muslim scholars. The idea of referring to empirical studies of Muslim women is not to be proscriptive, and suggest all Muslim women should wear headscarves, but merely to reflect the fact that many Muslim women wear headscarves and other articles of clothing *out of choice*.

There have been a number of cases of contestation over Muslim women's dress in Britain over recent years. This ranges from the British former Home Secretary Jack Straw's opinion in 2006 that women should not cover their faces in public, through to the sacking of a teaching assistant for wearing a veil in the school where she was employed, to a High Court appeal by a schoolgirl over her expulsion from a secondary school that originated in a dispute over dress codes. Moreover, verbal and physical attacks on Muslim women sometimes involve pulling off their veils, a symbolic act of humiliation.

In France, the issue of dress codes has been taken a step further and a law in 2004 enshrined the principle that ostentatious religious symbols could not be worn in public (that is, state) schools. It should be made clear that the republicans in France fought for centuries to have the Church formally separated from the State, and the principle of secular public institutions (*la laïcité*) is one of the founding values of the French republic, dating back to the law of 1905. The 2004 legislation came after repeated *affaires du foulard* (Headscarf Affairs), the first of which was in 1989, where stand-offs had taken place between pupils wearing Islamic headscarves and schools that prevented them from entering, on the grounds that the school was a secular space. Over the period 1994–2003, around 100 pupils were thus banned from returning to school if they continued to wear headscarves. The government had occasionally been forced to intervene, and as the courts overturned around half of these expulsions, it became clear that the existing laws and regulations were no longer feasible because they were open to too broad an interpretation (so that not every case ended up with the same outcome). After the Stasi Commission (Commission, 2003) had taken evidence, the government acted on the commission's report and introduced a law that was passed in March 2004. We are going to look at the response of one high-profile French feminist scholar, Christine Delphy[5] to the feminist discourse around the law, in order to draw some key points out, relating the way the problem was constructed.

In this particular article, Delphy (2006) concentrates only on the feminist discourse about wearing the veil and/or headscarf in France (1999–2004). She does so to tease out the issues of anti-sexism and anti-racism, which were presented implicitly as the two options (anti-sexism for those in favour of the law, and anti-racism for those opposed). Delphy's arguments are reminiscent of the criticisms made by black and minority women about Western feminism (see Chapter 3): minority women's voices were silenced or ignored; practices engaged in by all men were projected uniquely onto Muslims; French women assumed that they and their society was less sexist than that of Muslim women. Firstly, the headscarf itself, she argues, became the subject of a hyperbolic attack in which power was attributed to it that it does not possess. It is described in turns as 'diabolical', a very important form of oppression of women, and as a sign enabling other women to be identified for rape. Secondly, in a binary opposition, French society became an opposite of Muslim society, in that patriarchal relations and male violence toward women evaporated from it, so that all the negative things that happened to women in France were focused on Muslims. It should also be borne in mind that the places where violence toward women and their oppression take place, according to the discourse, is very heavily loaded with class interpretations. The *banlieues* (suburbs of major cities in which large-scale public housing is concentrated) represent a space of working-class, and underclass, crime, immorality and violence in the French collective imagination. Young people, substantial proportions of whom are descended from immigrants, from such places occasionally engage in political shows of strength (from the early 1990s to the riots of November 2005). We should note that by saying *banlieue* the focus is surreptitiously seeping into non-Muslim, non-immigrant working-class French people as well. During the period leading up to the passage of the law, the Commission heard evidence from very few Muslim women, and discussions in feminist circles included only those who were in favour of the law.

What happened in this process of distancing, argues Delphy, is that French feminists ended up reproducing the same set of relations as their opponents had in the past. First, the debates split women into two discrete groups: Muslims and non-Muslims. Then they read into this division a discrepancy of civilisation (modern (secular) vs backward (Muslim)), in which women are only victims. So, instead of looking at the intersection of 'race' and gender to see the specific position into which Muslim women are placed (simultaneously victims of racism and of sexism, but also agents), they placed them in a position where they were seen exclusively as victims of sexism, whose source was solely racialised men. Somehow, in this process, non-Muslim French society and its men had disappeared from the power equation. Indeed, some of most vehement advocates of sexual equality in the public discourse underlying this law were French men who had made no contribution to gender equality discourse prior to this. The background to this story, argues Delphy, was the cumulative power of a number of campaigns for solidarity with Muslim women in various parts of the world, alongside the post-2001 'War on Terror', which had made Muslim women into objects to be saved by French feminists. Indeed, the space in which to be French, Muslim and a woman (all at the same time), is virtually untenable given the parameters of the discussion Delphy describes. However, as Muslim responses show, this is exactly the identity prized by many people in contemporary France. Silverstein's coverage of the demonstrations held by Muslim women in January 2004 concludes:

> Alongside these evocations of freedom of choice, the protesting women embraced their simultaneous identity as Muslims and French citizens. Demonstrators throughout France carried French flags, marched with banners evoking 'Liberty, Equality, Fraternity, *laïcité*', released blue-white-and-red balloons, and even wore headscarves emblazoned with the French tricolor. They faultlessly sang the 'Marseillaise', including, as reporters remarked with amazement, verses seldom heard at national celebrations. The women likewise staked out their religious citizenship, declaring themselves to be 'proud to be French and Muslim'. (Silverstein, 2004)

Delphy's contribution to interrogating assumptions in public discourse on Islam in the West is rich and provocative, touching as it does on class, gender, 'race' and sexuality. However, one of the major aspects of the position of Muslims in the West is very often overlooked in the academic attention paid to the issue: socio-economic inequalities. The next section will look at this in relation to the UK.

Socio-economic indicators

One of the mechanisms through which racialisation functions is by suppressing difference *among* the majority and minority groups, and to express it all as the difference *between* majority and minority. Looking at some of the statistical indicators allows us to identify some patterns (see Box 11.1).

In terms of geographical distribution, 2.7 per cent of the UK population were Muslims at the 2001 Census, of whom 38 per cent lived in London, and 46 per cent were born in the UK. There are also concentrations of the Muslim population in Birmingham, Manchester, Leeds/Bradford and Lancashire towns such as Bolton, Preston and Oldham. Within London itself, where nearly 40 per cent of British Muslims live as opposed to 14 per cent of the British population (Mayor of London, 2006), it is clear that Muslims from different national origins are spatially distributed in different places: Middle Eastern in North London, Indian in West London and Bangladeshis in East and North London, while Pakistanis are split across the East and West of the city (ibid.: 18–33).

Box 11.1   Some statistics on UK Muslims (2001–6)

- Education – just over one-third (34 per cent) of Muslims are under 16 years of age, and 31 per cent of British Muslims leave school with no qualifications (c.f. 15 per cent of the total population). Compared with 52 per cent of White British pupils (and 67 per cent of Indian-origin pupils), only 48 per cent of Bangladeshi and 45 per cent of Pakistani pupils gained five or more grades A to C at GCSE (or equivalent).
- Poverty – Bangladeshi and Pakistani children (73 per cent) are at a much higher risk of living in households below the poverty line (defined as 60 per cent of the median income), than the average of 31 per cent. Moreover, 35 per cent of Muslim households have no adult in employment, which is double the national average.
- Housing – less than half the Muslim households were owner-occupiers compared to a national average of 67 per cent. There are also high levels of overcrowding, with one-third of households falling into that category. Compare that with the 6 per cent recorded by people who ticked the box 'Christian' in the 2001 Census.
- Employment – apart from the figure above, for households with no adults employed, there is also a very high level of youth unemployment. More than a quarter (28 per cent) of Muslims aged 16–24 are unemployed (compared to 11 per cent of Christians in that cohort), and nearly 70 per cent of adult women are economically inactive. Finally, 10 per cent of the UK prison population are Muslims, primarily young men aged between 18 and 30. Please see Appendix 1 – The National Youth Agency, for full details.

So on a number of indicators, Muslims in the UK are worse off than the average. Within those parameters, there are discrepancies between different groups, with Bangladeshis particularly over-represented near the bottom of the table. They were the newest migrant group as of the 2001 Census, and at the next, in 2011, another group might well be occupying a similar position.

What might all this tell us about Muslim experience in the UK? Firstly, that many experience life from a working-class and virtually always urban position. While there is a growing middle class, the majority experience is framed by the working-class positions that most migrants have come to in Britain.

While achievement is relatively low, conditions relatively poor and experiences of racism and a feeling of exclusion unfortunately typical, this provides a position of marginality that frames questions that are expressed exclusively in religious terms, as if 'Muslim' was one's sole identity, unaffected by gender, 'race', class, age, etc. For example, there are knock-on effects of having a principally urban-based and relatively young population, as is the case of British Muslims. Their 10 per cent incarceration rate is partly due to the youthful demographic, which puts a higher proportion of Muslims into the peak age cohort for offending, as well as the fact they are more likely to reside in urban areas which are subject to over-policing (Quraishi, 2005).

CONCLUSIONS

I think there is a strong case for using the term 'Islamophobia' to denote a separate form of racism targeted at Muslims, just as there is for using 'anti-Semitism' to focus on the precise pathology of racism directed against Jews. These are particular racisms having much in common with other strands but also their own historical and geopolitical pathologies. Islamophobia's 'closed' and 'open' definitions are a starting point for discussion, but no more than that. However, very few people may find themselves completely in either of its columns. People's opinions can be contradictory and irrational as well as logical and rational.

Islamophobia illustrates the intertwined nature of the physical and the cultural in recurring formations of 'race' and racism. As has been argued throughout this book, racism utilises ideas drawn from both the biological and the cultural domains. However, some extremely important structural and cultural issues are missed out by focusing on Islamophobia solely as a set of ideas about culture, even some as fascinating as the question of gendered dress, for example. Prejudice and the monopoly of the cultural realm distracts our attention from systemic processes that are revealed in patterns of employment, education and segregation. The obstacles to integration in various Western regimes, and cultural flashpoints around them, are not derived solely from ideas about religion.

Whatever definition of Islamophobia we end up with, it cannot prevent a progressive critique of social practices rationalised through specific *interpretations* of Islam which are clearly not the object of consensus among Muslims. These include, for example, political violence against civilians (this is obviously not only applicable to Islamists), anti-democratic government, and gendered punishments meted out for dress violations, adultery or other breaches of ethical codes. These ought to figure on a progressive agenda in any case, whether or not they are being carried out by people who are Muslims. Islam is engaged in an ongoing dialogue within itself as well as with other world faiths. The cry of 'Islamophobia' ought not be allowed to silence calls for social justice. However, as a point of principle, the essential starting point is not to see any of these things as *intrinsic* to Islam, and thus not prevalent in other religions or secular practices. The fight for democracy is not confined to the Islamic world, and it is only in relatively recent times that European nations that see themselves as the vanguard of rights gave the entitlement to vote to adult women, for example. There are still gendered discrepancies in the life chances, employment patterns, wages and pensions of men and women in the West, and levels of violence committed by men against women, as Delphy points out (2005, 2006), are still very high.

The way in which Islamophobia functions is precisely by collapsing a complex set of positions into one – a negative one, which is projected onto Muslims, and then evacuating the non-Muslim communities of any similar practices or norms. It operates, like all racisms, on binary principles (civilisation vs barbarity), where culture is one form of mediating such difference, but the actors are in more complex positionings than merely those defined by culture: they are also socially located by gender, class and education.

NOTES

1. I can only find it in the early 1980s, although Rana (2007) argues that it dates back to the 1970s.
2. Said can be seen talking about Orientalism on YouTube: uk.youtube.com/watch?v=_njKVdFL6Kw
3. One such key image is the Snake Charmer by Jean-Léon Gérôme, 1870, which adorns the cover of *Orientalism*. The painting can be seen at: www.jeanleongerome.org/Snake-Charmer.html
4. These civilisations are 'Western, Confucian, Japanese, Islamic, Hindu, Slavic-Orthodox, Latin American and possibly African' (Huntington, 1993: 25).
5. Christine Delphy was one of the founder members of the women's liberation movement in France in 1968, and published a very influential collection of essays on feminist organisation and theory, *L'ennemi principal* (1970). She went on to found the journal *Nouvelles Questions Féministes*, and is one of the leading figures in the French national research body, the CNRS.

Glossary of Terms

A8   In 2004, the European Union was enlarged to include 10 new member states: Poland, Lithuania, Latvia, Estonia, the Czech Republic, Slovakia, Slovenia, Malta, Cyprus and Hungary. In EU circles, these were called 'Accession States' in the period leading up to 2004, and of these, the eight for whom this new membership would enable nationals to access the labour markets of the existing member states without a visa for the first time (that is, all the above except Malta and Cyprus), were referred to as the A8 (A for Accession).

Apartheid   Between 1948 and 1994, the Republic of South Africa was officially governed according to the ideology of apartheid, an Afrikaans word meaning 'separateness'. The system, implemented by the National Party under Daniel Malan, involved the imposition of separate and parallel regimes of government for the various racialised strands of the population. Some African groups were allocated 'homelands' such as Transkei and KwaZulu in South Africa and occupied Namibia (then South-West Africa), while the main racial groups afforded legitimacy under apartheid – Whites, Coloureds, Indians and Blacks – had differential rights to geographical mobility, employment, housing, education, etc. Specifically, apartheid was a means of controlling the majority labour force and population, frequently with recourse to armed force, suspension of human rights and state terrorism. The small white population was the only one to enjoy the full range of democratic freedoms and had preferential access to the country's vast wealth. The bureaucracy created to oversee this system also created stable clerical work for white South Africans. Opposition to apartheid, which also came from the Communist Party and the Pan African Congress, soon took the shape of a national political party – the African National Congress (ANC), which waged a political and armed struggle against the apartheid system from the late 1950s. International sports boycotts from the 1960s, and anti-apartheid organisations in many countries, added to the pressure placed on South Africa to normalise its social relationships. On the back of the campaign to free ANC leader Nelson Mandela from captivity, which occurred in 1992, came the holding of free elections in 1994. The ANC won the elections with a landslide, and Mandela became the first post-apartheid President of South Africa.

Aryan   The term Aryan, borrowed from Sanskrit, was originally used to describe a set of languages originating in the India/Iran/Afghanistan regions. By the nineteenth century, it came to mean speakers of Indo-European languages. By the end of that century, scientists such as Thomas Huxley and Georges Vacher de Lapouge were speculating that the Aryan people were characterised by longer skulls than others, and had a leadership role in the modern world. This racial genealogy was reinvigorated by writers such as de Gobineau, who saw Nordic and Teutonic peoples as the basis of the Anglo-Saxon racial stock in the mid nineteenth-century, and most spectacularly by Houston Stewart Chamberlain whose writings on the Aryan race (*The Foundations of the Nineteenth Century*, 1911 [1899]) influenced Hitler. The Nazis used the term 'Aryan' to refer to those racialised as the authentic Germans, typically represented as tall, blue-eyed blondes, around which their social policies were based in the 1933–45 period (Burleigh and Wipperman, 1991).

burqa   A loose garment that goes on top of usual daily clothes. It is worn by some Muslim women and it is removed once the woman returns home.

Le foulard   The French word for 'headscarf'. The term is best known because of the *affaires du foulard*, or 'headscarf incidents', in which French Muslim girls were refused entry in to schools because they were wearing *foulards*. There were over 100 such incidents in the 1989–2003 period. The rationale for turning the schoolgirls away is that state schools are part of the secular public space that forms the basis of French republican values, according to which the private space can be religious but the public arena must be free of religious ideas, objects and symbolism. In 2004, a Special Commission was set up by the government to investigate the options for dealing with the situation (as half the decisions had been overturned by the courts). It recommended the drafting of a law against wearing 'conspicuous' religious items, such as the *foulard*, to school, which was passed in 2005. The public debate was very controversial, with various interlocutors accusing others of anti-republican values, sexism and racism, etc. The Law's opponents argue that although the wording specifies crucifixes and Jewish skull-caps as objects that must also not be worn conspicuously, the principal objective of the law is to prevent French Muslims from expressing their Muslim identities.

Hegemony   Italian Marxist Antonio Gramsci uses the concept of hegemony (literally meaning 'domination') to refer to the set of dominant ideas at any given time. The subtlety of Gramsci's hegemony is that it allows for people to recognise that the ideas may be untrue and/or unfair, without this being a barrier to those ideas being the dominant ones of an era, around which political discourse is based and normalised.

Hypodescent   This is also called the 'one-drop rule'. This American racial logic states that any person with any ancestors who are not white Europeans cannot be considered genuinely white, regardless of what that person looks like.

Intersectionality   This is an approach developed by Black American feminists in the late 1980s to analyse social relations by simultaneously taking into account multiple axes of identity, generally gender, class and 'race'.

Ius sanguinis   This refers to qualification through bloodlines (that is, parents' or grandparents' nationality) (see Box 2.2).

Ius soli   This refers to qualification for membership through birth within a given territory (see Box 2.2).

Jilbab   A loose garment covering the whole body except for the hands, face, feet and head, worn by some Muslim women. A headscarf or veil can also be worn with it. There is some discussion about whether the contemporary forms of *jilbab* are the same as what is referred to in the Qu'ran. There is an argument that it only appeared in the recent past as a form of identification with particular forms of political Islam, while others maintain it is exactly the same item that was worn in the seventh century.

'Jim Crow'   After the abolition of slavery and the Fourteenth Amendment had given former slaves the right to vote, there was a short period (1865–76, also known as the Reconstruction), during which black Americans enjoyed relatively improved status and were protected by Federal laws. However, in 1877, the last Federal troops were withdrawn from the Southern states, and the Democratic Party enacted a set of laws that established separate living and access to resources ordered by 'race' (segregation). This was institutionally recognised in a set of laws passed by state governments in the southern states of the USA. These included separate schooling, places to sit on trains and buses, restaurants, toilets, etc. Moreover, a series of amendments to voting rights effectively disenfranchised most black voters by the First World War. This set of laws was known as 'Jim Crow'. Such laws were by no means exclusive to the south. Laws segregating the 'races' were passed across the USA, and President Wilson even reintroduced segregated Federal Offices in 1913.

Additionally, the reaction to the short period of black progress in the South involved violence and extra-judicial acts of aggression to intimidate black Americans in order to prevent them reaching social equality with whites (Du Bois, 1998 [1935]). The Jim Crow laws were backed up by the accompanying extra-legal social realities of lynchings, beatings and rape. Jim Crow held sway formally in the southern states from around 1890 to the passage of the Civil Rights Act in 1965.

Limpieza de sangre   This fifteenth-century Spanish concept of purity of the blood referred originally to the class system of feudal Spain, particularly the lineage of nobles and state officials who had to have *limpieza de sangre* (bloodlines including no traceable Jewish or Muslim converts to Christianity). *Limpieza de sangre* was a resource for some Spaniards to defend against encroachment from the bloodlines of indigenous Americans and enslaved Africans.

Mestiçagem   This is the historical process of 'race mixing' in Portuguese.

Mixed-ness   The problems engendered by trying to talk about people as being the products of more than one racialised group are discussed in Chapter 6. There are vast numbers of words used to describe people whose parentage is 'mixed' in this way that derive from the colonial period of the Americas. In Spanish, for example, there is *mestizo, castizo, mulatto* and *zambo* (which denote a European-Amerindian, European and unspecified other, European-African and African-Amerindian mix respectively). (An example of such definitions and terminology used in New Spain (Mexico) can be found in Yelvington, 2005: 246.) In French, there is *métis, mulâtre, sang-mêlé* and *griffe*. In Portuguese, the equivalent to *mestizo* is *mestizaje*, while North American English developed a vocabulary to cover degrees of blackness: *quadroon* (someone with one black grandparent), *octoroon* (someone with one black great-grandparent), etc. Such terms typically refer to the animal world (*mulatto, mulâtre*), or fractions (half, quarter, etc.). Among the contemporary academic vocabulary one encounters in reading the US literature on bi-raciality/'mixed race' are terms such as the Hawaiian *hapa*, and the Japanese *haafu* (both of which are basically the word 'half'), chosen as less negative ways to approach the issue.

Niqab   A veil, worn by some Muslim women, that covers the face, leaving only a slit for the eyes.

Patriality   The concept introduced into British law by the 1968 Commonwealth Immigrants Act which makes accession to British nationality predicated on having one grandparent born in the UK. The objective was to override the previous *ius soli* practice of extending membership to people born on British territory when Britain's Empire lay across the world. In the context of the late 1960s, the introduction of patriality means an attempt to close off access to British citizenship for post-war migrants from outside the white dominions such as Canada, New Zealand and South Africa, especially those referred to as 'coloured' immigrants at that time (i.e. from the Anglophone Caribbean, the Indian subcontinent and West Africa).

Racial sciences   The branches of science that contributed to fixing 'race' as part of the intellectual landscape of the Western world from the late eighteenth century through to the mid-twentieth century. These could be natural sciences, like craniology or phrenology; elements of natural sciences that also focused on other things, like anthropometry; or streams within the social sciences, such as ethnology, anthropology and, to a degree, sociology. What makes a science 'racial' is not its entirety, but its embrace of the idea of 'race' and its contribution to legitimising discourse that makes a causal and circular link between physical appearance, cultural capacity for civilisation, intellect and innate characteristics.

Suttee   Also called *sati*. A minority practice within Hinduism of the widow either self-immolating or being forced to die on her husband's funeral pyre. The rationale is to purge the couple of all sin for the afterlife. The practice was banned by the British in the nineteenth century and again by the Indian government in the late twentieth century.

TCN   'Third Country National' (TCN) is a term developed in European Union discourse that refers to someone unfortunate enough not to be a national of an EU member state.

Unmah   Arabic word translated into English as 'community' or 'nation'. It is used as a collective term to describe the whole Muslim diaspora, as a community of believers.

Appendix: Statistics on Muslims in the UK

Demographics

- In 2001, there were 1.6 million Muslims living in the UK, compared to a total population of 58.7 people.
- Three quarters of Muslims (74%) were from an Asian ethnic background, predominantly Pakistani (43%).
- 46% of Muslims had been born in the UK.
- 34% of Muslims were under 16 years of age.
- A third of Muslim households (34%) contained more than five people, while 25% of households contained three or more dependent children.
- 38% of Muslims lived in London.

(*Source*: National Statistics, 2001 Census)

Education

- In 2001, there were 371,000 school-aged (5- to16-year-old) Muslim children in England. (*Source*: National Statistics)
- In 2004, 67% of Indian, 48% of Bangladeshi and 45% of Pakistani pupils gained five or more grades A* to C at GCSE (or equivalent), compared with 52% of white British pupils. (*Source*: Social Trends No. 36, 2006)
- 31% of young British Muslims leave school with no qualifications compared to 15% of the total population. (*Source*: National Statistics)

Poverty

- 35% of Muslim households have no adults in employment (more than double the national average). (*Source*: 'Muslim Housing Experience', Oxford Centre for Islamic Studies)
- Just under three-quarters of Bangladeshi and Pakistani children (73%) are living in households below the poverty line (60% of median income). This compares with under a third (31%) for children in all households. (*Source*: Department for Work and Pensions, Households Below Average Income 1994/5–2000/1)
- In 2001, 13% of Muslim men and 16% of Muslim women reported 'not good' health. These rates, which take account of the difference in age structures between the religious groups, were higher than those of Jewish and Christian people, who were the least likely to rate their health as 'not good'. (*Source*: National Statistics, 2001 Census)

Housing

- In 2001, 52% of Muslim households did not own their own home.
- 28% of Muslim households were living in social rented accommodation, that is accommodation rented from the council or a housing association.
- Muslim households were the most likely to experience overcrowding. One-third of Muslim households (32%) lived in overcrowded accommodation. This compares with just 6% of Christian households who experience over-crowding.
- Muslim households were the most likely to lack central heating (12%).

(*Source*: National Statistics, 2001 Census report on faith)

Employment

- In 2004, 28% of 16–24-year-old Muslims were unemployed. This compares with only 11% of Christians of the same age. (*Source*: National Statistics, 2001 Census report on faith)
- In 2004, a fifth of Muslims were self-employed. (*Source*: National Statistics)
- In 2004, almost seven in ten (69%) Muslim women of working age were economically inactive. (*Source*: Social Trends No. 36, 2006)

Crime

- 47% of Muslim students have experienced Islamophobia. (*Source*: FOSIS (Federation of Student Islamic Societies) survey, 2005)
- Almost 10% of the prison population are Muslim, two-thirds of whom are young men aged 18–30. (*Source*: Prison Service statistics, 2004)
- Between 2001 and 2003, there was a 302% increase in 'stop and search' incidents among Asian people, compared with 118% among white people. (*Source*: Home Office, Statistics on Race and the Criminal Justice System, 2004)

Source: The National Youth Agency website (www.nya.org. uk/information/100582/109652/100630/108761/ukmuslimcommunitystatistics/)

This information is reproduced with the kind permission of The National Youth Agency: www.nya.org.uk

References

Abbas, T. (2007) 'British Muslim Minorities Today: Challenges and Opportunities to Europeanism, Multiculturalism and Islamism', *Sociology Compass* 1(2): 720–36.

Adams, M. (2006) 'A New Definition of Racism', Townhall blogs: http://townhall.com/columnists/MikeSAdams/2006/04/10/a_new_definition_of_racism

Adams, M. and Burke, P.J. (2006) 'Recollections of September 11 in Three English Villages: Identifications and Self-Narrations', *Journal of Ethnic and Migration Studies* 32(6): 983–1003.

Adamson, W. (1986) 'Interview with Gayatri Spivak', *Thesis Eleven* 15: 91–7.

Agamben, G. (1998) *Homo Sacer: Sovereign Power and Bare Life*. Palo Alto, CA: Stanford University Press.

Agamben, G. (2005) *State of Exception*. Chicago: University of Chicago Press.

Ahmed, S. (2004) *The Cultural Politics of Emotion*. Edinburgh: Edinburgh University Press and New York: Routledge.

Ali, S. (2003) *Mixed-Race, Post-Race: Gender, New Ethnicities and Cultural Practice*. Oxford: Berg.

Allen, C. and Nielsen, J. (2002) *Summary Report on Islamophobia in the EU after 11 September 2001*. Vienna: European Union Monitoring Centre on Xenophobia and Racism.

American Society for Aesthetic Plastic Surgery (1999) *ASAPS 1999 Statistics on Cosmetic Surgery*. Available at: www.surgery.org/sites/default/files/ASAPS1999 Stats.pdf

American Society for Aesthetic Plastic Surgery (2003) *2003 ASAPS Statistics – 8.3 Million Cosmetic Procedures: American Society for Aesthetic Plastic Surgery Reports 20 Percent Increase*. Available at: www.surgery.org/sites/default/files/ 2003%20ASAPS%20Statistics-%208.3%20Million%20Cosmetic%20Procedures. pdf

American Society of Plastic Surgeons (2009) *2008 Cosmetic Demographics*. Available at: www.plasticsurgery.org/Media/stats/2008-cosmetic-procedure-demographics-ethnicity.pdf

Amos, V. and Parmar, P. (1984) 'Challenging Imperial Feminism', *Feminist Review* 17: 3–19.

Anderson, B. (1983) *Imagined Communities: Reflections on the Origin and Spread of Nationalism*. London: Verso.

Anderson, W. (2006) *The Cultivation of Whiteness: Science, Health and Racial Destiny in Australia*. Durham, NC: Duke University Press.

Anthias, F. (1990) 'Race and Class Revisited – Conceptualising Race and Racisms', *Sociological Review* 38: 19–43.

Anthias, F. (1999) 'Institutional Racism, Power and Accountability', *Sociological Research Online* 4(1): www.socresonline.org.uk/4/lawrence/anthias.html

Anthias, F. and Yuval-Davis, N. (1993) *Racialised Boundaries: Race, Nation, Gender, Colour and Class and the Anti-racist Struggle*. London: Routledge.

Appelbaum, N., MacPherson, A. and Rosemblatt, K. (2003) *Race and Nation in Modern Latin America*. Chapel Hill: University of North Carolina Press.

Appiah, A. (1990) 'Racisms', in D. Goldberg (ed.) *Anatomy of Racism*, pp. 3–17. Minneapolis: Minnesota University Press.

Aptheker, H. (1946) *The Negro People in America: A Critique of Gunnar Myrdal's 'An American Dilemma'*. New York: International Publishers.

Ardrey, R. (1967) *The Territorial Imperative*. London: Collins.

Armstrong, B. (1989) 'Racialisation and Nationalist Ideology: The Japanese Case', *International Sociology* 4(3): 329–43.

Armstrong, K. (2002) *The Battle for God: Fundamentalism in Judaism, Christianity and Islam*. New York: Alfred Knopf.

Association of Multiethnic Americans (AMEA) (2001) 'AMEA Responds to Multiracial Census Data', at www.ameasite.org/census/031201censusdata.asp

Atton, C. (2006) 'Far-right Media on the Internet: Culture, Discourse And Power', *New Media and Society* 8(4): 573–87.

Australian Human Rights Commission (1997) *Bring them Home: Report of the National Inquiry into the Separation of Aboriginal and Torres Strait Islander Children from Their Families*. Sydney: AHRC. Available at www.hreoc.gov.au/social_justice/bth_report/index.html

Back, L. (2002) 'Aryans Reading Adorno: Cyber-culture and Twenty-first Century Racism', *Ethnic and Racial Studies* 25(4): 628–51.

Baldwin, J. (1965) *Going to See the Man*. New York: Dial Press.

Baldwin, J. (1985) *The Price of the Ticket: Collected Non-fiction 1948–1985*. New York: St. Martin's Press.

Balibar, E. and Wallerstein, I. (1991) *Race, Class, Nation: Ambiguous Identities*. New York: Verso.

Ball, S. (1993) 'Education, Markets, Choice and Social Class: The Markets as a Class Strategy in the UK and the USA', *British Journal of the Sociology of Education* 14(1): 3–19.

Banton, M. (1977) *The Idea of Race*. London: Tavistock Press.

Banton, M. (1996) 'Racism', in E. Cashmore (ed.) *Dictionary of Race and Ethnic Relations*, 4th edn. London: Routledge.

Banton, M. (1997) *Ethnic and Racial Consciousness*. Harlow: Addison Wesley Longman.

Barker, M. (1981) *The New Racism: Conservatives and the Ideology of the Tribe*. London: Junction Books.

Barker, M. (1990) 'Biology and the New Racism', in D. Goldberg (ed.) *Anatomy of Racism*, pp. 18–37. Minneapolis: University of Minnesota Press.

Barot, R. and Bird, J. (2001) 'Racialisation: The Genealogy and Critique of a Concept', *Ethnic and Racial Studies* 24(4): 601–18.

Barrett, J. and Roediger, D. (1997) 'Inbetween Peoples: Race, Nationality and the "New Immigrant" Working Class', *Journal of American Ethnic History* Spring: 3–44.

Bauman, Z. (1989) *Modernity and the Holocaust*. Cambridge: Cambridge University Press.

Bauman, Z. (1993) *Life in Fragments*. Oxford: Blackwell.

Bauman, Z. (1998a) *Globalization: The Human Consequences*. Cambridge: Polity Press.

Bauman, Z. (1998b) *Work, Consumerism and the New Poor*. Buckingham: Open University Press.

Beck, U. (1992) *Risk Society: Toward a New Modernity*. London: Sage.

Beck, U. (2000) 'Living your own Life in a Runaway World: Individualisation, Globalisation and Politics', in W. Hutton and A. Giddens (eds) *On the Edge: Living with Global Capital*, pp. 164–74. New York: The New Press.

Bhattacharyya, G. (2008) *Dangerous Brown Men: Exploiting Sex, Violence and Feminism in the War on Terror*. London: Zed.

Billig, M. (1995) *Banal Nationalism*. London: Sage.

Bishop, R. and Robinson, L. (1998) *Night Market: Sexual Cultures and the Thai Economic Miracle*. New York: Routledge.

Bobo, L. (2004) 'Inequalities that Endure? Racial Ideology, American Politics and the Peculiar Role of the Social Sciences', in M. Krysan and A. Lewis (eds) *The Changing Terrain of Race and Ethnicity*, pp. 13–42. New York: Russell Sage Foundation.

Bobo, L., Kluegel, J. and Smith, R. (1997) 'Laissez-Faire Racism: The Crystallization of a Kinder, Gentler, Anti-Black Ideology', in S. Tuch and J. Martin (eds) *Racial Attitudes in the 1990s: Continuity and Change*, pp. 15–44. *Westport*, CT: Praeger.

Bonacich, E. (1975) 'A Theory of Middleman Minorities', *American Sociological Review* 38: 583–94.

Bonilla-Silva, E. (2002) 'We are all Americans!: The Latin Americanization of Racial Stratification in the USA', *Race and Society* 5(1): 3–16.

Bonilla-Silva, E. (2006) *Racism Without Racists: Color-Blind Racism and the Persistence of Racial Inequality in the United States*. Lanham, MD: Rowman and Littlefield.

Bourdieu, P. (1977) *Outline of a Theory of Practice*. Cambridge: Cambridge University Press.

Bourdieu, P. (1984) *Distinction: A Social Critique of the Judgement of Taste*. London: Routledge.

Bourdieu, P. (1986) 'The Forms of Capital', in J.G. Richardson (ed.) *The Handbook of Theory: Research for the Sociology of Education*, pp. 241–58. New York: Greenwood Press.

Bowes, A., Ferguson, I. and Sims, D. (2009) 'Asylum Policy and Asylum Experiences: Interactions in a Scottish Context', *Ethnic and Racial Studies* 32(1): 23–43.

Brah, A. (1996) *Cartographies of Diaspora: Contesting Identities*. London: Routledge.

Broberg, G. and Roll-Hansen, N. (2005) *Eugenics and the Welfare State: Sterilization Policy in Norway, Sweden, Denmark, and Finland*. East Lansing, MI: Michigan State University Press.

Bruce, S. (2000) *Fundamentalism*. Cambridge: Polity Press.

Brunsma, D. (ed.) (2006) *Mixed Messages: Multiracial Identities in the 'Color-Blind' Era*. Boulder, CO: Lynne Rienner Press.

Buchanan, S. and Grillo, B. (2004) 'What's the Story? Reporting on Asylum in the British Media', *Forced Migration Review* 19(1): 41–3.

Burleigh, M. (2001) *A New History of the Third Reich*. London: Pan.

Burleigh, M. and Wipperman, W. (1991) *The Racial State: Nazi Germany, 1933–45*. Cambridge: Cambridge University Press.

Burnett, A. and Peel, M. (2001) 'Asylum Seekers and Refugees in Britain: Health Needs of Asylum Seekers and Refugees', *British Medical Journal* 322: 544–7.

Buruma, I. and Margalit, A. (2004) *Occidentalism: The West in The Eyes of its Enemies*. New York: Penguin.

Byrne, B. (2006) *White Lives: The Interplay of 'Race', Class and Gender in Everyday Life*. London: Routledge.

Calhoun, C. (1997) *Nationalism*. Milton Keynes: Open University Press.

Camiscioli, E. (2001) 'Producing Citizens, Reproducing the "French Race": Immigration, Demography and Pronatalism in Early Twentieth-Century France', *Gender and History*, 13(3): 593–621.

Carby, H. (1982) 'White Woman Listen! Black Feminism and the Boundaries of Sisterhood', in *The Empire Strikes Back*, pp. 212–31. Centre for Contemporary Cultural Studies, London: Hutchinson.

Carmichael, S. and Hamilton, C. (1967) *Black Power: The Politics of Liberation*. New York: Random House.

Carr, L. (1997) *Color-Blind Racism*. Thousand Oaks, CA: Sage.

Carrier, J. (1992) 'Occidentalism: The World Turned Upside-Down', *American Ethnologist* 19(2): 195–212.

Cartwright, S. (1860) 'Slavery in the Light of Ethnology', in E. Elliott (ed.) *Cotton is King and Pro-Slavery Arguments*. Augusta, GA: Pritchard, Abbott and Loomis.

Chamberlain, H. (1911 [1899]) *The Foundations of the Nineteenth Century* (trans. John Lees). London and New York: John Lane.

Chang, I. (2004) *The Chinese in America: A Narrative History*. New York: Penguin.

Childs, E. (2005) *Navigating Interracial Borders: Black–White Couples and Their Social Worlds*. Brunswick, NJ: Rutgers University Press.

Christian, M. (2004) 'Assessing Multiracial Identity', in J. Ifekwunigwe (ed.) *Mixed Race Studies: A Reader*, pp. 303–12. London: Routledge.

Clarke, S. and Garner, S. (2009) *White Identities*. London: Pluto.

Combahee River Collective (1977/1982) 'A Black Feminist Statement', in G. Hull, P. Scott and B. Smith (eds) *All the Women are White, All the Blacks are Men, But Some of Us Are Brave: Black Women Studies*, pp. 13–22. Old Westbury, NY: The Feminist Press.

Commission on British Muslims and Islamophobia (1997) *Islamophobia: A Challenge for Us All*. London: Runnymede Trust.

Commission for Racial Equality (1998) *Culture of Suspicion*. London: CRE. Available at http://193.113.211.175/pdfs/cultsus.pdf

Commission de Réflexion sur l'Application du Principe de Laïcité dans la République (2003) *Rapport au Président de la République*. Paris: La Documentation Française. Available at http://lesrapports.ladocumentationfrancaise.fr/BRP/034000725/0000.pdf

Condor, S. (2000) 'Pride and Prejudice: Identity Management in English People's Talk about "this Country"', *Discourse and Society* 11: 163–93.

Cox, O.C. (1948) *Caste, Class and Race*. New York: Doubleday.

Crawley, H. (2005) *Evidence on Attitudes to Asylum and Immigration: What We Know, Don't Know and Need to Know*. Centre on Migration, Policy and Society, Working Paper No. 23, University of Oxford.

Crenshaw, K. (1989) 'Demarginalising the Intersection of Race and Sex: A Black Feminist Critique of Anti-discrimination Doctrine, Feminist Theory and Anti-Racist Politics', *University of Chicago Legal Forum* 139: 383–94. Available at http://lic.law.ufl.edu/~hernandez/Women/crenshaw.pdf

Crenshaw, K. (1991) 'Mapping the Margins: Intersectionality, Identity Politics, and Violence against Women of Color', *Stanford Law Review* 43(6): 1241–99.

Crenshaw, K. (1997) 'Color-Blind Dreams and Racial Nightmares: Reconfiguring Racism in the Post-Civil Rights Era', in, T. Morrison and C. Lacour (eds) *Birth of a Nation'hood*, pp. 97–168. New York: Pantheon Books.

Cutler, D., Glaeser, E. and Vigdor, J. (1999) 'The Rise and Decline of the American Ghetto', *Journal of Political Economy* 107(3): 455–506.

Dalmage, H. (2000) *Tripping on the Color Line: Black-White Multiracial Families in a Racially Divided World*. New Brunswick, NJ: Rutgers University Press.

Daniels, J. (1997) *White Lies: Race, Class, Gender, and Sexuality in White Supremacist Discourse*. New York: Routledge.

Davenport, C. (1911) *Heredity in Relation to Eugenics*. New York: Henry Holt & Co.

Dávila, J. (2003) *Diploma of Whiteness: Race and Social Policy in Brazil, 1917–1945*. Durham, NC: Duke University Press.

Davis, A. (2001) *Women, Race and Class*. London: Virago.

Davis, F.J. (1991) *Who is Black? One Nation's Definition*. Park: Pennsylvania State University.

Davis, F.J. (2006) 'Defining Race: Comparative Perspectives', in D. Brunsma (ed.) *Mixed Messages*, pp. 15–32. Boulder, CO: Lynne Rienner Press.

Davis, M. (1992) *City of Quartz: Excavating the Future in Los Angeles*. New York: Vintage.

Davis, M. (2001) *Late Victorian Holocausts: El Niño Famines and the Making of the Third World*. New York: Verso.

Dawkins, R. (1976) *The Selfish Gene*. Oxford: Oxford University Press.

Delgado, R. and Stefancic, J. (1995) *Critical Race Theory: The Cutting Edge*. Philadelphia: Temple University Press.

Delphy, C. (1970) 'L'ennemi principal', *Partisan*, 54–55.

Delgado, R. and Stefancic, J. (1997) *Critical White Studies: Looking Behind the Mirror*. Philadelphia: Temple University Press.

Delphy, C. (2005) 'Gender, Rage and Racism: The Ban of the Islamic Headscarf in France', in M. Thapan (ed.) *Transnational Migration and the Politics of Identity*, pp. 228–51. London: Sage.

Delphy, C. (2006) 'Antisexisme or anti-racisme? Un Faux dilemme', *Nouvelles Questions Féministes* 25(1): 59–83.

Denis, A. (2008) 'Review Essay: Intersectional Analysis', *International Sociology* 23(5): 677–94.

Dhami, R., Squires, J. and Modood, T. (2006) *Developing Positive Action Policies: Learning from the Experiences of Europe and North America*. Department of Work and Pensions Research Report no. 406. Leeds: Department of Work and Pensions. Available at www.bris.ac.uk/sociology/ethnicitycitizenship/employment. pdf

Doane, A. (2006) 'What is Racism? Racial Discourse and Racial Politics', *Critical Sociology* 32(2–3): 255–74.

Douglas, M. (1966) *Purity and Danger: An Analysis of Concepts of Pollution and Taboo*. London: Routledge.

Douglass, R. (2000) 'Upgrading America's Conversations on Race: The Multi-Race Option for Census 2000', Association of Multi Ethnic Americans, June 2000. Available at www.ameasite.org/census/upgrade2k.asp

Du Bois, W.E.B. (1998 [1935]) *Black Reconstruction in the United States, 1860–1880*. New York: Free Press.

Duster, T. (1990) *Backdoor to Eugenics*. New York: Routledge.

Duster, T. (2006) 'Lessons from History: Why Race and Ethnicity Have Played a Major Role in Biomedical Research', *Journal of Law, Medicine and Ethics* 34(3): 487–96.

Dwyer, C. (1999) 'Veiled Meanings: Young British Muslim Women and the Negotiation of Differences', *Gender, Place and Culture* 6(1): 5–26.

Dyer, R. (1997) *White*. London: Routledge.

Edmonds, A. (2007) 'Triumphant Miscegenation: Reflections on Beauty and Race in Brazil', *Journal of Intercultural Studies* 28(1): 83–97.

Ehrenreich, B. and Hochschild, A. (eds) (2003) *Global Woman: Nannies, Maids, and Sex Workers in the New Economy*. New York: Metropolitan Books.

Eisenstadt, S. (1995) 'Fundamentalism, Phenomenology, and Comparative Dimensions', in M.E. Marty and R.S. Appleby (eds) *Fundamentalisms Comprehended*, pp. 259–76. Chicago: University of Chicago Press.

Elliott, A. (2008) *Making the Cut: How Cosmetic Surgery is Transforming Our Lives*. London: Reaktion Books.

Ellison, R. (1952) *Invisible Man*. New York: Random House.

Equality Authority (2006) *Annual Report 2006*. Dublin: Equality Authority.

European Union (2000) 'Council Directive 2000/78/EC of 27 November 2000: Establishing a General Framework for Equal Treatment in Employment and Occupation.' Available at http://eur-lex.europa.eu/LexUriServ/LexUriServ.do?uri=CELEX:32000L0078: EN:HTML

Eze, E. (1997) *Race and the Enlightenment: A Reader*. Boston: Blackwell.

FAIR (Forum Against Islamophobia and Racism) 'Defining Islamophobia.' Available at www.fairuk.org/docs/defining%20islamophobia.pdf

Fanon, F. (1967) *Black Skin, White Masks*. New York: Grove Press.

Fanon, F. (1967) *The Wretched of the Earth*. New York: Grove Press.

Farough, S. (2004) 'The Social Geographies of White Masculinities', *Critical Sociology* 30(2): 241–64.

Feagin, J. (2006) *Systemic Racism: A Theory of Oppression*. New York: Routledge.

Fenton, S. (2003) *Ethnicity*. Cambridge: Polity Press.

Finney, N. (2004) 'Asylum Seeker Dispersal: Public Attitudes and Press Portrayals around the UK', PhD thesis, University of Wales, Swansea.

Finney, N. and Peach, E. (2005) *Attitudes towards Asylum Seekers*. Centre for Asylum Seekers and Refugees (ICAR), CRE.

Forman, T. (2004) 'Color-Blind Racism and Racial Indifference: The Role of Racial Apathy in Facilitating Enduring Inequalities', in M. Krysan and A. Lewis (eds) *The Changing Terrain of Race and Ethnicity*, pp. 43–66. New York: Russell Sage Foundation.

Forman, T. and Lewis, A. (2006) 'Racial Apathy and Hurricane Katrina: The Social Anatomy of Prejudice in the Post-Civil Rights Era', *Du Bois Review* 3(1): 175–202.

Foucault, M. (1977) *Discipline and Punish: The Birth of the Prison* (trans. Alan Sheridan). New York: Vintage.

Foucault, M. (2003) *Society Must Be Defended: Lectures at the Collège De France, 1975–76*. London: Allen Lane.

Frankenberg, R. (1994) *White Women, Race Matters*. Madison: University of Wisconsin Press.

Frankenberg, R. (1997) *Displacing Whiteness: Essays in Social and Cultural Criticism*. Durham, NC: Duke University Press.

Fraser, S. (ed.) (1995) *The Bell Curve Wars: Race, Intelligence, and the Future of America*. New York: Basic Books.

Frederickson, G. (1988) *The Arrogance of Race*. Hanover, NH: Wesleyan University Press.

Freimuth, V., Crouse Quinn, S., Thomas, S., Colea, G., Zook, E. and Duncan, T. (2001) 'African Americans' Views on Research and the Tuskegee Syphilis Study', *Social Science and Medicine* 52: 797–808.

Fukuyama, F. (1992) *The End of History and the Last Man*. New York: Free Press.

Fuller, T. (2006) 'A Vision of Pale Beauty Carries Risks for Asia's Women', *New York Times*, 14 May. Available at www.nytimes.com/2006/05/14/world/asia/14thailand.html?pagewanted=2&_r=2&sq=skin%20whitening&st=nyt&scp=7

Gallagher, C. (2003) 'Color-Blind Privilege: The Social and Political Functions of Erasing the Color Line in Post Race America', *Race, Gender and Class* 10(4): 1–17.

Gallagher, C. and Twine, F.W. (2007) 'The Future of Whiteness: A Map of the "Third Wave"', *Ethnic and Racial Studies* 31(1): 4–24.

Galton, F. (1905) 'Eugenics: Its Definition, Scope and Aims', *Sociological Papers* 1: 45–51.

Garner, S. (2004) *Racism in the Irish Experience*. London: Pluto.

Garner, S. (2007a) *Whiteness: An Introduction*. London: Routledge.

Garner, S. (2007b) 'The European Union and the Racialisation of Immigration, 1986–2006', *Race/Ethnicity: Multidisciplinary Global Contexts*, 1(1): 61–87.

Garner, S. (2007c) 'Babies, Blood and Entitlement: Gendered Citizenship and Asylum in the Republic of Ireland', *Parliamentary Affairs* 60(4): 137–51.

Garner, S. (2009a) 'Empirical Research into White Racialized Identities in Britain', *Sociology Compass*. 2(6): 1–14.

Garner, S. (2009b) 'Ireland: From Racism without "Race", to "Racism without Racists"', *Radical History Review*, no. 104. 41–56.

Giddens, A. (1984) *The Constitution of Society: Outline of a Theory of Structuration*. Cambridge: Polity Press.

Giddings, P. (1984) *When and Where I Enter: The Impact of Black Women on Race and Sex in America*. New York: William Morrow.

Gillborn, D. (2005) 'Education Policy as an Act of White Supremacy: Whiteness, Critical Race Theory and Education Reform', *Journal of Education Policy* 20(4): 485–505.

Gilman, S. (1991) *The Jew's Body*. New York: Routledge.

Gilroy, P. (1987) *Ain't no Black in the Union Jack*. London: Hutchinson.

Gilroy, P. (2000) *Against Race: Imagining Political Culture Beyond the Color Line*. Cambridge, MA: The Belknap Press of Harvard University Press.

Glenn, E. (2008) 'Yearning for Lightness: Transnational Circuits in the Marketing and Consumption of Skin Lighteners', *Gender and Society* 22(3): 281–302.

Gobineau, Arthur (1853–55) *Essai sur l'inégalité des races humaines*. Paris: Firmin Didot.

Goldberg, D. (2000) *The Racial State*. Boston: Blackwell.

Goldberg, D. (2005) 'On Racial Americanization', in K. Murji and J. Solomos (eds) *Racialisation: Studies in Theory and Practice*, pp. 87–102. Oxford: Oxford University Press.

Goodhart, D. (2004) 'Too Diverse' *Prospect*, 95: www.prospect-magazine.co.uk/article_details.php?id=5835

Gordon, L. (1997) *Her Majesty's Other Children*. Lanham, MD: Rowman and Littlefield.

Gotham, K. (2000) 'Urban Space, Restrictive Covenants and the Origins of Racial Residential Segregation in a US City, 1900–50', *International Journal of Urban and Regional Research* 24(3): 616–33.

Gramsci, A. (1971) *Selections from the Prison Notebooks of Antonio Gramsci* (ed./trans. by Q. Hoare and G. Nowell-Smith). New York: International Books.

Grant, M. (1915) *The Passing of the Great Race*. New York: Charles Scribner's Sons.

Green, D. (ed.) (2000) *Institutional Racism in the Police Force: Fact or Fiction*. London: Civitas. Available at www.civitas.org.uk/pdf/cs06.pdf

Grieco, E. and Cassidy, R. (2001) 'Overview of Race and Hispanic Origin: Census 2000 Briefs' US Census Bureau'. Available at www.census.gov/cprod/2001 pubs/c2kbro1-1.pdf

Halkias, A. (2003) 'Money, God and Race: The Politics of Reproduction and the Nation in Modern Greece', *European Journal of Women's Studies*, 10(2): 211–32.

Hall, S. (1988) 'New Ethnicities', in K. Mercer (ed.) *Black Film Black Cinema*, pp. 27–31. London: Institute of Contemporary Arts.

Halliday, F. (1999) 'Islamophobia Reconsidered', *Ethnic and Racial Studies* 22(5): 892–902.

Hanchard, M. (1998) *Orpheus and Power: The Movimento Negro of Rio de Janeiro and Sao Paulo, Brazil, 1945–1988*. Princeton, NJ: Princeton University Press.

Hanchard, M. (1999) (ed.) *Racial Politics in Contemporary Brazil*. Durham, NC: Duke University Press.

Haraway, D. (1988) 'Situated Knowledges: The Science Question in Feminism and the Privilege of Partial Perspective', *Feminist Studies* 14(3): 575–99.

Harding, S. (1991) *Whose Science? Whose Knowledge? Thinking from Women's Lives*. Ithaca, NY: Cornell University Press.

Harris, C. (1993) 'Whiteness as Property', *Harvard Law Review* 106(8): 1707–93.

Hartigan, J. (1997) 'Locating White Detroit', in R. Frankenberg (ed.) *Displacing Whiteness*, pp. 180–213. Durham, NC: Duke University Press.

Hartigan, J. (1999) *Racial Situations: Class Predicaments of Whiteness in Detroit*. Princeton, NJ: Princeton University Press.

Hartigan, J. (2005) *Odd Tribes: Toward a Cultural Analysis of White People*. Durham, NC: Duke University Press.

Haywood, K. and Yar, M. (2006) 'The "Chav" Phenomenon: Consumption, Media and the Construction of a New Underclass', *Crime, Media, Culture* 2(1): 9–28.

Herder, J.G. (1784–91) *Ideas for a Philosophy of a History of Humanity*, cited in E. Eze (1997) *Race and Enlightenment: A Reader*. Boston: Blackwell.

Herrnstein, R. and Murray, C. (1994) *The Bell Curve: Intelligence and Class Structure in American Life*. New York: Free Press.

Hill-Collins, P. (1990) *Black Feminist Thought*. New York: Routledge.

Hillyard, P. (1993) *Suspect Community*. London: Pluto.

Hiro, D. (2002) *War without End: The Rise of Islamist Terrorism and the Global Response*. London: Routledge.

Hobsbawm, E. and Ranger, T. (1983) *The Invention of Tradition*. Cambridge: Cambridge University Press.

Hoggett, P., Garner, S., Wilkinson, H., Cowles, J., Lung, B. and Beedell, P. (2008) *Race, Class and Cohesion: A Community Profile of Hillfields (Bristol)*. Bristol: Bristol City Council/UWE, Centre for Psychosocial Studies. Available at www.uwe. ac.uk/hlss/research/cpss/research_reports/Hillfields.pdf

hooks, b. (1982) *Ain't I a Woman? Black Women and Feminism*. Boston: South End Press.

hooks, b. (1992) *Black Looks: Race and Representation*. Boston: South End Press.

hooks, b. (2000) *Where We Stand: Class Matters*. New York: Routledge.

Horsman, R. (1981) *Race and Manifest Destiny: The Origins of American Anglo-Saxonism*. Cambridge: Cambridge University Press.

Horton, H.D. (2006) 'Racism, Whitespace and the Rise of the Neo-Mulattos', in D. Brunsma (ed.) *Mixed Messages: Multiracial Identities in the 'Color-Blind' Era*, pp. 117–21. Boulder, CO: Lynne Rienner Press.

Hubbard, P. (2005) '"Inappropriate and Incongruous": Opposition to Asylum Centres in the English Countryside', *Journal of Rural Studies* 21: 3–17.

Hunter, M. (2007) 'The Persistent Problem of Colorism: Skin Tone, Status, and Inequality', *Sociology Compass* 1(1): 237–54.

Huntington, S. (1993) 'The Clash of Civilizations and the Remaking of World Order', *Foreign Affairs* 72(3): 22–49.

Huntington, S. (1996) *The Clash of Civilizations and the Remaking of World Order*. New York: Simon and Schuster.

Husbands, C. (1987) 'British Racisms: The Construction of Racial Ideologies', in C. Husbands (ed.) *'Race' in Britain*. London: Hutchinson.

Hussain, Y. and Bagguley, P. (2005) 'Citizenship, Ethnicity and Identity: British Pakistanis after the 2001 "Riots"', *Sociology* 39(3): 407–25.

Hylton, K. (2005) '"Race", Sport and Leisure: Lessons From Critical Race Theory', *Leisure Studies* 24(1): 81–98.

Ifekwunigwe, J. (1999) *Scattered Belongings: Cultural Paradoxes of 'Race', Nation and Gender*. London: Routledge.

Ifekwunigwe, J. (2001) 'Re-Membering "Race": On Gender, Mixed Race and Family in the African Diaspora', in D. Parker and M. Song (eds) *Rethinking 'Mixed Race'*, pp. 42–64. London: Pluto.

Ifekwunigwe, J. (2004) *Mixed Race Studies: A Reader*. London: Routledge.

Ignatieff. M. (2000) 'Less Race, Please', in D. Green (ed.) *Institutional Racism and the Police: Fact or Fiction?*, pp. 21–4. London: Institute for the Study of Civil Society.

Institute on Race and Poverty (IRP) (2002) 'Long Island Fair Housing: A State of Inequity.' Available at www.eraseracismny.org/downloads/reports/ERASE_Housing Monograph.pdf

International Council on Human Rights Protection (2000) 'The Persistence and Mutation of Racism.' Available at www.ichrp.org/files/reports/26/112_report_ en.pdf

Jacobson, M. (1998) *Whiteness of A Different Colour: European Immigrants and the Alchemy of Race*. Cambridge, MA: Harvard University Press.

Jempson, M. (2007) 'Portrayal and Participation of Minorities in the Media', paper delivered at the INCORE Race and Media Conference, University of Ulster, 3 October.

Johnson, J.W. ([1990] 1917) *Autobiography of an Ex-Colored Man*. New York: Penguin.

Johnson, H. and Shapiro, T. (2003) 'Good Neighborhoods, Good Schools: Race and the "Good Choices" of White Families', in A. Doane and E. Bonilla-Silva (eds) *White Out: The Continuing Significance of Racism*, pp. 173–88. New York: Routledge.

Jones, D. M. (1997) 'Darkness Made Visible: Law, Metaphor and the Racial Self', in R. Delgado and J. Stefancic (eds) *Critical White Studies: Looking Behind the Mirror*, pp. 66–78. Philadelphia: Temple University Press.

Jones, J. (1993) *Bad Blood: The Tuskegee Syphilis Experiment*. New York: Free Press.

Jones, S. (1994) *The Language of the Genes: Biology, History and the Evolutionary Future*. London: Flamingo.

Joppke, C. (1999) 'How Immigration is Changing Citizenship: A Comparative View', *Ethnic and Racial Studies* 22(4): 629–52.

Jordan, B., Stråth, B. and Triandafyllidou, A. (2003) 'Comparing Cultures of Discretion', *Journal of Ethnic and Migration Studies* 29(2): 373–95.

Joseph, P. (ed.) (2006) *The Black Power Movement: Rethinking the Civil Rights–Black Power Era*. New York: Routledge.

Kahn, J. (2006) 'Race, Pharmacogenomics, and Marketing: Putting BiDil in Context', *The American Journal of Bioethics* 6(5): W1–W5.

Kahn, J. (2007a) 'Race-ing Patents/Patenting Race: An Emerging Political Geography of Intellectual Property in Biotechnology', *Iowa Law Review* 92: 354–416.

Kahn, J. (2007b) 'Race in a Bottle', *Scientific American*, July: www.sciam.com/article.cfm?id=race-in-a-bottle

Kefalas, M. (2003) *Working-class Heroes: Protecting Home, Community and Nation in a Chicago Neighborhood*. Berkeley: UCLA Press.

Kenny, L. (2000) *The Daughters of Suburbia: Growing up White, Middle Class and Female*. New Brunswick, NJ: Rutgers University Press.

Knox, R. (1850) *The Races of Men: A Philosophical Inquiry into the Influence of Race over the Destinies of Nations*. London: Henry Renshaw.

Kushner, T. (2005) 'Racialisation and "White European" Immigration to Britain', in K. Murji and J. Solomos (eds) *Racialisation: Studies in Theory and Practice*, pp. 207–26. Oxford: Oxford University Press.

Lacy, K. (2007) *Blue-chip Black: Race, Class, and Status in the New Black Middle Class*. Berkeley: University of California Press.

Ladson-Billings, G. and Tate, W. (1995) 'Toward a Critical Race Theory of Education', *Teacher's College Record* 97(1): 47–68.

Lamont, M. (2000) *The Dignity of Working Men*. Cambridge, MA: Harvard University Press.

Larsson, G. (2005) 'The Impact of Global Conflicts on Local Contexts: Muslims in Sweden after 9/11 – the Rise of Islamophobia, or New Possibilities?', *Islam and Christian-Muslim Relations* 16(1): 29–42.

Lawler, S. (2005) 'Disgusted Subjects: The Making of Middle-class Identities', *Sociological Review* 53(3): 429–46.

Leclerc, G.-L. (1748–1804) *A Natural History, General and Particular*, cited in E. Eze (1997) *Race and Enlightenment: A Reader*. Boston: Blackwell.

Lentin, R. (2004) 'From Racial State to Racist State: Ireland on the Eve of the Citizenship Referendum', *Variant* 20: www.variant.randomstate.org/20texts/raciststate.html

Lentin, A. and Lentin, R. (eds) (2006) *Race and State*. Newcastle: Cambridge Scholar's Press.

Lentin, R. and McVeigh, R. (2006) *After Optimism: Ireland, Racism and Globalisation*. Dublin: Metro Eireann.

Lewis, A. (2003) *Race in the Schoolyard: Negotiating the Color Line in Classrooms and Communities*. New Brunswick, NJ: Rutgers University Press.

Lewis, B. (1990) 'The Roots Of Muslim Rage: Why so Many Muslims Deeply Resent the West, and Why their Bitterness will not Easily be Mollified', *Atlantic Online*, September: http://tonyinosaka.googlepages.com/muslimrage-atlantic.pdf

Lewis, M. (2005) *Asylum: Understanding Public Attitudes*. London: IPPR.

Linnaeus (1735) *The System of Nature*, cited in E. Eze (1997) *Race and Enlightenment: A Reader*. Boston: Blackwell.

Lipsitz, G. (1995) 'The Possessive Investment in Whiteness: Racialised Social Democracy and the "White" Problem in American Studies', *American Quarterly* 47(3): 369–87.

Lipsitz, G. (1998) *The Possessive Investment in Whiteness: How White People Profit from Identity Politics*. Philadelphia: Temple University Press.

Lombroso, C. (1876) *L'Uomo Delinquente*. Milan: Hoepli.

Lukács, G. (1971) *History and Class Consciousness*. Boston: MIT Press.

Luibhéid, E. (2004) 'Childbearing Against the State? Asylum Seeker Women in the Irish Republic', *Women's Studies International Forum* 27: 335–49.

Mac an Gháill, M. (1999) *Contemporary Racisms and Ethnicities: Social and cultural transformations*. Buckingham: Open University Press.

MacPherson, W. (1999) *The Stephen Lawrence Inquiry: Report of an Inquiry by Sir William MacPhersan of Cluny* (CM 4262-I). HMSO online: www.archive.official-documents.co.uk/document/cm42/4262/4262.htm

Mahtani, M. (2002a) 'What's in a Name? Exploring the Employment of "Mixed Race" as an Identification', *Ethnicities* 2(4): 469–90.

Mahtani, M. (2002b) 'Interrogating the Hyphen-Nation: Canadian Multicultural Policy and "Mixed Race" Identities', *Social Identities* 8(1): 67–90.

Mahtani, M. and Moreno, A. (2001) 'Same Difference', in D. Parker and M. Song (eds) *Rethinking 'Mixed Race'*, pp. 65–75. London: Pluto.

Malik, K. (2005) 'The Islamophobia Myth.' Available at www.kenanmalik.com/essays/islamophobia_prospect.html

Malthus, T. (1798) *Essay on the Principle of Population*. London: J. Johnson.

Massey, D. and Denton, N. (1994) *American Apartheid: Segregation and the Making of the Underclass*. Cambridge, MA: Harvard University Press.

Mayor of London (2006) *Muslims in London*. London: Greater London Authority.

McCall, L. (2001a) 'Sources of Racial Wage Inequality in Metropolitan Labor Markets: Racial, Ethnic, and Gender Differences', *American Sociological Review* 66(4): 520–41.

McCall, L. (2001b) *Complex Inequality: Gender, Race, and Class in the New Economy*. New York: Routledge.

McCall, L. (2005) 'The Complexity of Intersectionality', *Journal of Women in Culture and Society* 30: 1771–800.

McDonald, K. (2002) 'From s11 to September 11 – Implications for Sociology', *Journal of Sociology* 38(3): 229–36.

McIntosh, P. (1988) 'White Privilege and Male Privilege: A Personal Account of Coming to See Correspondences through Work in Women's Studies', Working Paper 189, Wellesley College.

McKinney, K. (2004) *Being White: Stories of Race and Racism*. New York: Routledge.

McLaren, L. and Johnson, M. (2007) 'Resources, Group Conflict and Symbols: Explaining Anti-Immigration Hostility in Britain', *Political Studies* 55: 709–24.

Mengel, L. (2001) 'Triples – the Social Evolution of an Asian Pan-ethnicity', in D. Parker and M. Song (eds) *Rethinking 'Mixed Race'*, pp. 99–116. London: Pluto.

Meer, N. (2006) '"Get Off Your Knees": Print Media Public Intellectuals and Muslims in Britain', *Journalism Studies* 7(1): 35–59.

Melwani, L. (2008) 'The White Complex', *Little India*, 18 August. Available at www.littleindia.com/news/134/ARTICLE/1828/2007-08-18.html

Miles, R. (1987) *Racism*. London: Routledge.

Miles, R. (1982) *Racism and Migrant Labour*. London: Routledge.

Miles, R. and Brown, M. (2003) *Racism*. London: Routledge.

Miller, M. (2004) *Rise and Fall of the Cosmic Race: The Cult of Mestizaje in Latin America*. Austin: University of Texas Press.

Mills, C.W. (1997) *The Racial Contract*. Ithaca, NY: Cornell University Press.

Mills, C.W. (2003) *From Class to Race: Essays in White Marxism and Black Radicalism*. Oxford: Rowman and Littlefield.

Mills, C.W. (2004) 'Racial Exploitation and the Wages of Whiteness', in G. Yancy (ed.), *What White Looks Like: African-American Philosophers on the Whiteness Question*, pp. 25–54. New York: Routledge.

Mills, C.W. and Pateman, C. (2007) *Contract and Domination*. Cambridge: Polity Press.

Millward, P. (2008) 'Rivalries and Racisms: "Closed" and "Open" Islamophobic Dispositions Amongst Football Supporters', *Sociological Research Online* 13(6): www.socresonline.org.uk/13/6/5.html

Milne, S. (2008) 'This Persecution of Gypsies is now the Shame of Europe', *The Guardian*, 10 July.

Mire, A. (2005) 'Pigmentation and Empire: The Emerging Skin-Whitening Industry', *Counterpunch*, 28 July: www.counterpunch.org/mire07282005.html

Modood, T. (1992) *Not Easy Being British: Colour, Culture and Citizenship*. Stoke: Runnymede Trust and Trentham Books.

Modood, T. (1997) 'Introduction: The Politics of Multiculturalism in the New Europe', in T. Modood and P. Werbner (eds) *The Politics of Multiculturalism in the New Europe: Racism, Identity and Community*. London: Zed Books.

Modood, T. (2004) 'Muslims and the Politics of Difference', *The Political Quarterly* 74(1): 100–15.

Modood, T. (2005) *Multicultural Politics: Racism, Ethnicity and Muslims in Britain*. Edinburgh: Edinburgh University Press.

Modood, T. (2007) *Multiculturalism A Civic Idea*. Cambridge: Polity Press.

Modood, T., Berthoud, R., Lakey, J., Nazroo, J., Smith, P., Virdee, S. and Beishon, S. (1997) *Ethnic Minorities in Britain: Diversity and Disadvantage – Fourth National Survey of Ethnic Minorities*. London: PSI.

Mohanty, C. (1988) 'Under Western Eyes: Feminist Scholarship and Colonial Discourses', *Feminist Review* 30: 61–88.

Moon, K. (1997) *Sex Among Allies: Military Prostitution in US–Korea Relations*. New York: Columbia University Press.

Morris, D. (1968) *The Naked Ape*. London: Corgi.

Morrison, T. (1970) *The Bluest Eye*. New York: Holt, Rinehart and Wilson.

Morrison, T. (1993) *Playing in the Dark: Whiteness and the Literary Imagination*. New York: Vintage.

Morton, S. (1839) *Crania Americana: A Comparative View of the Skulls of Various Aboriginal Natives of North and South America, to which is Prefixed an Essay on the Variety of Human Species*. Philadelphia: J. Dobson.

Murji, K. and Solomos, J. (eds) (2005a) *Racialisation: Studies in Theory and Practice*. Oxford: Oxford Univesity Press.

Murji, K. and Solomos, J. (2005b) 'Introduction', in Murji and Solomos (eds) *Racialisation: Studies in Theory and Practice*, pp. 1–28. Oxford: Oxford University Press.

Nagel, J. (2003) *Race, Ethnicity and Sexuality: Intimate Intersections, Forbidden Frontiers*. New York: Oxford University Press.

Nahman, M. (2008) 'Nodes of Desire: Romanian Egg Sellers, "Dignity" and Feminist Alliances in Transnational Ova Exchanges', *European Journal of Women's Studies* 15(2): 65–82.

Nayak, A. (2003) 'Ivory Lives: Economic Restructuring and the Making of Whiteness in a Post-industrial Youth Community', *European Journal of Cultural Studies* 6(3): 305–25.

Nayak, A. (2007) 'Critical Whiteness Studies', *Sociology Compass* 1(2): 737–55.

Nye, R. (1949) *Fettered Freedom: Civil Liberties and the Slavery Controversy, 1830–1860*. East Lansing, MI: Michigan State College Press.

O'Keeffe, G. (2007) 'The Irish in Britain – Towards Greater Visibility?', in W. Huber, M. Böss, C. Malignant and H. Schwall (eds) *Irish Studies in Europe*, pp. 121–32. EFACIS: The European Federation of Associations and Centres of Irish Studies.

Oakley, A. (1974) *The Sociology of Housework*. London: Martin Robertson.

Oliver, M. and Shapiro, T. (1995) *Black Wealth/White Wealth: A New Perspective on Racial Inequality*. New York: Routledge.

Omi, M. (2001) 'The Changing Meaning of Race', in N. Smelser, W.J. Wilson and F. Mitchell (eds) *America Becoming: Racial Trends and Their Consequences, Volume 1*, pp. 243–63. Washington, DC: National Research Council.

Omi, M., and Winant, H. (1994[1986]) *Racial Formation in the US: from the 1960s to the 1980s*. New York: Routledge

Owen, C. (2001) 'Mixed Race in Official Statistics', in D. Parker and M. Song (eds) *Rethinking 'Mixed Race'*, pp. 134–53. London: Pluto.

Parekh, B. (1991) *The Concept of Fundamentalism* (Meghraj Lecture, 1991). Coventry/Leeds: University of Warwick/Peepal Tree Press.

Parker, D. and Song, M. (eds) (2001) *Rethinking 'Mixed Race'*. London: Pluto.

Parker, D. and Song, M. (2006) 'New Ethnicities Online: Reflexive Racialisation and the Internet', *The Sociological Review* 54(3): 575–94.

Pateman, C. (1988) *The Sexual Contract*. Cambridge: Polity.

Pearson, K. (1930) *Life, Letters and Labours of Francis Galton, Volume Three A: Correlation, Personal Identification and Eugenics*. Cambridge: Cambridge University Press.

Peiss, K. (1999) *Hope in a Jar: The Making of America's Beauty Culture*. New York: Holt.

Phillips, D. (2006) 'Parallel Lives? Challenging Discourses of British Muslim Self-segregation', *Environment and Planning D: Society and Space* 24(1): 25–40.

Phoenix, A. (1996) 'I'm White – so What? The Construction of Whiteness for Young Londoners', in M. Fine (ed.) *Off White*, pp. 187–97. New York: Routledge.

Phoenix, A. (2005) 'Remembered Racialization: Young People and Positioning in Different Understandings', in K. Murji and J. Solomos (eds) *Racialisation: Studies in Theory and Practice*, pp. 103–22. Oxford: Oxford University Press.

Pickering, C. (1854) *The Races of Men: And Their Geographical Distribution*. London: H.G. Bohn.

Putnam, R. (2000) *Bowling Alone: The Collapse and Revival of the American Community*. New York: Simon and Schuster.

Putnam, R. (2007) 'E Pluribus Unum: Diversity and Community in the Twenty-first Century – The 2006 Johan Skytte Prize Lecture', *Journal of Scandinavian Political Studies* 30(2): 137–74.

Quraishi, M. (2005) *Muslims and Crime: A Comparative Study*. Aldershot: Ashgate.

Qureshi, R. (2007) 'Something Remarkable', *The Guardian*, 13 April.

Raimon, E.A. (2004) *The 'Tragic Mulatta' Revisited: Race and Nationalism in Nineteenth-Century Antislavery Fiction*. New Brunswick, NJ: Rutgers University Press.

Rana, J. (2007) 'The Story of Islamophobia', *Souls* 9(2): 148–61.

Rattansi, A. (2005) 'The Uses of Racialisation: The Time–Spaces and Subject–Objects of the Raced Body', in K. Murji and J. Solomos (eds) *Racialisation: Studies in Theory and Practice*, pp. 271–302. Oxford: Oxford University Press.

Reay, D., Hollingworth, S., Williams, K., Jamieson, F., Crozier, G., James, D. and Beedell, P. (2007) '"A Darker Shade of Pale?" Whiteness, the Middle Classes and Multi-Ethnic Inner City Schooling', *Sociology* 41(6): 1041–60.

Renan, E. (1992 [1882]) *Qu'est-qu'une Nation?: Et Autres Essais Politiques*. Paris: Agora.

Rex, J. (1970) *Race Relations in Sociological Theory*. London: Routledge.

Rich, P. (1990) *Race and Empire in British Politics*. Cambridge: Cambridge University Press.

Richardson, J. (2004) *(Mis)Representing Islam: The Racism and Rhetoric of British Broadsheet Newspapers*. Amsterdam: John Benjamins.

Rinaldo, R.A. (2007) 'High Heels and Headscarves: Women's Clothing and Islamic Piety in Indonesia', paper presented at the annual meeting of the American Sociological Association, New York, 11 August. Available at www. allacademic. com//meta/p_mla_apa_research_citation/1/8/2/5/8/pages182584/p182584-1.php

Robinson, C. (1983) *Black Marxism: The Making of the Black Radical Tradition*. London: Zed Books.

Robinson, V. (2003) *Spreading the 'Burden'? A Review of Policies to Disperse Asylum Seekers and Refugees*. Bristol: Policy Press.

Rockquemore, K.A. (2002) 'Negotiating the Color Line: The Gendered Process Of Racial Identity Construction among Black/White Biracial Women', *Gender and Society* 16(4): 485–503.

Rockquemore, K.A. and Arend, P. (2002) 'Opting for White: Choice, Fluidity and Racial Identity Construction in Post Civil-rights America', *Race and Society* 5: 49–64.

Rockquemore, K.A. and Laszloffy, T. (2005) *Raising Biracial Children*. Lanham, MD: Altamira.

Roediger, D. (1991) *The Wages of Whiteness: Race and the Making of the American Working* Class. London: Verso.

Rojek, C. and Turner, B. (2001) *Society and Culture*. London: Sage.

Roosevelt, T. (1906) *State of the Union*. Available at www.theodore-roosevelt. com/sotu6.html

Root, M. (1996) 'The Multiracial Experience: Racial Borders as Significant Frontier in Race Relations', in M. Root (ed.) *The Multiracial Experience*. Thousand Oaks: Sage.

Ropp, S. (2004) 'Do Multicultural Subjects Really Challenge Race?: Mixed Race Asians in the United States and the Caribbean', in J. Ifekwunigwe (ed.) *Mixed Race Studies: A Reader*, pp. 263–70. London: Routledge.

Said, E. (1979) *Orientalism*. New York: Vintage.

Said, E. (2001) 'Clash of Ignorance', *The Nation*. Available at www.thenation. com/doc/20011022/said

Sanchez, G. (2004) 'Y Tù qué?: Latino History in the New Millennium', in J. Ifekwunigwe (ed.) *Mixed Race Studies: A Reader*, pp. 276–82. London: Routledge.

San Juan, E. (2001) 'Problems in the Marxist Project of Theorising Race', in E. Cashmore and R. Jennings (eds) *Racism: Essential Readings*, pp. 225–46. London: Sage.

Satzewitch, V. (1987) 'Racisms: The Reactions to Chinese Migrants in Canada at the Turn of the Century', *International Sociology* 4(3): 311–27.

Saxton, A. (1990) *The Rise and Fall of the White Republic: Class Politics and Mass Culture in Nineteenth Century America*. New York: Verso.

Scarman, L. (1986) *Scarman Report: The Brixton Disorders, 10–12 April, 1981*. London: Pelican.

Senna, D. (2004) 'The Mulatto Millennium', in J. Ifekwunigwe (ed.) *Mixed Race Sudies: A Reader*, pp. 204–9. London: Routledge.

Sheridan, L.P. (2006) 'Islamophobia Pre- and Post-September 11th, 2001', *Journal of Interpersonal Violence* 21(3): 317–36.

Sibley, D. (1995) *Geographies of Exclusion: Society and Difference in the West*. London: Routledge.

Silverstein, P. (2004) 'Headscarves and the French Tricolor', *Middle East Report*, 30 January. Available at www.merip.org/mero/mero013004.html

Silverstein, P. (2005) 'Immigrant Racialisation and the New Savage Slot: Race, Migration, and Immigration in the New Europe', *Annual Review of Anthropology* 34: 363–84.

Sims, J. (2007) *Mixed Heritage: Identity, Policy and Practice*. London: Runnymede Trust.

Sivanandan, A. (1990) *Communities of Resistance*. London: Verso.

Skeggs, B. (1997) *Formations of Class and Gender: Becoming Respectable*. London: Sage.

Skeggs, B. (2005) *Class, Self and Culture*. London: Routledge.

Skeggs, B. and Wood, H. (2008) 'Spectacular Morality: Reality Television and the Re-making of the Working Class', in D. Hesmondhalgh and J. Toynbee (eds) *Media and Social Theory*, pp. 177–94. London: Routledge.

Skinner, D. (2006) 'Racialised Futures: Biologism and the Changing Politics of Identity', *Social Studies of Science* 36(3): 459–88.

Small, S. (1994) *Racialised Barriers: The Black Experience in the United States and England in the 1980s*. London: Routledge.

Small, S. (2001) 'Colour, Culture and Class: Interrogating Interracial Marriage and People of Mixed Descent in the United States', in D. Parker and M. Song (eds) *Rethinking 'Mixed Race'*, pp. 117–33. London: Pluto.

Sowell, T. (1990) *Preferential Policies*. New York: William Morrow.

Spencer, H. (1864) *Principles of Biology, Volume. 1.* London: Williams and Norgate.

Spencer, J.M. (2000) *The New Colored People: The Mixed-Race Movement in America*. New York: New York University Press.

Spencer, R. (2006) 'New Racial Identities, Old Arguments: Continuing Biological Reification', in D. Brunsma (ed.) *Mixed Messages*, pp. 83–116. Boulder, CO: Lynne Rienner Press.

Spruill, J.C. (1938) *Women's Life and Work in the Southern Colonies*. New York and London: W.W. Norton & Company.

Stepan, N. (1991) *The Hour of Eugenics: Race, Gender, and Nation in Latin America*. Ithaca, NY: Cornell University Press.

Stoddard, W. (1922) *Revolt Against Civilization*. New York: Scribner.

Stonequist, E. (1937) *The Marginal Man: A Study in Personality and Culture Conflict*. New York: Charles Scribner's Sons.

Taguieff, P.A. (1990) 'The New Cultural Racism in France', *Telos* 83: 109–22.

Taguieff, P.A. (2001) *The Force of Prejudice: On Racism and Its Doubles* (trans. Hassan Melehy). Minneapolis: University of Minnesota Press.

Tizard, B. and Phoenix, A. (2002) *Black, White or Mixed Race? Race and Racism in the Lives of Young People of Mixed Parentage*, 2nd edn. London: New York.

Twinam, A. (2006) 'Purchasing Whiteness: Conversations on the Essence of Pardo-ness and Mulatto-ness at the End of Empire', paper presented at Lockmiller seminar, Emory University, 29 March.

Twine, F.W. (1996) 'Brown-skinned White Girls: Class, Culture and the Construction of White Identity in Suburban Communities', *Gender, Place and Culture* 3: 205–24.

Tyler, I. (2008) '"Chav Mum, Chav Scum": Class Disgust in Contemporary Britain', *Feminist Media Studies* 8(1): 17–34.

Tyler, K. (2003) 'The Racialised and Classed Constitution of Village Life', *Ethnos* 68(3): 391–412.

Tyler, K. (2006) 'Village People: Race, Class, Nation and the Community Spirit', in S. Neal and J. Agyeman (eds) *The New Countryside: Ethnicity, Nation and Exclusion in Contemporary Rural Britain*, pp. 129–48. Bristol: Polity Press.

United Nations (1965) *International Convention on the Elimination of All Forms of Racial Discrimination: adopted and opened for signature and ratification by General Assembly resolution 2106 (XX) of 21 December 1965*: www2.ohchr.org/english/law/pdf/cerd.pdf

United Nations High Commission for Refugees (UNHCR) (2008) *Statistical Yearbook 2007: Trends in Displacement, Protection and Solutions*. Geneva: UNHCR.

Van Deburg, W. (1992) *New Day in Babylon: The Black Power Movement and American Culture, 1965–1975*. Chicago: University of Chicago Press.

Voegelin, E. (2000 [1933]) *Race and State* (trans. Ruth Heim). Baton Rouge and London: Louisiana State University Press.

Voegelin, E. (1940) 'The Growth of the Race Idea', *The Review of Politics*. July: 283–317.

Watanabe, K. (1995) 'Trafficking in Women's Bodies, Then and Now: the Issue of Military Comfort Women', *Peace and Change*, 20: 501–14.

Watt, P. and Stenson, K. (1998) 'The Street: "It's a Bit Dodgy Around There": Safety, Danger, Ethnicity and Young People's Use of Public Space', in T. Skelton and G. Valentine (eds) *Cool Places: Geographies of Youth Cultures*, pp. 249–66. London: Routledge.

Weber, M. (1946) *Essays in Sociology* (ed./trans./intro.H.H. Gerth and C. Wright Mills,). Oxford: Oxford University Press.

Weinstein, B. (2003) 'Racialising Regional Difference: Sao Paulo versus Brazil, 1932', in N. Appelbaum, A. MacPherson and K. Rosemblatt (eds) *Race and Nation in Modern Latin America*, pp. 237–62. Chapel Hill: University of North Carolina Press.

Weis, L. (2006) 'Masculinity, Whiteness, and the New Economy: An Exploration of Privilege and Loss', *Men and Masculinities* 8(3): 262–72.

Wells, I. (1893) Lynch Law (excerpt available at: www.historyisaweapon.com/defcon1/wellslynchlaw.html)

Werbner, P. (2005) 'Islamophobia: Incitement to Religious Hatred – Legislating for a New Fear?', *Anthropology Today* 21(1): 5–9.

Wieviorka, M. (1995) *The Arena of Racism*. New York: Sage.

Wilson, E. (1976) *Sociobiology – The New Synthesis*. Cambridge, MA: Harvard University Press.

Wolfe, P. (2002) 'Race and Racialisation: Some Thoughts', *Postcolonial Studies* 5(1): 51–62.

Wray, M. (2006) *Not Quite White: White Trash and the Boundaries of Whiteness*. Durham, NC: Duke University Press.

X, Malcolm, and Haley, A. (1969) *The Autobiography of Malcolm X*. New York: Random House.

Yancy, G. (2001) 'A Foucauldian (Genealogical) Reading of Whiteness: The Production of the Black Body/Self and the Racial Deformation of Pecola Breedlove in Toni Morrison's *The Bluest Eye*', *Radical Philosophy Review* 4(1–2): 1–29.

Yelvington, K. (2005) *Understanding Contemporary Latin America*. Boulder, CO: Lynne Rienner Press.

Young, R. (1995) *Colonial Desire: Hybridity in Theory, Culture and Race*. London: Routledge.

Yuval-Davis, N. (1997) *Gender and Nation*. London: Routledge.

Zack, N. (1993) *Race and Mixed Race*. Philadelphia: Temple University Press.

Zappone, K. (ed.) (2003) *Re-thinking Equality: The Challenge of Diversity*. Dublin: Equality Authority.

Žižek, S. (1989) *The Sublime Object of Ideology*. London: Verso.

Index